Cooking Light.
dinner's
ready!

Cooking Light

dinner's ready!

Oxmoor House

ISBN-13: 978-0-8487-3820-4
ISBN-10: 0-8487-3820-9
Library of Congress Control Number: 2012942587

Printed in the United States of America
First Printing 2012

Be sure to check with your health-care provider before making any changes in your diet.

Oxmoor House

Editorial Director: Leah McLaughlin
Creative Director: Felicity Keane
Brand Manager: Michelle Turner Aycock
Senior Editors: Heather Averett; Andrea C. Kirkland, MS, RD
Managing Editor: Rebecca Benton

Cooking Light® Dinner's Ready!

Art Director: Claire Cormany
Project Editor: Emily Chappell
Assistant Designer: Allison Sperando Potter
Director, Test Kitchen: Elizabeth Tyler Austin
Assistant Directors, Test Kitchen: Julie Christopher, Julie Gunter
Recipe Developers and Testers: Wendy Ball, RD; Victoria E. Cox; Stefanie Maloney; Callie Nash; Leah Van Deren
Recipe Editor: Alyson Moreland Haynes
Food Stylists: Margaret Monroe Dickey, Catherine Crowell Steele
Photography Director: Jim Bathie
Senior Photo Stylist: Kay E. Clarke
Senior Photographer: Hélène Dujardin
Photo Stylist: Katherine Eckert Coyne
Assistant Photo Stylist: Mary Louise Menendez
Assistant Production Manager: Diane Rose

Contributors

Designer: Teresa Cole
Project Editor: Lacie Pinyan
Recipe Developers and Testers: Martha Condra, Tamara Goldis, Erica Hopper, Kathleen Royal Phillips
Copy Editor: Erica Midkiff
Proofreader: Jacqueline Giovanelli
Indexer: Mary Ann Laurens
Nutritional Analyses: Wendy Ball, RD; Keri Matherne, RD
Interns: Susan Kemp, Emily Robinson, Katie Strasser, Maria Sanders
Photographers: Johnny Autry, Beau Gustafson, Beth Hontzas, Mary Britton Senseney
Photo Stylists: Mindi Shapiro Levine, Lydia DeGaris Pursell

Time Home Entertainment Inc.

Publisher: Jim Childs
Vice President, Strategy & Business Development: Steven Sandonato
Executive Director, Marketing Services: Carol Pittard
Executive Director, Retail & Special Sales: Tom Mifsud
Director, Bookazine Development & Marketing: Laura Adam
Executive Publishing Director: Joy Butts
Associate Publishing Director: Megan Pearlman
Finance Director: Glenn Buonocore
Associate General Counsel: Helen Wan

Cooking Light®

Editor: Scott Mowbray
Creative Director: Carla Frank
Executive Managing Editor: Phillip Rhodes
Executive Editor, Food: Ann Taylor Pittman
Special Publications Editor: Mary Simpson Creel, MS, RD
Senior Food Editors: Timothy Q. Cebula, Julianna Grimes
Senior Editor: Cindy Hatcher
Assistant Editor, Nutrition: Sidney Fry, MS, RD
Assistant Editors: Kimberly Holland, Phoebe Wu
Test Kitchen Director: Vanessa T. Pruett
Assistant Test Kitchen Director: Tiffany Vickers Davis
Recipe Testers and Developers: Robin Bashinsky, Adam Hickman, Deb Wise
Art Directors: Fernande Bondarenko, Shawna Kalish
Senior Deputy Art Director: Rachel Cardina Lasserre
Senior Designer: Anna Bird
Designer: Hagen Stegall
Assistant Designer: Nicole Gerrity
Photo Director: Kristen Schaefer
Assistant Photo Editor: Amy Delaune
Senior Photographer: Randy Mayor
Senior Photo Stylist: Cindy Barr
Photo Stylist: Leigh Ann Ross
Chief Food Stylist: Kellie Gerber Kelley
Food Styling Assistant: Blakeslee Wright
Copy Chief: Maria Parker Hopkins
Assistant Copy Chief: Susan Roberts
Research Editor: Michelle Gibson Daniels
Production Director: Liz Rhoades
Production Editor: Hazel R. Eddins
Assistant Production Editor: Josh Rutledge
Administrative Coordinator: Carol D. Johnson
CookingLight.com Editor: Allison Long Lowery
CookingLight.com Nutrition Editor: Holley Johnson Grainger, MS, RD
CookingLight.com Associate Editor/Producer: Mallory Daugherty Brasseale

To order additional publications, call 1-800-765-6400 or 1-800-491-0551

For more books to enrich your life, visit **oxmoorhouse.com**

To search, savor, and share thousands of recipes, visit **myrecipes.com**

Cover: Caribbean Black Bean Soup (page 238)
Back cover (clockwise from top left): Salmon, Asparagus, and Orzo Salad with Lemon-Dill Vinaigrette (page 111), Cilantro-Lime Chicken with Avocado Salsa (page 53), Strawberries with Crunchy Almond Topping (page 407), Seashell Salad with Buttermilk-Chive Dressing (page 115), Pork and Slaw Sandwiches (page 280), and Gruyère-Bacon Dip (page 337)

introduction

Whether you're looking for something hearty and healthy to feed your family or wanting a special dish to impress your guests, you'll find everything you need in *Cooking Light Dinner's Ready!* From filling pastas to savory soups and stews, this collection of test kitchen–approved favorites has something for everyone.

With more than 250 great-tasting and good-for-you recipes, this collection proves that you don't have to sacrifice time or flavor to prepare something the whole family can agree on. Tempt your taste buds with classic favorites like **Chicken Cacciatore** (page 301) or **Steak Tips with Peppered Mushroom Gravy** (page 129). Or spice up your usual weeknight fare with global flavors in dishes like **Sausage Jambalaya** (page 271), **Mexican Turkey Stew** (page 217), or **Indian Lamb Curry** (page 283).

And because you want more than just a collection of recipes, we've also included a Cooking Class with each main-dish chapter highlighting everything from how to make soup stocks from scratch, the pros and cons of dried and fresh pasta, to purchasing and safety instructions for chicken and quick slow-cooker cleanup.

In *Cooking Light Dinner's Ready!*, our dedicated staff of culinary professionals and registered dietitians gives you all the tools and recipes you'll need to prepare healthful, delicious meals any night of the week. Let these kitchen-tested recipes breathe new life into your dinner tonight.

The *Cooking Light* Editors

contents

chicken tonight!

cooking class

Chicken is a perennial favorite among *Cooking Light* readers—and with good reason. It is versatile, straightforward, and in our recipes, always delicious. With this Cooking Class highlighting all the ins and outs of cooking chicken, you'll be ready for chicken tonight!

Chicken Safety

Chicken is highly perishable and should be handled carefully to prevent food-borne illness. Check the "sell by" date on the package label before purchasing. This shows the last day the product should be sold.

Storing: Refrigerate raw chicken for up to two days and cooked chicken for up to three days. Raw skinless, boneless chicken can marinate in the refrigerator for up to 8 hours; raw chicken pieces with skin and bone can marinate for up to one day. Freeze uncooked chicken up to six months and cooked chicken up to three months.

Thawing: You can thaw frozen chicken in the refrigerator or in cold water. Allow about five hours per pound of frozen chicken to thaw in the refrig-

erator. For the cold-water method, submerge the chicken—still in its wrapping—in a sink or pot of cold water, and change the water every 30 minutes until it's thawed.

Handling: Wash your hands well with hot water and plenty of soap before and after handling raw chicken. Use hot water and soap to wash the cutting board and any utensils that come in contact with the chicken.

Cooking: To prevent food-borne illnesses, chicken must be cooked to 165°. For whole birds, use an instant-read thermometer inserted in the thickest part of the thigh to confirm the temperature. For breasts, legs, and thighs, pierce with the tip of a knife—when it's done, the flesh should be opaque, and the juices should run clear.

Chicken Glossary

Here's our guide to commonly purchased chicken.

Broiler-fryers: Broiler-fryers are about seven weeks old, and they weigh 3 to 4 pounds. They're good for making stock (they're not as meaty as roasters) and will work in any recipe that calls for a cut-up fryer.

Roasters: At three to five months old, roasters weigh 4 to 7 pounds. If you want to bake a whole chicken, look for a roaster—they have the highest meat-to-bone ratio.

Stewing hens: At 10 months to 1½ years old, stewing hens are literally tough old birds. They're best used for chicken and dumplings or soup; when roasted, they're almost jaw-exhausting.

Cornish game hen: The term Cornish game hen is a misnomer. These small birds are actually a cross between Cornish game roosters and White Rock hens; despite the gender-specific name, both male and female birds are sold. At a month old, they weigh about 1½ to 2 pounds. Roasting works best for these petite birds.

Boneless, skinless chicken breasts: We often use this cut in our Test Kitchen because chicken breasts are lean and versatile. You can buy them with the skin on, but be sure to remove the skin before eating the chicken—you can easily remove the skin and fat with kitchen shears.

Chicken thighs: Either bone-in or skinless, chicken thighs are higher in fat than breasts, but they have a succulent and hearty flavor and a firmer flesh that work well in dishes with a longer cook time.

Dark meat is higher in fat and generally works better in recipes that cook slowly.

Chicken roaster

The white meat, with the skin removed, contains the leanest meat.

Purchasing Info

When purchasing chicken there are many options. Let the ingredients list for the recipe be your guide.

Fresh whole chicken (broiler-fryers, roasters, and stewing hens): For more information on whole chickens see the chicken glossary on page 12.

Organic and free-range chicken: Organic and free-range chickens have a "cleaner" chicken flavor and a better texture than conventionally farmed chicken. The thing you need to consider is whether you believe they are worth the extra expense. Unless you're cooking simple roasted chicken, probably not.

Fresh chicken pieces (breasts, tenders, and thighs): Fresh chicken comes packaged in many ways. Read the labels carefully to check for specific pieces, size and weight, and for added flavor enhancers.

Frozen chicken: Individually frozen portions of bone-in and boneless breast halves, tenders, thighs, and drumsticks are readily available. They are frozen individually and packed loosely in resealable bags. Remove what you need for a given recipe, and keep the remainder frozen.

Precooked chicken: If your recipe calls for cooked chicken and you don't have any leftovers to use, you have options: poached chicken breasts, refrigerated or frozen cooked chicken, or store-cooked chicken. The store-cooked chicken (also known as deli-roasted or rotisserie chicken) is our favorite option. A rotisserie chicken keeps for three days in the refrigerator and is great to keep on hand for a quick meal.

Rotisserie chicken

Cooking Techniques

Sautéing

Chicken breasts are a staple of healthful cooking because they're lean and cook in a flash. Cook chicken breasts, deglaze the caramelized juice and browned bits in the pan with liquid, add a few other seasonings, and you're ready for supper in less than 30 minutes. For the best results, use a nonstick skillet, and scrape up the sauce thoroughly from the bottom of the pan to get the concentrated flavor left behind by sautéing.

How to sauté skinless, boneless chicken breasts and make pan sauce:

1. Trim away the fat and any small pieces of meat.
2. Place the breast between plastic wrap. Pound to a ½-inch thickness so it cooks quickly and evenly.
3. To tell if the chicken is done, pierce it with a fork. If the juices run clear, it's done.
4. After adding liquid to the pan, scrape the bottom to loosen the browned bits. This will add flavor to the sauce.
5. Pour the sauce into a measuring cup to be sure that it has reduced enough.

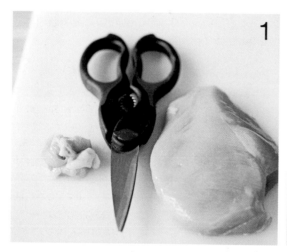

Consider your sautéed chicken a blank canvas. All you need to dress it up are pan and no-cook sauces. Here are six high-flavor options.

White Wine Sauce: Heat a skillet over medium-high heat. Coat pan with cooking spray. Add ⅓ cup finely chopped onion to pan; sauté 2 minutes, stirring frequently. Stir in ½ cup fat-free, lower-sodium chicken broth, ¼ cup dry white wine, and 2 tablespoons white wine vinegar; bring to a boil. Cook until reduced to ¼ cup (about 5 minutes). Remove from heat; stir in 2 tablespoons butter and 2 teaspoons finely chopped fresh chives. Yield: 6 tablespoons (serving size: 1½ tablespoons).

CALORIES 59; FAT 5.7g (sat 3.6g, mono 1.5g, poly 0.2g); PROTEIN 0.6g; CARB 1.6g; FIBER 0.4g; CHOL 15mg; IRON 0.2mg; SODIUM 90mg; CALC 8mg

Spicy Orange Sauce: Heat a skillet over medium-high heat; coat with cooking spray. Add 1 tablespoon grated ginger; sauté 1 minute, stirring constantly. Stir in ⅔ cup fat-free, lower-sodium chicken broth, 3 tablespoons orange marmalade, and 1½ tablespoons lower-sodium soy sauce; bring to a boil. Cook until mixture is slightly thick. Stir in 1½ teaspoons fresh lemon juice and ¾ teaspoon sambal oelek (or other hot chile sauce). Yield: about ¾ cup (serving size: about 3 tablespoons).

CALORIES 45; FAT 0.1g (sat 0g, mono 0.1g, poly 0g); PROTEIN 0.8g; CARB 11.2g; FIBER 0.4g; CHOL 0mg; IRON 0.2mg; SODIUM 273mg; CALC 10mg

Tangy Mustard Sauce: Heat 2 teaspoons olive oil in a skillet over medium-high heat. Add 2 minced garlic cloves to pan; sauté 30 seconds, stirring constantly. Stir in ¼ cup dry white wine, ¼ cup fat-free, lower-sodium chicken broth, 2 tablespoons maple syrup, and 2 tablespoons Dijon mustard; bring to a boil. Cook until reduced to ¼ cup (about 5 minutes), stirring occasionally. Stir in ¾ teaspoon chopped fresh rosemary and ½ teaspoon freshly ground black pepper. Yield: ¼ cup (serving size: 1 tablespoon).

CALORIES 54; FAT 2.3g (sat 0.3g, mono 1.7g, poly 0.3g); PROTEIN 0.3g; CARB 8.2g; FIBER 0.2g; CHOL 0mg; IRON 0.3mg; SODIUM 87mg; CALC 13mg

Parsley Pesto: Place 2 cups fresh flat-leaf parsley leaves, 2 tablespoons toasted pine nuts, 1½ tablespoons grated fresh Parmigiano-Reggiano cheese, 1 teaspoon extra-virgin olive oil, and ¼ teaspoon salt in a food processor; process until smooth. Yield: ½ cup (serving size: 2 tablespoons).

CALORIES 59; FAT 4.8g (sat 0.7g, mono 1.9g, poly 1.6g); PROTEIN 2.3g; CARB 2.8g; FIBER 1.2g; CHOL 2mg; IRON 2.1mg; SODIUM 211mg; CALC 64mg

Creamy White Sauce: Combine ¼ cup canola mayonnaise, 2 teaspoons white vinegar, 1 teaspoon fresh lemon juice, ½ teaspoon freshly ground black pepper, ¼ teaspoon salt, and 1 minced garlic clove, stirring well. Yield: about ⅓ cup (serving size: about 4 teaspoons).

CALORIES 47; FAT 4.5g (sat 0g, mono 2.5g, poly 1.5g); PROTEIN 0.1g; CARB 0.5g; FIBER 0.1g; CHOL 0mg; IRON 0mg; SODIUM 238mg; CALC 2.4mg

Classic Vinaigrette: Combine 1½ tablespoons red wine vinegar, 1 tablespoon chopped shallots, ¼ teaspoon salt, 1 tablespoon Dijon mustard, and ⅛ teaspoon pepper. Gradually add 3 tablespoons extra-virgin olive oil, stirring until incorporated. Yield: 6 tablespoons (serving size: 1½ tablespoons).

CALORIES 94; FAT 10.1g (sat 1.4g, mono 7.4g, poly 1.1g); PROTEIN 0.1g; CARB 0.7g; FIBER 0g; CHOL 0mg; IRON 0.1mg; SODIUM 178mg; CALC 2mg

Pan-Frying and Oven-Frying

Pan-frying entails cooking food in a moderate amount of fat in an uncovered pan. It's similar to sautéing but requires more fat and often lower temperatures. Oven-frying utilizes the oven to mimic deep-frying by breading foods and then baking using a moderate amount of oil. The coating of flour and breadcrumbs helps create the desired crisp crust and also insulates the chicken breast to prevent it from overcooking.

How to bread a chicken breast:

1. Pound chicken breast between 2 sheets of heavy-duty plastic wrap.

2. Working with 1 chicken breast at a time, dredge breast in flour, turning to coat. Shake off excess flour.

3. Dip floured chicken breast in egg mixture.

4. Dredge chicken breast in breadcrumb mixture.

Braising

Long, slow cooking is essential to success with this technique. This process marries the flavors, and the moist heat tenderizes inexpensive cuts of meat.

How to braise chicken:

1. Use a large deep skillet so the heat is diffused and food cooks evenly. The diameter of the base should be about three times the height of the sides. If it's too shallow, moisture will evaporate easily, and the food can dry out as it cooks. Check periodically, and if the liquid dips too far down, top it off. Start with large pieces of meat. Here we're using bone-in chicken pieces because they take longer to cook than boneless. Brown the meat in the skillet.

2. Begin to build flavor in the dish by adding vegetables, spices, and herbs. Add hearty ingredients like tough root vegetables, spices, and dried herbs to the skillet early, and allow them to cook and flavor the dish. It's best to garnish with delicate chopped fresh herbs just before serving.

3. Create a bouquet garni by wrapping ingredients such as sprigs of fresh herbs, peppercorns, or bay leaves in cheesecloth. Place the bundle in the skillet to infuse the cooking liquid and meat as the dish simmers.

4. To achieve the best results, partially submerge the meat in a flavorful liquid as it cooks. Broth, milk, cream, cider, beer, wine, or spirits are all good options. Plain water is also useful in casseroles.

Roasting

Few entrées are as familiar and welcoming as a succulent roasted chicken. It can be the star of both homey weeknight suppers and company-worthy dinners. Roasted chicken's broad appeal is well deserved because its neutral-tasting meat harmonizes with many flavors.

How to roast chicken and make gravy:

1. Separate the skin from the meat, and rub the seasoning mixture directly on the meat.

2. Tie the legs of the chicken together with kitchen twine for a professional presentation.

3. The bird cooks more evenly when it's elevated off the pan atop vegetables or a rack.

4. Insert the thermometer into the meaty part of the thigh to get an accurate temperature reading. This is the slowest-cooking part of the bird.

5. For a substantial fat savings, remove and discard the skin before serving.

6. Use a sharp knife to remove the legs first.

7. Hold the knife parallel to the chicken breast, and slice thinly.

8. Combine the pan drippings with a liquid, such as broth or wine, and drain off the fat.

9. Place the roasting pan over medium-high heat, and pour the liquid (along with the remaining drippings) back into the pan, scraping to loosen all the delicious browned bits. Add a bit of flour and a little more liquid, and cook until thick.

1

2

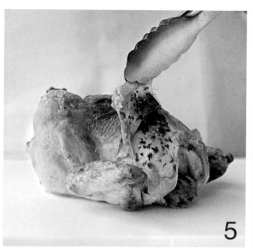

3

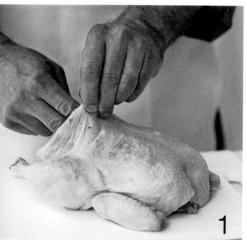

4

5

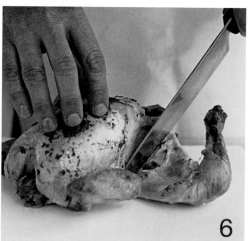

6

Grilling

Grilling chicken is an easy way to transform this humble food. You'll get the best results if you let the chicken stand out at room temperature before grilling.

How to grill chicken:

1. Prepare the grill for indirect grilling with one hot side and one side without a direct source of heat.

2. If you plan to baste with a glaze as the chicken cooks, remove the skin before cooking; this allows the flesh to absorb the flavor of the glaze and brown nicely at the same time. (Chicken that is not glazed should be grilled with the skin on to shield the meat and keep it moist.)

3. Brown the chicken over direct heat. Then cook it over indirect heat, brushing it with glaze (if using) each time it's turned. Be sure to let the chicken stand 10 minutes before serving.

Hot Chicken and Chips Retro

This recipe has a nostalgic appeal that harks back to the 1950s and '60s. If you make it ahead, don't add the potato chips until it's time to bake the casserole, or they'll become soggy.

Yield: 6 servings

4 cups chopped roasted skinless, boneless chicken breast (about 4 breasts)

¼ cup chopped green onions

¼ cup chopped red bell pepper

2 tablespoons finely chopped fresh flat-leaf parsley

1 (8-ounce) can sliced water chestnuts, drained and chopped

½ cup low-fat mayonnaise

¼ cup reduced-fat sour cream

2 tablespoons fresh lemon juice

2 teaspoons Dijon mustard

½ teaspoon salt

½ teaspoon freshly ground black pepper

Cooking spray

¾ cup (3 ounces) shredded Swiss cheese

¾ cup crushed baked potato chips (about 2 ounces)

1. Preheat oven to 400°.

2. Combine chicken and next 4 ingredients in a large bowl; stir well. Combine low-fat mayonnaise and next 5 ingredients in a small bowl, stirring with a whisk. Add mayonnaise mixture to chicken mixture; stir well to combine. Spoon chicken mixture into an 11 x 7–inch baking dish coated with cooking spray, and sprinkle with cheese. Top cheese evenly with chips. Bake at 400° for 13 minutes or until filling is bubbly and chips are golden.

CALORIES 321; FAT 10.9g (sat 4.1g, mono 2.6g, poly 1g); PROTEIN 34.3g; CARB 20.4g; FIBER 2.6g; CHOL 96mg; IRON 11.4mg; SODIUM 606mg; CALC 175mg

QUICK TIP

To crush baked potato chips for the casserole topping, place the chips in a large zip-top plastic bag. With a meat mallet or rolling pin, crush the chips by lightly pounding or rolling until you achieve the desired size and texture. This method makes clean-up a breeze and keeps crumbs in the bag.

Chicken Chilaquiles

For even more heat, add ¼ teaspoon ground red pepper to the tomatillo mixture. You can have this from kitchen to table in 45 minutes. Serve with coleslaw and fruit on the side.

Yield: 4 servings (serving size: 1½ cups)

2 cups shredded cooked chicken breast

½ cup chopped green onions

½ cup (2 ounces) shredded Monterey Jack cheese with jalapeño peppers, divided

2 tablespoons grated Parmesan cheese

1 teaspoon chili powder

¼ teaspoon salt

¼ teaspoon black pepper

¾ cup 1% low-fat milk

¼ cup chopped fresh cilantro

1 (11-ounce) can tomatillos, drained

1 (4.5-ounce) can chopped green chiles, drained

12 (6-inch) corn tortillas

Cooking spray

1. Preheat oven to 375°.

2. Combine cooked chicken, onions, ¼ cup Monterey Jack cheese, Parmesan, chili powder, salt, and pepper in a medium bowl. Place milk and next 3 ingredients in a blender or food processor; process until smooth.

3. Heat tortillas according to package directions. Pour ⅓ cup tomatillo mixture into bottom of an 11 x 7–inch baking dish coated with cooking spray. Arrange 4 corn tortillas in dish, and top with half of chicken mixture. Repeat layers with remaining tortillas and chicken mixture, ending with tortillas.

4. Pour remaining 1½ cups tomatillo mixture over tortillas; sprinkle with remaining ¼ cup Monterey Jack cheese. Bake at 375° for 20 minutes or until bubbly.

CALORIES 347; FAT 10.9g (sat 4.5g, mono 2.9g, poly 1.9g); PROTEIN 30.9g; CARB 33.3g; FIBER 5.9g; CHOL 79mg; IRON 1.5mg; SODIUM 560mg; CALC 272mg

Herbed Chicken and Dumplings

Fluffy herb-flecked dumplings, tender vegetables, and rich dark-meat chicken combine in this soul-satisfying comfort dish. Garnish each serving with a fresh sprig of parsley, if desired. This is a perfect, cozy dinner for two on a chilly night.

Yield: 2 servings (serving size: 2 cups)

Cooking spray

8 ounces skinless, boneless chicken thighs, cut into bite-sized pieces

¾ cup (¼-inch) diagonally cut celery

½ cup (¼-inch) diagonally cut carrot

½ cup chopped onion

⅛ teaspoon dried thyme

3 fresh parsley sprigs

1 bay leaf

3 cups fat-free, lower-sodium chicken broth

2.25 ounces all-purpose flour (about ½ cup)

1 tablespoon chopped fresh parsley

¼ teaspoon baking powder

¼ teaspoon salt

¼ cup 1% low-fat milk

1. Heat a large saucepan over medium-high heat. Coat pan with cooking spray. Add chicken to pan; cook 4 minutes, browning on all sides. Remove chicken from pan; keep warm. Add celery and next 5 ingredients to pan; sauté 5 minutes or until onion is tender. Return chicken to pan; cook 1 minute. Add broth to pan; bring mixture to a boil. Cover, reduce heat, and simmer 30 minutes.

2. Lightly spoon flour into a dry measuring cup; level with a knife. Combine flour, chopped parsley, baking powder, and salt in a medium bowl. Add milk, stirring just until moist. Spoon by heaping teaspoonfuls into broth mixture; cover and simmer 10 minutes or until dumplings are done. Discard parsley sprigs and bay leaf.

CALORIES 285; FAT 5.2g (sat 1.5g, mono 1.9g, poly 1.2g); PROTEIN 25g; CARB 35.2g; FIBER 3.1g; CHOL 55mg; IRON 3.4mg; SODIUM 596mg; CALC 133mg

Weeknight Coq au Vin

Serve this robust French classic over egg noodles to round out the meal.

Yield: 4 servings (serving size: 1 thigh, 1 drumstick, and ¾ cup sauce)

2 bacon slices, chopped

4 (4-ounce) bone-in chicken thighs, skinned

4 (4-ounce) chicken drumsticks, skinned

½ teaspoon salt

½ teaspoon freshly ground black pepper

¼ cup finely chopped fresh flat-leaf parsley, divided

1½ cups sliced cremini mushrooms

1½ cups dry red wine

1 cup chopped carrot

½ cup chopped shallots

½ cup fat-free, lower-sodium chicken broth

1 tablespoon brandy

1 teaspoon minced fresh thyme

2 teaspoons tomato paste

1 garlic clove, minced

1. Cook bacon in a large Dutch oven over medium-high heat 2 minutes. Sprinkle chicken with salt and pepper. Add chicken to pan; cook 2 minutes. Stir in 3 tablespoons parsley, mushrooms, and remaining ingredients; bring to a boil. Cover, reduce heat, and simmer 25 minutes or until chicken is done.

2. Remove chicken with a slotted spoon; keep warm. Bring cooking liquid to a boil; cook until reduced to 3 cups (about 6 minutes). Return chicken to pan; cook 1 minute or until thoroughly heated. Sprinkle with remaining 1 tablespoon parsley.

CALORIES 345; FAT 12.7g (sat 3.7g, mono 4.7g, poly 2.7g); PROTEIN 43.7g; CARB 11g; FIBER 1.6g; CHOL 150mg; IRON 3.3mg; SODIUM 595mg; CALC 60mg

INGREDIENT TIP

A good rule of thumb when cooking with wine is to use a wine that is the same or has similar qualities to the wine

you'll serve with the meal. For this traditional French dish, a dry red wine works well, particularly a Burgundy or pinot noir.

Chicken with Dark Beer

Residents of southern France like their chicken cooked in wine, preferably a rich red, but those living in the North go for the caramel intensity of dark beer laced with plenty of onions. The sweetness of the beer is enhanced with a spicing of juniper berries and a shot of gin. The traditional accompaniment would be mashed or boiled potatoes.

Yield: 4 servings

3 tablespoons all-purpose flour

½ teaspoon salt

¼ teaspoon freshly ground black pepper

2 bone-in chicken breast halves, skinned

2 bone-in chicken thighs, skinned

2 chicken drumsticks, skinned

2 tablespoons butter

1 tablespoon canola oil

3 tablespoons dry gin

¾ cup chopped celery

¾ cup chopped peeled carrot

½ cup chopped shallots (about 3 medium)

3 juniper berries, crushed

1 (8-ounce) package mushrooms, halved

3 sprigs fresh thyme

3 sprigs fresh flat-leaf parsley

1 bay leaf

1 cup dark beer

¼ cup whole-milk Greek yogurt

2 teaspoons white wine vinegar

1 tablespoon chopped fresh flat-leaf parsley

1. Combine first 3 ingredients; sprinkle evenly over both sides of chicken. Heat butter and oil in a large, deep skillet over medium-high heat. Add chicken to pan; sauté 5 minutes on each side or until browned. Remove pan from heat. Pour gin into one side of pan; return pan to heat. Ignite gin with a long match; let flames die down. Remove chicken from pan; set aside and keep warm.

2. Add celery, carrot, shallots, and juniper berries to pan; sauté 5 minutes or until vegetables are tender, stirring occasionally. Add mushrooms. Place thyme, parsley, and bay leaf on a double layer of cheesecloth. Gather edges of cheesecloth together; tie securely. Add cheesecloth bag to pan. Return chicken to pan, nestling into vegetable mixture. Stir in beer; bring to a simmer. Cover, reduce heat, and simmer 45 minutes or until a thermometer inserted in the meaty parts of chicken registers 165°. (Breasts may cook more quickly. Check them after 35 minutes, and remove them when they're done; keep warm.)

3. Discard cheesecloth bag. Remove chicken from pan; keep warm. Place pan over medium heat; stir in yogurt. Cook 1 minute or until thoroughly heated (do not boil, as the yogurt may curdle). Remove from heat; stir in vinegar. Taste and adjust seasoning, if desired. Place 1 chicken breast half or 1 drumstick and 1 thigh on each of 4 plates; top each serving with about ¾ cup sauce and vegetable mixture. Sprinkle with chopped parsley.

CALORIES 370; FAT 16g (sat 6.6g, mono 5g, poly 3g); PROTEIN 30.8g; CARB 15.1g; FIBER 1.4g; CHOL 103mg; IRON 2mg; SODIUM 465mg; CALC 55mg

MAKE-AHEAD TIP

The chicken can be prepared ahead and refrigerated in its sauce up to three days or frozen up to one month. Thaw, reheat, and add the yogurt and vinegar before serving.

Sherry-Soy Glazed Chicken

Pair this entrée with a simple rice pilaf: Heat 1 tablespoon canola oil in a large sauce-pan over medium-high heat. Add ½ cup chopped onion and 2 teaspoons grated peeled fresh ginger to pan; sauté 2 minutes. Stir in 1 cup water, ½ cup long-grain rice, and ¼ teaspoon salt; bring to a boil. Cover, reduce heat, and simmer 12 minutes or until liquid is absorbed. Remove from heat; stir in 2 tablespoons chopped fresh cilantro.

Yield: 4 servings (serving size: about ¾ cup)

3 tablespoons lower-sodium soy sauce, divided

2 tablespoons dry sherry

4 teaspoons cornstarch, divided

1 pound skinless, boneless chicken breast, cut into bite-sized pieces

½ cup fat-free, lower-sodium chicken broth

2 tablespoons oyster sauce

1 tablespoon honey

2 teaspoons sesame oil, divided

¾ cup chopped onion

½ cup chopped celery

½ cup chopped red bell pepper

1 tablespoon grated peeled fresh ginger

2 garlic cloves, minced

½ cup chopped green onions (about 3 green onions)

¼ cup chopped unsalted dry-roasted cashews

1. Combine 1 tablespoon soy sauce, sherry, 2 teaspoons corn-starch, and chicken in a bowl; toss well to coat. Combine remaining 2 tablespoons soy sauce, remaining 2 teaspoons cornstarch, broth, oyster sauce, and honey in a small bowl.

2. Heat 1 teaspoon oil in a large nonstick skillet over medium-high heat. Add chicken mixture to pan; sauté 3 minutes. Remove from pan. Heat remaining 1 teaspoon oil in pan. Add onion, celery, and bell pepper to pan; sauté 2 minutes. Add ginger and garlic; sauté 1 minute. Stir in broth mixture. Bring to a boil; cook 1 minute, stirring constantly. Remove from heat. Return chicken to pan. Sprinkle with green onions and cashews.

CALORIES 257; FAT 9g (sat 1.9g, mono 4.2g, poly 2.3g); PROTEIN 26g; CARB 17g; FIBER 1.9g; CHOL 63mg; IRON 2mg; SODIUM 584mg; CALC 45mg

Spicy Asian Noodles with Chicken

Add a snow pea sauté to complete the meal: Heat 2 teaspoons canola oil in a large nonstick skillet over medium-high heat. Add 2 minced garlic cloves; sauté 15 seconds. Add 2 cups trimmed fresh snow peas and 1 cup drained sliced canned water chestnuts; sauté 3 minutes or until crisp-tender. Remove from heat; stir in 1 tablespoon lower-sodium soy sauce.

Yield: 4 servings (serving size: 1¾ cups)

1 tablespoon dark sesame oil, divided

1 tablespoon grated peeled fresh ginger

2 garlic cloves, minced

2 cups chopped roasted chicken breast

½ cup chopped green onions

¼ cup chopped fresh cilantro

3 tablespoons lower-sodium soy sauce

2 tablespoons rice vinegar

2 tablespoons hoisin sauce

2 teaspoons sambal oelek (ground fresh chile paste)

1 (6.75-ounce) package thin rice sticks (rice-flour noodles)

2 tablespoons chopped dry-roasted peanuts

1. Heat 2 teaspoons oil in a small skillet over medium-high heat. Add ginger and garlic to pan; cook 45 seconds, stirring constantly. Place in a large bowl. Stir in remaining 1 teaspoon oil, chicken, and next 6 ingredients.

2. Cook noodles according to package directions. Drain and rinse under cold water; drain. Cut noodles into smaller pieces. Add noodles to bowl; toss well to coat. Sprinkle with peanuts.

CALORIES 381; FAT 8.1g (sat 1.5g, mono 3.2g, poly 2.7g); PROTEIN 27.5g; CARB 47.1g; FIBER 2.3g; CHOL 60mg; IRON 3.1mg; SODIUM 614mg; CALC 55mg

Curried Chicken and Cashews

Madras curry powder delivers more intensity than regular curry powder. For less heat, leave the chiles whole when you add them to the wok with the curry powder.

Yield: 4 servings (serving size: 1 cup chicken mixture and ¾ cup rice)

Sauce:

⅓ cup fat-free, lower-sodium chicken broth

3 tablespoons water

1½ tablespoons fish sauce

1 teaspoon sugar

1 teaspoon rice vinegar

Remaining Ingredients:

¾ pound skinless, boneless chicken breast

2 tablespoons canola oil, divided

1½ cups vertically sliced onion

1 tablespoon minced peeled fresh ginger

1 tablespoon minced garlic

1 teaspoon Madras curry powder

3 small dried hot red chiles, broken in half

⅓ cup chopped fresh cilantro

¼ cup chopped dry-roasted salted cashews

3 cups hot cooked short-grain rice

1. To prepare sauce, combine first 5 ingredients; set aside.

2. Cut chicken across grain into ¼-inch slices; cut slices into ½-inch-wide strips. Cut strips into 3-inch-long pieces.

3. Heat a 14-inch wok over high heat. Add 1 tablespoon oil to wok, swirling to coat. Add half of chicken to wok; stir-fry 2 minutes. Spoon cooked chicken into a bowl. Repeat procedure with 2 teaspoons oil and remaining chicken.

4. Add remaining 1 teaspoon oil to wok, swirling to coat. Add onion, ginger, and garlic to wok; stir-fry 1 minute or until lightly browned. Add curry powder and chiles; stir-fry 30 seconds. Add sauce and chicken to wok; stir-fry 1 minute. Spoon into a serving dish. Sprinkle with cilantro and cashews. Serve over rice.

CALORIES 439; FAT 13g (sat 1.7g, mono 6.9g, poly 3.2g); PROTEIN 26g; CARB 52.6g; FIBER 3.2g; CHOL 49mg; IRON 3.9mg; SODIUM 669mg; CALC 37mg

INGREDIENT TIP

Madras curry powder, named for a city in southern India, is hotter than standard curry powder. It quickly loses its pungency, so store it in an airtight container, and use it within two months.

Barley, Wild Rice, and Chicken Pilaf

This recipe has some of the creamy texture of a risotto but requires far less stirring.

Yield: 4 servings (serving size: 1 cup)

½ cup hot water

¼ cup dried porcini mushrooms, chopped

1 tablespoon olive oil

1 cup finely chopped onion (about 1 medium)

3 garlic cloves, minced

¾ cup uncooked pearl barley

¼ cup wild rice

2 teaspoons chopped fresh thyme

1 (14-ounce) can fat-free, lower-sodium chicken broth

2 cups chopped cooked chicken breast

½ cup (2 ounces) grated fresh Parmesan cheese

¼ cup chopped fresh parsley

¼ teaspoon salt

¼ teaspoon freshly ground black pepper

1. Combine ½ cup hot water and mushrooms; let stand 10 minutes or until mushrooms are tender. Set aside.

2. Heat oil in a large nonstick skillet over medium heat. Add onion; cook 1 minute, stirring frequently. Add garlic; cook 30 seconds, stirring frequently. Add barley, rice, and thyme; cook 5 minutes or until lightly browned, stirring frequently. Stir in mushroom mixture and broth. Cover, reduce heat, and simmer 40 minutes or until barley is tender. Stir in chicken and cheese; cook 5 minutes or until thoroughly heated. Stir in parsley, salt, and pepper.

CALORIES 409; FAT 12.4g (sat 3.9g, mono 5.6g, poly 2g); PROTEIN 31.6g; CARB 42.8g; FIBER 7.7g; CHOL 68mg; IRON 2.7mg; SODIUM 515mg; CALC 160mg

WINE TIP

A chicken breast does not always demand to be paired with white wine, especially when it's accompanied by porcini mushrooms and wild rice. Serve an easy-drinking wine, like a pinot noir.

Spiedini of Chicken and Zucchini with Almond Salsa Verde

Spiedini is Italian for "little skewers." These grilled kebabs are paired with a zesty sauce of herbs, nuts, citrus, and capers.

Yield: 6 servings (serving size: 2 spiedini and 2½ tablespoons salsa)

Salsa:

1 cup chopped fresh parsley

2 tablespoons chopped almonds, toasted

2 tablespoons chopped fresh chives

3 tablespoons capers, chopped

½ teaspoon grated lemon rind

3 tablespoons fresh lemon juice

1 tablespoon extra-virgin olive oil

½ teaspoon chopped fresh thyme

½ teaspoon chopped fresh oregano

¼ teaspoon kosher salt

⅛ teaspoon freshly ground black pepper

1 garlic clove, minced

Spiedini:

1½ pounds skinless, boneless chicken breast, cut into 1-inch pieces

6 small zucchini, cut into 1-inch slices (about 1¼ pounds)

Cooking spray

¼ teaspoon kosher salt

⅛ teaspoon freshly ground black pepper

1. Soak 12 (10-inch) wooden skewers in water 30 minutes to prevent burning.

2. Prepare grill to medium-high heat.

3. To prepare salsa, combine first 12 ingredients; set aside.

4. To prepare spiedini, thread chicken and zucchini alternately onto each of 12 (10-inch) skewers. Coat spiedini with cooking spray; sprinkle evenly with ¼ teaspoon salt and ⅛ teaspoon pepper. Place on grill rack; grill 6 minutes or until done, turning once. Serve with salsa.

CALORIES 187; FAT 5.5g (sat 0.9g, mono 2.9g, poly 1.1g); PROTEIN 28.7g; CARB 6.3g; FIBER 2.2g; CHOL 66mg; IRON 2.1mg; SODIUM 376mg; CALC 56mg

MAKE-AHEAD TIP

For a backyard barbecue, prepare the salsa up to a day ahead, and assemble the skewers earlier in the day. Coat with cooking spray and seasonings just before grilling.

Lemon-Grilled Chicken Breasts

To round out your meal, serve this versatile grilled chicken with a couscous and pine nut pilaf and grilled asparagus. Garnish with grilled lemon slices, if desired.

Yield: 7 servings (serving size: 1 chicken breast half)

3 tablespoons fresh lemon juice

2 tablespoons extra-virgin olive oil

2 garlic cloves, minced

7 (6-ounce) skinless, boneless chicken breast halves

½ teaspoon kosher salt

½ teaspoon freshly ground black pepper

Cooking spray

1. Prepare grill to medium-high heat.

2. Combine first 4 ingredients in a large zip-top plastic bag; seal. Marinate in refrigerator 30 minutes, turning occasionally. Remove chicken from bag; discard marinade. Sprinkle chicken evenly with salt and pepper.

3. Place chicken on grill rack coated with cooking spray; grill 6 minutes on each side or until done.

CALORIES 159; FAT 3.5g (sat 0.7g, mono 1.8g, poly 0.6g); PROTEIN 29.5g; CARB 0.5g; FIBER 0.1g; CHOL 74mg; IRON 1mg; SODIUM 218mg; CALC 16mg

Grilled Cumin Chicken with Fresh Tomatillo Sauce

Bring the heat of the Southwest to the weeknight dinner table with this delicious take on chicken. Serve with chipotle rice: Combine 1 cup long-grain rice and 2 cups fat-free, lower-sodium chicken broth in a medium saucepan; bring to a boil. Cover, reduce heat, and simmer 15 minutes or until liquid is absorbed. Stir in ¼ cup thinly sliced green onions and ½ teaspoon minced chipotle chile, canned in adobo sauce.

Yield: 4 servings (serving size: 1 chicken breast half and about 5 tablespoons sauce)

2 teaspoons olive oil

½ teaspoon ground cumin

⅛ teaspoon freshly ground black pepper

2 garlic cloves, minced

4 (6-ounce) skinless, boneless chicken breast halves

½ pound tomatillos

½ cup fat-free, lower-sodium chicken broth

¼ cup cilantro leaves

¼ cup chopped green onions

2 tablespoons fresh lime juice

½ teaspoon sugar

¼ teaspoon salt

1 garlic clove, chopped

1 jalapeño pepper, seeded and chopped

¼ teaspoon salt

Cooking spray

1. Prepare grill to medium-high heat.

2. Combine first 4 ingredients in a large zip-top plastic bag. Add chicken to bag; seal and let stand 15 minutes.

3. Discard husks and stems from tomatillos. Combine tomatillos and broth in a small saucepan over medium-high heat; cover and cook 8 minutes. Drain and cool slightly. Place tomatillos, cilantro, and next 6 ingredients in a food processor; process until smooth.

4. Remove chicken from bag; discard marinade. Sprinkle chicken evenly with ¼ teaspoon salt. Place on a grill rack coated with cooking spray; grill 6 minutes on each side or until chicken is done. Serve with tomatillo sauce.

CALORIES 237; FAT 5.1g (sat 1g, mono 2.3g, poly 1g); PROTEIN 40.4g; CARB 6g; FIBER 1.5g; CHOL 99mg; IRON 1.9mg; SODIUM 465mg; CALC 35mg

INGREDIENT TIP

Tomatillos are an apple-green fruit with tangy flavor and a papery husk that splits  *open as the fruit matures. They're easy to find at most supermarkets and add authentic Southwestern flavor to recipes.*

Marinated Grilled Chicken Breasts with Watermelon-Jalapeño Salsa

Sweet watermelon perfectly complements the earthy spices—oregano, chili powder, and cumin—used to marinate juicy chicken breasts.

Yield: 4 servings (serving size: 1 chicken breast half and 1 cup salsa)

1 tablespoon chopped fresh oregano

1 tablespoon extra-virgin olive oil

1 teaspoon chili powder

¾ teaspoon ground cumin

½ teaspoon salt

3 garlic cloves, minced

4 (6-ounce) skinless, boneless chicken breast halves

Cooking spray

2 cups (½-inch) cubed seeded watermelon

1 cup (½-inch) cubed peeled ripe mango

¼ cup finely chopped red onion

2 tablespoons chopped fresh cilantro

2 tablespoons finely chopped seeded jalapeño pepper (about 1 small)

1 tablespoon fresh lime juice

½ teaspoon sugar

¼ teaspoon salt

1. Combine first 6 ingredients in a large zip-top plastic bag. Add chicken to bag; seal. Marinate in refrigerator up to 4 hours, turning bag occasionally.
2. Prepare grill.
3. Place chicken on grill rack coated with cooking spray. Grill 5 minutes on each side or until done. Combine watermelon and remaining ingredients. Serve watermelon mixture with chicken.

CALORIES 304; FAT 8.3g (sat 1.8g, mono 4.1g, poly 1.4g); PROTEIN 40.7g; CARB 15.9g; FIBER 1.5g; CHOL 108mg; IRON 1.8mg; SODIUM 540mg; CALC 44mg

SAFETY TIP

When cutting or seeding hot peppers, wear rubber gloves to prevent your hands from being burned. To seed the peppers, slice off the stem end, and cut the pepper in half lengthwise. Remove the seeds with a knife or by running your finger along the inside of the vein, scraping off the seeds. Stack the two pepper halves on top of each other, and cut into irregular pieces about the size of peas.

Marinated Grilled Chicken Legs

Here's a recipe that's sure to be a hit at your next cookout. It's quick and easy and is made with ingredients you're likely to already have on hand. For a variation, consider substituting pineapple juice for the orange juice, or lime juice for the lemon.

Yield: 4 servings (serving size: 2 drumsticks)

1 cup fresh orange juice

2 tablespoons fresh lemon juice

4 teaspoons lower-sodium soy sauce

1 tablespoon dry sherry

1½ teaspoons minced garlic

1½ teaspoons balsamic vinegar

1½ teaspoons basil oil

1 teaspoon onion powder

1 teaspoon dark sesame oil

½ teaspoon salt

¼ teaspoon hot pepper sauce

8 chicken drumsticks (about
2¼ pounds), skinned

Cooking spray

Green onion strips (optional)

1. Combine first 11 ingredients in a large zip-top plastic bag. Add chicken to bag; seal. Marinate in refrigerator 2 hours, turning bag occasionally.
2. Prepare grill.
3. Remove chicken from bag, reserving marinade. Place reserved marinade in a small saucepan; cook over medium heat 3 minutes. Place chicken on grill coated with cooking spray; grill 30 minutes or until chicken is done, turning and basting occasionally with reserved marinade. Garnish with green onion strips, if desired.

CALORIES 215; FAT 7.5g (sat 1.8g, mono 2.8g, poly 1.8g); PROTEIN 30g; CARB 4.4g; FIBER 0.1g; CHOL 97mg; IRON 1.5mg; SODIUM 339mg; CALC 18mg

Spiced Chicken Kebabs

Yield: 8 servings (serving size: 1 kebab and about 2 tablespoons raita)

Kebabs:

¾ cup plain low-fat yogurt

1 tablespoon grated peeled fresh ginger

2 teaspoons ground coriander

2 teaspoons paprika

1 teaspoon ground cumin

¼ teaspoon ground cardamom

¼ teaspoon ground turmeric

¼ teaspoon saffron threads, crushed

⅛ teaspoon ground cinnamon

⅛ teaspoon ground cloves

3 garlic cloves, minced

2 pounds skinless, boneless chicken thighs, cut into 1-inch chunks

1 red onion, cut into 1-inch chunks

1 large red bell pepper, cut into 1-inch chunks (about 8 ounces)

1 medium zucchini, cut into 1-inch chunks (about 8 ounces)

Cooking spray

½ teaspoon salt

½ teaspoon freshly ground black pepper

Raita:

½ cup plain low-fat yogurt

⅓ cup diced seeded tomato

¼ cup cucumber, peeled, seeded, grated, and squeezed dry

¼ cup reduced-fat sour cream

1 tablespoon minced seeded jalapeño

1½ teaspoons chopped fresh cilantro

¼ teaspoon ground cumin

¼ teaspoon salt

1. Soak 8 (12-inch) wooden skewers in water 30 minutes to prevent burning.

2. To prepare kebabs, combine first 12 ingredients in a large zip-top plastic bag; seal and marinate in refrigerator overnight, turning bag occasionally.

3. Prepare grill.

4. Remove chicken from bag; discard marinade. Thread chicken, onion, bell pepper, and zucchini alternately on each of 8 (12-inch) wooden skewers. Coat kebabs with cooking spray, and sprinkle with ½ teaspoon salt and black pepper. Place kebabs on grill rack coated with cooking spray. Grill 25 minutes or until chicken is done, turning occasionally. Remove from grill; keep warm.

5. To prepare raita, combine ½ cup yogurt and remaining ingredients in a small bowl. Serve with kebabs.

CALORIES 189; FAT 6g (sat 2g, mono 1.7g, poly 1.3g); PROTEIN 24.9g; CARB 8.5g; FIBER 1.7g; CHOL 99mg; IRON 1.7mg; SODIUM 344mg; CALC 81mg

INGREDIENT TIP

Saffron has always been the world's most expensive spice, but you need only a few dried stigmas to color a dish golden yellow and impart a warm, aromatic quality.

Grilled Chicken with Sriracha Glaze

Dense, bone-in chicken leg quarters benefit from long, slow cooking over indirect heat. The less intense heat also prevents the sweet glaze from burning. Customize the glaze according to what you have on hand; try pineapple preserves or apple jelly in place of mango jam, for example, or hot pepper sauce instead of Sriracha. Serve with a simple slaw of cabbage, carrots, lime juice, and sugar.

Yield: 4 servings (serving size: 1 leg-thigh quarter and 1 tablespoon mango mixture)

⅔ cup mango jam

2 tablespoons finely chopped fresh chives

2 tablespoons rice vinegar

2 tablespoons Sriracha

1 tablespoon olive oil

4 (12-ounce) bone-in chicken leg-thigh quarters, skinned

½ teaspoon kosher salt

¼ teaspoon freshly ground black pepper

1. Prepare grill for indirect grilling. If using a gas grill, heat one side to medium-high and leave one side with no heat. If using a charcoal grill, arrange hot coals on either side of charcoal grate, leaving an empty space in the middle.

2. Combine mango jam, chives, vinegar, and Sriracha, stirring until smooth. Reserve ¼ cup mango mixture; set aside.

3. Brush oil evenly over chicken. Sprinkle chicken with salt and pepper.

4. Carefully remove grill rack. Place a disposable foil pan on unheated part of grill. Carefully return grill rack to grill. Place chicken on grill rack over unheated part. Brush chicken with about 2 tablespoons remaining mango mixture. Close lid; grill 90 minutes or until a thermometer inserted into meaty part of thigh registers 165°, turning chicken and brushing with about 2 tablespoons mango mixture every 20 minutes. Transfer the chicken to a platter. Drizzle chicken with reserved ¼ cup mango mixture.

CALORIES 326; FAT 10.4g (sat 2.3g, mono 4.7g, poly 2.1g); PROTEIN 38.7g; CARB 18.2g; FIBER 2.7g; CHOL 154mg; IRON 4.5mg; SODIUM 515mg; CALC 102mg

INGREDIENT TIP

Sriracha is a moderately hot and spicy chili sauce that's reminiscent of barbecue sauce. The most common brand, Huy

Fong, comes in a clear plastic squeeze bottle with a rooster on the label and a bright green cap.

Chicken, Mushroom, and Gruyère Quesadillas

Build on the traditional Mexican classic by adding fun new ingredients like sliced mushrooms and a different creamy cheese. Watermelon-jicama salad is a refreshing side for this easy summer dish: Combine 4 cups (½-inch) cubed seedless watermelon, 1½ cups (½-inch) cubed peeled jicama, 1 cup chopped English cucumber, and ½ cup chopped red onion. Add 2 tablespoons fresh lemon juice, 2 teaspoons sugar, and 1 teaspoon olive oil; toss well.

Yield: 4 servings (serving size: ½ quesadilla)

1 teaspoon olive oil

1 cup presliced mushrooms

½ cup thinly sliced onion

⅛ teaspoon salt

⅛ teaspoon freshly ground black pepper

1 teaspoon minced garlic

1 tablespoon sherry or red wine vinegar

2 (10-inch) fat-free flour tortillas

1 cup shredded cooked chicken breast (about 8 ounces)

1 cup arugula

½ cup (2 ounces) shredded Gruyère cheese

Cooking spray

1. Heat a large nonstick skillet over medium-high heat. Add olive oil to pan; swirl to coat. Add mushrooms, sliced onion, salt, and pepper to pan; sauté 5 minutes. Stir in garlic, and sauté 30 seconds. Add vinegar; cook 30 seconds or until liquid almost evaporates.

2. Arrange half of mushroom mixture over half of each tortilla. Top each tortilla with ½ cup chicken, ½ cup arugula, and ¼ cup cheese; fold tortillas in half.

3. Wipe pan clean with a paper towel. Heat pan over medium heat. Coat pan with cooking spray. Add tortillas to pan. Place a heavy skillet on top of tortillas; cook 2 minutes on each side or until crisp.

CALORIES 270; FAT 8.9g (sat 3.7g, mono 3g, poly 0.8g); PROTEIN 25.2g; CARB 20.3g; FIBER 3g; CHOL 64mg; IRON 1.7mg; SODIUM 391mg; CALC 242mg

INGREDIENT TIP

Use baby spinach in place of arugula, if you like.

Fiesta Chicken Tacos with Mango and Jicama Salad

Try this with a side of chipotle *refritos:* Combine 1 tablespoon fresh lime juice, 1 teaspoon minced canned chipotle chile in adobo sauce, 1 (16-ounce) can refried beans, and 1 minced garlic clove in a saucepan. Cook over medium heat 5 minutes or until thoroughly heated. Sprinkle with 2 teaspoons chopped fresh cilantro.

Yield: 4 servings (serving size: 2 tacos)

Salad:

¾ cup (3-inch) julienne-cut peeled jicama

½ cup sliced peeled ripe mango

¼ cup presliced red onion

1 tablespoon fresh lime juice

½ teaspoon sugar

1½ teaspoons chopped fresh cilantro

¼ teaspoon salt

Dash of black pepper

Tacos:

1 tablespoon olive oil, divided

1 pound skinless, boneless chicken breast, cut into thin strips

½ teaspoon chili powder

½ teaspoon ground cumin

⅛ teaspoon ground chipotle chile pepper

1 cup presliced red bell pepper

1 cup presliced red onion

¼ teaspoon salt

8 (6-inch) corn tortillas

1 cup mixed salad greens

1. To prepare salad, combine first 8 ingredients.

2. To prepare tacos, heat 2 teaspoons oil in a large nonstick skillet over medium-high heat. Sprinkle chicken evenly with chili powder, cumin, and chipotle pepper. Add chicken mixture to pan; sauté 3 minutes. Remove from pan.

3. Heat remaining 1 teaspoon oil in pan. Add bell pepper and 1 cup onion; cook 3 minutes or until crisp-tender. Return chicken mixture to pan; cook 2 minutes or until chicken is done. Sprinkle with ¼ teaspoon salt.

4. Heat tortillas according to package directions. Arrange 2 table-spoons mixed greens, about ⅓ cup chicken mixture, and about 2 tablespoons salad in each tortilla; fold over.

CALORIES 320; FAT 6.4g (sat 1.1g, mono 3.2g, poly 1.3g); PROTEIN 30.4g; CARB 36.1g; FIBER 5.8g; CHOL 66mg; IRON 2.2mg; SODIUM 471mg; CALC 129mg

INGREDIENT TIP

Find jicama year-round in the produce section of many supermarkets and Latin American markets. Select firm, dry jicama roots. Skin should not appear shriveled, bruised, or blemished.

Chicken Scaloppine with Broccoli Rabe

If you can't find cutlets, place chicken breast halves between two sheets of heavy-duty plastic wrap, and pound to ¼-inch thickness using a meat mallet. Broccoli florets can be substituted for broccoli rabe; the cooking time may be a little longer, though. Add a side of roasted potato wedges and carrots, if desired.

Yield: 4 servings (serving size: 1 cutlet and ½ cup broccoli rabe mixture)

1 tablespoon olive oil

⅓ cup Italian-seasoned breadcrumbs

¼ teaspoon black pepper

4 (6-ounce) skinless, boneless chicken breast cutlets

½ cup dry white wine

½ cup fat-free, lower-sodium chicken broth

3 tablespoons fresh lemon juice

1 teaspoon butter

1 pound broccoli rabe (rapini), cut into 3-inch pieces

2 tablespoons chopped fresh parsley

2 tablespoons capers, rinsed and drained

4 lemon slices (optional)

Parsley sprigs (optional)

1. Heat oil in a large nonstick skillet over medium-high heat.

2. Combine breadcrumbs and pepper in a shallow dish; dredge chicken in breadcrumb mixture. Add chicken to pan; cook 3 minutes on each side or until done. Remove from pan; keep warm.

3. Add wine, broth, juice, and butter to pan, scraping pan to loosen browned bits. Stir in broccoli rabe; cover and cook 3 minutes or until broccoli rabe is tender. Stir in chopped parsley and capers. Serve chicken over broccoli rabe mixture. Garnish with lemon slices and parsley sprigs, if desired.

CALORIES 318; FAT 7.4g (sat 1.7g, mono 3.3g, poly 1g); PROTEIN 44.3g; CARB 14g; FIBER 3.9g; CHOL 101mg; IRON 2.9mg; SODIUM 577mg; CALC 102mg

Chicken with Provençal Sauce

Capturing every morsel of chicken flavor is the secret to this quick-to-prepare dinner favorite. The tiny browned bits that remain in the skillet after the chicken is cooked are key. Serve with roasted potato wedges.

Yield: 4 servings (serving size: 1 chicken breast half and about 2 tablespoons sauce)

4 (6-ounce) skinless, boneless chicken breast halves

¼ teaspoon salt

¼ teaspoon freshly ground black pepper

1½ tablespoons olive oil

1 garlic clove, minced

1 cup fat-free, lower-sodium chicken broth

1½ teaspoons dried herbes de Provence

1 teaspoon butter

1 teaspoon fresh lemon juice

Thyme sprigs (optional)

1. Place each chicken breast half between 2 sheets of heavy-duty plastic wrap; pound to ½-inch thickness using a meat mallet or rolling pin. Sprinkle chicken evenly with salt and pepper.

2. Heat oil in a large nonstick skillet over medium heat. Add chicken; cook 6 minutes on each side or until done. Remove chicken from pan; keep warm.

3. Add garlic to pan; cook 1 minute, stirring constantly. Add broth and herbes de Provence; bring to a boil, scraping pan to loosen browned bits. Cook until broth mixture is reduced to ½ cup (about 3 minutes). Remove from heat; add butter and lemon juice, stirring until butter melts. Serve sauce over chicken. Garnish with thyme sprigs, if desired.

CALORIES 248; FAT 8.2g (sat 1.8g, mono 4.5g, poly 1g); PROTEIN 40.2g; CARB 1g; FIBER 0.3g; CHOL 101mg; IRON 1.5mg; SODIUM 376mg; CALC 32mg

INGREDIENT TIP

With a heady combination of dried basil, thyme, marjoram, rosemary, lavender, and sage, herbes de Provence is a classic French seasoning. Try it in other Mediterranean dishes, such as pasta sauce or baked black olives.

Sesame-Orange Chicken

Ground sesame seeds thicken the sauce as it cooks. Serve with a salad and bread.

Yield: 4 servings (serving size: 1 chicken breast half and 3 tablespoons sauce)

2 tablespoons sesame seeds, toasted

1 tablespoon grated orange rind

¼ teaspoon salt, divided

Dash of ground red pepper

4 (6-ounce) skinless, boneless chicken breast halves

2 teaspoons canola oil

1 teaspoon butter

1 cup fat-free, lower-sodium chicken broth

⅓ cup orange juice

1 tablespoon whipping cream

1. Place sesame seeds, rind, ⅛ teaspoon salt, and pepper in a food processor; process until mixture resembles coarse meal.
2. Place each chicken breast half between 2 sheets of heavy-duty plastic wrap; pound to ¼-inch thickness using a meat mallet or rolling pin. Sprinkle chicken evenly with ⅛ teaspoon salt.
3. Heat oil and butter in a large nonstick skillet over medium heat until butter melts. Add chicken; cook 6 minutes on each side or until done. Remove chicken from pan; keep warm.
4. Add ground sesame mixture to pan, stirring with a whisk. Add broth, and bring to a boil, scraping pan to loosen browned bits. Cook broth mixture until reduced to ⅔ cup (about 3 minutes). Add orange juice and cream; cook 30 seconds, stirring constantly. Serve sauce over chicken.

CALORIES 271; FAT 9.1g (sat 2.5g, mono 3.4g, poly 2.2g); PROTEIN 41.1g; CARB 4g; FIBER 0.7g; CHOL 106mg; IRON 1.9mg; SODIUM 377mg; CALC 70mg

QUICK TIP

Pounding chicken breast halves cuts the cooking time in half while leaving the chicken moist and tender. To easily pound a chicken breast, place each breast

between two sheets of heavy-duty plastic wrap; pound to desired thickness— usually ¼- to ½-inch thick—using a meat mallet or rolling pin.

Moroccan Chicken with Fruit and Olive Topping

The pairing of dried fruit and olives is also characteristic of other North African cuisines, such as Tunisian and Algerian. Serve over Israeli couscous, a pearl-like pasta; sprinkle with chopped green onions.

Yield: 4 servings (serving size: 1 chicken breast half and about ⅓ cup fruit mixture)

1 tablespoon olive oil, divided

½ teaspoon salt

¼ teaspoon black pepper

¼ teaspoon dried thyme

4 (6-ounce) skinless, boneless chicken breasts

½ cup prechopped onion

2 teaspoons minced garlic

¾ cup dried mixed fruit

½ cup dry white wine

½ cup fat-free, lower-sodium chicken broth

¼ cup chopped pitted green olives

⅛ teaspoon salt

⅛ teaspoon black pepper

1. Heat 2 teaspoons oil in a large nonstick skillet over medium-high heat. Sprinkle ½ teaspoon salt, ¼ teaspoon pepper, and thyme evenly over chicken. Add chicken to pan; cook 4 minutes on each side or until done. Remove from pan; cover and keep warm.

2. Heat remaining 1 teaspoon oil in pan. Add onion to pan; sauté 2 minutes until tender. Add garlic to pan; sauté 30 seconds. Add fruit and remaining ingredients to pan; cook 5 minutes or until liquid almost evaporates. Serve over chicken.

CALORIES 346; FAT 7.5g (sat 1g, mono 4.3g, poly 1.3g); PROTEIN 40.6g; CARB 26g; FIBER 2.1g; CHOL 99mg; IRON 2.4mg; SODIUM 591mg; CALC 45mg

INGREDIENT TIP

Pearl-like Israeli couscous, also known as maftoul, *has larger-sized grains than regular couscous and takes on the consistency of macaroni when prepared. It cooks longer than regular couscous due*

to its size, but its size allows it to absorb plenty of liquid and flavor. Look for it in specialty and Middle Eastern markets.

Chicken with Dried Plums and Sage

Add quick-cooking whole wheat couscous and steamed green beans.

Yield: 4 servings (serving size: 1 chicken breast half and about ½ cup sauce)

4 (6-ounce) skinless, boneless chicken breast halves

2 tablespoons chopped fresh sage, divided

½ teaspoon salt

¼ teaspoon black pepper, divided

4 teaspoons olive oil, divided

2 cups thinly sliced onion (about 1 large)

½ cup dry white wine

½ cup fat-free, lower-sodium chicken broth

12 pitted dried plums, halved

1½ teaspoons balsamic vinegar

1. Place each chicken breast half between 2 sheets of heavy-duty plastic wrap; pound to ½-inch thickness using a meat mallet or small heavy skillet. Sprinkle chicken with 1 tablespoon sage, salt, and ⅛ teaspoon pepper.

2. Heat 2 teaspoons oil in a large nonstick skillet over medium heat. Add chicken to pan; cook 3 minutes on each side or until done. Remove chicken from pan; keep warm. Heat remaining 2 teaspoons oil in pan. Add onion to pan; cook 3 minutes or until tender. Stir in wine and broth; bring to a boil. Add remaining 1 tablespoon sage and dried plums to pan; cook 4 minutes or until mixture thickens. Stir in remaining ⅛ teaspoon pepper and vinegar. Serve with chicken.

CALORIES 301; FAT 8.7g (sat 1.8g, mono 4.7g, poly 1.4g); PROTEIN 35.4g; CARB 19.8g; FIBER 2.3g; CHOL 94mg; IRON 1.6mg; SODIUM 438mg; CALC 49mg

Cilantro-Lime Chicken with Avocado Salsa

Here's a terrific recipe for a busy weeknight or for a casual alfresco dinner party. It's especially wonderful in the summer since it's so simple and flavorful. Serve with saffron rice to round out the meal.

Yield: 4 servings (serving size: 1 chicken breast half and about ¼ cup salsa)

Chicken:

2 tablespoons minced fresh cilantro

2½ tablespoons fresh lime juice

1½ tablespoons olive oil

4 (6-ounce) skinless, boneless chicken breast halves

¼ teaspoon salt

Cooking spray

Salsa:

1 cup chopped plum tomato (about 2)

2 tablespoons finely chopped onion

2 teaspoons fresh lime juice

¼ teaspoon salt

⅛ teaspoon freshly ground black pepper

1 avocado, peeled and finely chopped

1. To prepare chicken, combine first 4 ingredients in a large bowl; toss and let stand 3 minutes. Remove chicken from marinade; discard marinade. Sprinkle chicken evenly with ¼ teaspoon salt. Heat a grill pan over medium-high heat. Coat pan with cooking spray. Add chicken to pan; cook 6 minutes on each side or until done.

2. To prepare salsa, combine tomato and next 4 ingredients in a medium bowl. Add avocado; stir gently to combine. Serve salsa over chicken.

CALORIES 289; FAT 13.2g (sat 2.4g, mono 7.5g, poly 1.9g); PROTEIN 35.6g; CARB 6.6g; FIBER 3.6g; CHOL 94mg; IRON 1.6mg; SODIUM 383mg; CALC 29mg

FLAVOR TIP

A three-minute dip in a pungent marinade is all that's needed to deliver big flavor to these chicken breasts. In addition, just-squeezed citrus brightens the taste of the chicken and adds zip to the simple toss-together salsa.

Citrus Chicken

This spicy sauce works equally well with fish or pork.

Yield: 4 servings

¼ **cup orange juice**

½ **teaspoon grated lime rind**

2 **tablespoons fresh lime juice**

2 **tablespoons chopped fresh thyme**

2 **teaspoons minced garlic**

1 **teaspoon grated orange rind**

¼ **teaspoon salt**

⅛ **teaspoon ground red pepper**

1 **pound skinless, boneless chicken breast cutlets**

1 **tablespoon olive oil**

Cooking spray

6 **cups bagged prewashed baby spinach**

1. Combine first 8 ingredients in a small bowl, stirring well with a whisk. Pour ¼ cup juice mixture into a large zip-top plastic bag. Add chicken to bag. Seal; let stand 5 minutes. Add oil to remaining juice mixture; stir well with a whisk.

2. Heat a large nonstick skillet over medium-high heat. Coat pan with cooking spray. Remove chicken from bag; discard marinade. Add chicken to pan; cook 4 minutes on each side or until done. Place 1½ cups spinach on each of 4 plates. Divide chicken evenly among servings; top each serving with 1 tablespoon juice mixture.

CALORIES 183; FAT 4.9g (sat 0.9g, mono 2.8g, poly 0.7g); PROTEIN 27.4g; CARB 7.1g; FIBER 2.1g; CHOL 66mg; IRON 2.3mg; SODIUM 278mg; CALC 50mg

INGREDIENT TIP

Be sure to wash the limes before grating or squeezing. When grating, remove only the colored part of the peel; the white part is bitter. You'll get more juice out of a lime if you bring it to room temperature before squeezing.

Peanut-Crusted Chicken with Pineapple Salsa

Serve with steamed broccoli and warm rolls to complete the dinner.

Yield: 4 servings (serving size: 1 cutlet and ¼ cup salsa)

1 cup chopped fresh pineapple

2 tablespoons chopped fresh cilantro

1 tablespoon finely chopped red onion

⅓ cup unsalted dry-roasted peanuts

1 (1-ounce) slice white bread

½ teaspoon salt

⅛ teaspoon black pepper

4 (4-ounce) chicken breast cutlets

1½ teaspoons canola oil

Cooking spray

Cilantro sprigs (optional)

1. Combine first 3 ingredients in a small bowl, tossing well.

2. Place peanuts and bread slice in a food processor; process until finely chopped. Sprinkle salt and pepper evenly over chicken. Dredge chicken in breadcrumb mixture.

3. Heat oil in a large nonstick skillet coated with cooking spray over medium-high heat. Add chicken to pan; cook 2 minutes on each side or until done. Serve chicken with pineapple mixture. Garnish with cilantro sprigs, if desired.

CALORIES 219; FAT 7.4g (sat 1.1g, mono 3.4g, poly 2.1g); PROTEIN 28.9g; CARB 9.1g; FIBER 1.3g; CHOL 66mg; IRON 1.2mg; SODIUM 398mg; CALC 27mg

QUICK TIP

Pick up a container of fresh pineapple chunks in the produce section of the supermarket; chop into ½-inch pieces for the salsa.

Pan-Fried Chicken

The key to success with this recipe is even heat. If the oil gets too hot, the chicken may brown too quickly before fully cooking. You can lower the heat, or brown the chicken on the stovetop and then cook in a 350° oven until done. If the oil is not hot enough, the chicken will absorb too much of it. Omit spices in the breading, if you prefer.

Yield: 4 servings (serving size: 1 chicken breast half or 1 thigh and 1 drumstiok)

4.5 ounces all-purpose flour (about 1 cup)

2.25 ounces whole-wheat flour (about ½ cup)

1 teaspoon ground ginger

½ teaspoon hot paprika

½ teaspoon ground cinnamon

½ teaspoon freshly ground nutmeg

½ teaspoon fine sea salt

2 bone-in chicken breast halves, skinned

2 bone-in chicken thighs, skinned

2 chicken drumsticks, skinned

¼ cup peanut oil

1. Sift together first 6 ingredients; place mixture in a large zip-top plastic bag. Sprinkle salt evenly over chicken. Add chicken, one piece at a time, to bag; seal. Shake bag to coat chicken. Remove chicken from bag, shaking off excess flour. Place chicken on a cooling rack; place rack in a jelly-roll pan. Reserve remaining flour mixture. Loosely cover chicken; chill 1½ hours. Let chicken stand at room temperature 30 minutes. Return chicken, one piece at a time, to flour mixture, shaking bag to coat chicken. Discard excess flour mixture.

2. Heat peanut oil in a large skillet over medium-high heat. Add chicken to pan. Reduce heat to medium-low, and cook 25 minutes or until done, carefully turning every 5 minutes.

3. Line a clean cooling rack with brown paper bags; arrange chicken in a single layer on bags. Let stand 5 minutes.

CALORIES 245; FAT 10.1g (sat 2g, mono 4.1g, poly 3g); PROTEIN 28.2g; CARB 9g; FIBER 0.8g; CHOL 87mg; IRON 1.8mg; SODIUM 240mg; CALC 17mg

Chicken with 40 Cloves of Garlic

Roasting softens the flavor of garlic and makes it easy to spread over the baguette slices. Serve with steamed asparagus.

Yield: 8 servings (serving size: about 4 ounces chicken, 2 tablespoons sauce, 5 garlic cloves, and 3 bread slices)

2 (3-pound) whole chickens

1 tablespoon butter

1 tablespoon extra-virgin olive oil

½ teaspoon salt

¼ teaspoon freshly ground black pepper

40 garlic cloves, peeled

1¼ cups fat-free, lower-sodium chicken broth

1 cup dry white wine

24 (¼-inch-thick) slices diagonally cut French bread baguette

Chopped fresh flat-leaf parsley (optional)

1. Remove and discard giblets and neck from chickens. Rinse chickens with cold water; pat dry. Trim excess fat; remove skin. Cut each chicken into 8 pieces. Combine butter and oil in a 12-inch nonstick skillet over medium-high heat. Sprinkle salt and pepper evenly over chicken pieces. Add half of chicken pieces to pan; cook 2 minutes on each side or until golden. Remove chicken from pan; keep warm. Repeat procedure with remaining chicken.

2. Reduce heat to medium. Add garlic; cook 1 minute or until garlic begins to brown, stirring frequently. Arrange chicken on top of garlic. Add broth and wine; cover and cook 25 minutes or until chicken is done.

3. Remove chicken from pan; keep warm. Increase heat to medium-high; cook 10 minutes or until liquid is reduced to about 1 cup. Serve sauce and garlic with chicken and bread. Garnish with chopped parsley, if desired.

CALORIES 343; FAT 13.7g (sat 3.6g, mono 4.9g, poly 3.4g); PROTEIN 29.6g; CARB 24.2g; FIBER 2g; CHOL 111mg; IRON 2.3mg; SODIUM 468mg; CALC 58mg

INGREDIENT TIP

One of the basic tenets of French cuisine is making full use of ingredients—hence, whole chickens in this recipe. In a pinch, you can substitute 6 pounds of chicken pieces.

Three-Cheese Chicken Penne Florentine

Fresh spinach, chicken, and a combination of cheeses make this dish comforting enough for the last days of winter yet fresh enough for the first days of spring.

Yield: 8 servings (serving size: about 1 cup)

1 teaspoon olive oil

Cooking spray

3 cups thinly sliced mushrooms

1 cup chopped onion

1 cup chopped red bell pepper

3 cups chopped fresh spinach

1 tablespoon chopped fresh oregano

¼ teaspoon freshly ground black pepper

1 (16-ounce) carton 2% low-fat cottage cheese

4 cups hot cooked penne (about 8 ounces uncooked tube-shaped pasta)

2 cups shredded roasted skinless, boneless chicken breast

1 cup (4 ounces) shredded reduced-fat sharp cheddar cheese, divided

½ cup (2 ounces) grated fresh Parmesan cheese, divided

½ cup 2% reduced-fat milk

1 (10¾-ounce) can condensed reduced-fat, reduced-sodium cream of chicken soup, undiluted

1. Preheat oven to 425°.

2. Heat olive oil in a large nonstick skillet coated with cooking spray over medium-high heat. Add mushrooms, onion, and bell pepper; sauté 4 minutes or until tender. Add spinach, oregano, and black pepper; sauté 3 minutes or just until spinach wilts.

3. Place cottage cheese in a food processor; process until very smooth. Combine spinach mixture, cottage cheese, pasta, chicken, ¾ cup cheddar cheese, ¼ cup Parmesan cheese, milk, and soup in a large bowl. Spoon mixture into a 2-quart baking dish coated with cooking spray. Sprinkle with remaining ¼ cup cheddar cheese and remaining ¼ cup Parmesan cheese. Bake at 425° for 25 minutes or until lightly browned and bubbly.

CALORIES 345; FAT 9.7g (sat 5.1g, mono 3.1g, poly 1g); PROTEIN 31.7g; CARB 32.9g; FIBER 2.1g; CHOL 56mg; IRON 2mg; SODIUM 532mg; CALC 275mg

QUICK TIP

You can also cook the pasta mixture in individual 8-ounce ramekins; bake for 15 minutes.

Chicken Enchiladas with Salsa Verde

A squeeze of lime juice brightens the flavor of this hearty Mexican dish. The enchiladas are mild, so serve with hot sauce, if desired. If you can't find queso fresco, use ¼ cup shredded Monterey Jack cheese or Monterey Jack with jalapeño peppers.

Yield: 4 servings (serving size: 2 enchiladas and 1 lime wedge)

1 cup chopped onion

¼ cup chopped fresh cilantro

2 garlic cloves, minced

1 (7-ounce) bottle salsa verde

2 cups shredded cooked chicken breast

⅓ cup (3 ounces) ⅓-less-fat cream cheese, softened

1 cup fat-free, lower-sodium chicken broth

8 (6-inch) corn tortillas

Cooking spray

¼ cup (1 ounce) crumbled queso fresco

½ teaspoon chili powder

4 lime wedges

Cilantro sprigs (optional)

1. Preheat oven to 425°.

2. Place first 4 ingredients in a blender; process until smooth. Combine chicken and cream cheese in a large bowl. Stir in ½ cup salsa mixture. Reserve remaining salsa mixture.

3. Bring broth to a simmer in a medium skillet. Working with one tortilla at a time, add tortilla to pan; cook 20 seconds or until moist, turning once. Remove tortilla; drain on paper towels. Spoon about ¼ cup chicken mixture down center of tortilla; roll up. Place tortilla, seam side down, in an 11 x 7–inch baking dish coated with cooking spray. Repeat procedure with remaining tortillas, broth, and chicken mixture.

4. Pour remaining salsa mixture over enchiladas; sprinkle evenly with queso fresco and chili powder. Bake at 425° for 18 minutes or until thoroughly heated. Serve with lime wedges. Garnish with cilantro sprigs, if desired.

CALORIES 327; FAT 9.5g (sat 4.4g, mono 2.9g, poly 1.3g); PROTEIN 28.5g; CARB 31g; FIBER 3.3g; CHOL 78mg; IRON 1.8mg; SODIUM 493mg; CALC 149mg

QUICK TIP

Buy a rotisserie chicken at the supermarket, and use the breast meat for this recipe. Use any leftover meat for sandwiches.

Feta, Herb, and Sun-Dried Tomato-Stuffed Chicken

Sun-dried tomatoes and fresh basil temper tangy feta in a savory chicken breast stuffing. Serve with quick-cooking orzo pasta tossed with fresh parsley.

Yield: 4 servings (serving size: 1 packet)

2 cups water

½ cup sun-dried tomatoes, packed without oil

½ cup (2 ounces) crumbled feta cheese

2 teaspoons chopped fresh basil

1 teaspoon chopped fresh oregano

½ teaspoon minced garlic

¾ teaspoon freshly ground black pepper, divided

4 (6-ounce) skinless, boneless chicken breast halves

½ teaspoon kosher salt

2 tablespoons butter

½ teaspoon grated lemon rind

¼ cup fat-free, lower-sodium chicken broth

2 teaspoons thinly sliced fresh basil (optional)

1. Preheat oven to 425°

2. Bring 2 cups water to a boil in a small saucepan; add tomatoes. Remove from heat; cover and let stand 5 minutes. Drain and slice into thin strips. Combine tomatoes, cheese, 2 teaspoons chopped basil, oregano, garlic, and ¼ teaspoon pepper in a small bowl.

3. Place chicken breast halves between 2 sheets of heavy-duty plastic wrap, and pound each piece to an even thickness using a meat mallet or small heavy skillet. Cut a horizontal slit through one side of each chicken breast half to form a deep pocket. Stuff ¼ cup tomato mixture into each pocket. Sprinkle both sides of chicken with salt and remaining ½ teaspoon pepper.

4. Fold 4 (16 x 12–inch) sheets of heavy-duty foil in half crosswise. Open foil; place 1½ teaspoons butter on half of each foil sheet. Lay one stuffed chicken breast half on top of each portion of butter. Place ⅛ teaspoon grated lemon rind on top of each stuffed chicken breast half, and drizzle each serving with 1 tablespoon chicken broth. Fold foil over chicken, and tightly seal edges. Place packets on a baking sheet. Bake packets at 425° for 20 minutes. Remove from oven, and let stand 5 minutes. Unfold packets carefully, and thinly slice each chicken breast half. Garnish each serving with ½ teaspoon sliced basil, if desired. Serve immediately.

CALORIES 311; FAT 10.1g (sat 5.7g, mono 2g, poly 0.7g); PROTEIN 43g; CARB 8.2g; FIBER 2.5g; CHOL 121mg; IRON 1.6mg; SODIUM 572mg; CALC 77mg

INGREDIENT TIP

Sun-dried tomatoes add a burst of vivid flavor and nutrition to many dishes. Drying intensifies the naturally sweet taste of Roma or plum tomatoes. Their slightly chewy texture adds richness to the consistency of a dish.

Vanilla Balsamic Chicken

After scraping the seeds for the sauce, add the vanilla bean pod to a canister of sugar. The scent of the bean will permeate the sugar. Serve the chicken with a tossed green salad.

Yield: 8 servings (serving size: 2 thighs)

½ cup fat-free, lower-sodium chicken broth

½ cup balsamic vinegar

¼ cup finely chopped shallots

¼ cup packed brown sugar

¼ teaspoon grated orange rind

¼ cup fresh orange juice

1 (2-inch) piece vanilla bean, split lengthwise

¾ teaspoon salt, divided

16 skinless, boneless chicken thighs (about 2 pounds)

Cooking spray

½ teaspoon freshly ground black pepper

Orange rind strips (optional)

1. Preheat oven to 450°.

2. Combine first 6 ingredients in a small saucepan. Scrape seeds from vanilla bean; stir seeds into broth mixture, reserving the bean for another use. Bring to a boil. Reduce heat, and simmer until reduced to ½ cup (about 20 minutes). Stir in ¼ teaspoon salt.

3. Arrange chicken in a single layer in the bottom of a roasting pan coated with cooking spray. Sprinkle chicken evenly with remaining ½ teaspoon salt and pepper. Bake at 450° for 10 minutes.

4. Brush half of broth mixture over chicken; bake 5 minutes. Brush remaining broth mixture over chicken; bake 15 minutes or until a thermometer registers 180°. Garnish with orange rind, if desired.

CALORIES 209; FAT 5.5g (sat 1.4g, mono 1.7g, poly 1.4g); PROTEIN 27.5g; CARB 10.9g; FIBER 0.2g; CHOL 115mg; IRON 1.8mg; SODIUM 371mg; CALC 29mg

Honey-Pomegranate Roasted Chicken Thighs

You can find pomegranate molasses in Middle Eastern and specialty stores. Serve these succulent thighs warm or at room temperature. Garnish with chives, if desired.

Yield: 8 servings (serving size: 2 thighs)

¾ cup honey

⅓ cup finely chopped shallots

¼ cup fresh lemon juice (about 3 small lemons)

1 tablespoon grated lemon rind

2 tablespoons pomegranate molasses

1 teaspoon Worcestershire sauce

1 teaspoon hot sauce

6 garlic cloves, minced

16 chicken thighs (about 4 pounds), skinned

1 tablespoon cornstarch

1 tablespoon water

Cooking spray

1 teaspoon salt

¼ teaspoon freshly ground black pepper

1. Combine first 9 ingredients in a large bowl; marinate in refrigerator 2 hours, stirring occasionally.

2. Preheat oven to 425°.

3. Remove chicken from bowl, reserving marinade. Combine cornstarch and water in a small bowl. Place reserved marinade in a small saucepan; bring to a boil. Stir in cornstarch mixture, and cook 3 minutes or until thickened, stirring frequently. Remove from heat. Place chicken on a broiler pan coated with cooking spray; sprinkle with salt and pepper. Bake at 425° for 30 minutes or until chicken is done, basting with reserved marinade every 10 minutes.

CALORIES 378; FAT 13.1g (sat 3.7g, mono 5g, poly 3g); PROTEIN 31.7g; CARB 33.8g; FIBER 0.3g; CHOL 114mg; IRON 2.6mg; SODIUM 416mg; CALC 36mg

Spiced Roasted Chicken

While it's easy enough to buy a rotisserie chicken, roasting chicken at home allows you to control the sodium, flavorings, and quality of ingredients. Preparation is simple, while cooking is hands-off. Serve with a quick carrot-raisin salad and mashed potatoes.

Yield: 4 servings (serving size: about 5 ounces chicken)

1 (3¾-pound) whole roasting chicken

1 teaspoon dried oregano

1 teaspoon cumin seed, crushed

1 teaspoon minced garlic

2 teaspoons olive oil

½ teaspoon salt

½ teaspoon ground cumin

Cooking spray

1. Preheat oven to 375°.

2. Remove and discard giblets and neck from chicken; trim excess fat. Starting at neck cavity, loosen skin from breasts and drumsticks by inserting fingers, gently pushing between skin and meat.

3. Combine oregano, cumin seed, garlic, oil, salt, and ground cumin in a small bowl. Rub seasoning mixture under loosened skin and over breasts and drumsticks. Tie ends of legs together with twine. Lift wing tips up and over back; tuck under chicken. Place chicken, breast side up, on a rack coated with cooking spray, and place rack in a roasting pan.

4. Bake at 375° for 40 minutes.

5. Increase oven temperature to 450° (do not remove chicken from oven); bake an additional 12 minutes or until a thermometer inserted in the meaty part of thigh registers 165°. Remove chicken from pan; let stand 15 minutes. Remove skin from chicken; discard.

CALORIES 185; FAT 6.4g (sat 1.3g, mono 2.9g, poly 1.2g); PROTEIN 29g; CARB 0.8g; FIBER 0.3g; CHOL 92mg; IRON 2.1mg; SODIUM 403mg; CALC 27mg

Herb Roast Chicken

Start with the best-quality chicken you can find. We chose a fresh organic bird. Make your meal complete with smashed potatoes and haricots verts.

Yield: 4 servings (serving size: 1 chicken breast half or 1 thigh and 1 drumstick, and 1 tablespoon drippings)

1 (4½-pound) whole roasting chicken

¾ teaspoon fine sea salt, divided

¾ teaspoon freshly ground black pepper, divided

1 lemon, halved

2 tablespoons butter, softened

2 tablespoons minced shallots

2 teaspoons chopped fresh rosemary

2 teaspoons chopped fresh thyme

Cooking spray

¾ cup water

1. Preheat oven to 450°.

2. Remove giblets and neck from chicken cavity; discard. Trim excess fat from chicken. Loosen skin from breast and drumsticks by inserting fingers, gently pushing between skin and meat. Sprinkle ¼ teaspoon salt and ½ teaspoon pepper inside body cavity. Squeeze lemon juice into body cavity; place lemon halves in body cavity. Combine softened butter, minced shallots, rosemary, and thyme, stirring with a fork until well blended. Combine remaining ½ teaspoon salt and remaining ¼ teaspoon pepper in a small bowl; rub salt mixture evenly under skin over breast and drumstick meat. Rub butter mixture evenly under skin over breast and drumstick meat. Tie ends of legs together with twine. Lift wing tips up and over back, and tuck under chicken.

3. Place chicken, breast side up, on a rack coated with cooking spray; place rack in a roasting pan. Pour ¾ cup water into roasting pan. Bake chicken at 450° for 1 hour or until a thermometer inserted in meaty part of thigh registers 165°. Remove chicken from pan; let stand, breast side down, 15 minutes. Remove skin; discard.

4. Place a large zip-top plastic bag inside a 4-cup glass measure. Pour drippings through a sieve into bag; discard solids. Let drippings stand 10 minutes (fat will rise to the top). Seal bag; carefully snip off 1 bottom corner of bag. Drain drippings into a medium bowl, stopping before fat layer reaches opening; discard fat. Carve chicken; serve with drippings.

CALORIES 222; FAT 11.4g (sat 5.2g, mono 3.5g, poly 1.5g); PROTEIN 26.6g; CARB 2.3g; FIBER 0.2g; CHOL 97mg; IRON 1.3mg; SODIUM 548mg; CALC 23mg

Chicken and Feta Tabbouleh

Delicious when eaten right away, the flavors in this meal stand up admirably when it's prepared ahead—making this a good take-to-work lunch, too. Serve with toasted pita wedges or flatbread.

Yield: 4 servings (serving size: 1½ cups)

¾ cup uncooked bulgur

1 cup boiling water

2 cups chopped skinless, boneless rotisserie chicken breast

1 cup chopped plum tomato

1 cup chopped English cucumber

¾ cup chopped fresh parsley

½ cup (2 ounces) crumbled feta cheese

⅓ cup finely chopped green onions

¼ cup chopped fresh mint

2 tablespoons fresh lemon juice

1 tablespoon extra-virgin olive oil

1 teaspoon minced garlic

¼ teaspoon salt

¼ teaspoon ground cumin

¼ teaspoon black pepper

1. Place bulgur in a medium bowl; cover with 1 cup boiling water. Let stand 15 minutes or until liquid is absorbed.

2. Combine chicken and remaining ingredients in a large bowl. Add bulgur to chicken mixture; toss gently to combine.

CALORIES 296; FAT 9.5g (sat 3.4g, mono 4.1g, poly 1.2g); PROTEIN 28.2g; CARB 25.6g; FIBER 6.4g; CHOL 72mg; IRON 2.7mg; SODIUM 344mg; CALC 128mg

QUICK TIP

For a speedier version, use prechopped onions and tomato, precrumbled cheese, and chopped cooked chicken breast.

Roast Chicken Salad with Peaches, Goat Cheese, and Pecans

Fresh peaches and goat cheese headline this simple no-cook salad recipe. The 8-ingredient vinaigrette, made with pantry staples, takes minutes to make and is a delicious complement to the other ingredients in the salad. Use a store-bought rotisserie chicken to save time in the kitchen. Serve with herbed bread.

Yield: 4 servings (serving size: about 1¾ cups salad and 1½ teaspoons cheese)

2½ tablespoons balsamic vinegar

1½ tablespoons extra-virgin olive oil

1½ tablespoons minced shallots

2½ teaspoons fresh lemon juice

2½ teaspoons maple syrup

¾ teaspoon Dijon mustard

¼ teaspoon kosher salt

¼ teaspoon freshly ground black pepper

2 cups shredded skinless, boneless rotisserie chicken breast

2 cups sliced peeled peaches

½ cup vertically sliced red onion

¼ cup chopped pecans, toasted

1 (5-ounce) package gourmet salad greens

2 tablespoons crumbled goat cheese

1. Combine first 8 ingredients; stir with a whisk.

2. Combine chicken and remaining ingredients except cheese in a large bowl. Add vinegar mixture; toss gently. Sprinkle with cheese.

CALORIES 285; FAT 14g (sat 2.4g, mono 7.8g, poly 2.8g); PROTEIN 24.6g; CARB 16g; FIBER 2.9g; CHOL 61mg; IRON 1.9mg; SODIUM 203mg; CALC 54mg

INGREDIENT TIP

Although we absolutely love the sweet freshness peaches add to this summer-*time salad, apricots or nectarines make a good substitute, too. Just be sure to use the freshest fruits you have on hand.*

Chicken and Farfalle Salad with Walnut Pesto

To make sure the walnut pesto ingredients are evenly minced, stop the food processor halfway through processing, and scrape down the sides.

Yield: 4 servings (serving size: 1½ cups salad and 1 lettuce leaf)

Salad:

2 cups uncooked farfalle (bow tie pasta; about 6 ounces)

2 cups cubed cooked skinless, boneless chicken breast

1 cup quartered cherry tomatoes

2 tablespoons chopped pitted kalamata olives

Walnut Pesto:

1 cup basil leaves

½ cup fresh parsley leaves

3 tablespoons coarsely chopped walnuts, toasted

1½ tablespoons extra-virgin olive oil

1 tablespoon white wine vinegar

½ teaspoon salt

1 garlic clove, peeled

Remaining Ingredient:

4 curly leaf lettuce leaves

1. To prepare salad, cook pasta according to package directions, omitting salt and fat. Drain; rinse with cold water. Combine pasta, chicken, tomatoes, and olives in a large bowl.

2. To prepare walnut pesto, place basil and next 6 ingredients in a food processor; pulse 6 times or until finely minced. Add pesto to pasta mixture, tossing gently to coat. Place 1 lettuce leaf on each of 4 plates; top each serving with salad mixture.

CALORIES 374; FAT 12.5g (sat 2g, mono 5.5g, poly 3.9g); PROTEIN 29.4g; CARB 36.3g; FIBER 3g; CHOL 60mg; IRON 3.6mg; SODIUM 393mg; CALC 62mg

INGREDIENT TIP

Keep kalamata olives on hand to add zesty saltiness to salads, sandwiches, and spreads.

Arugula Salad with Chicken and Apricots

This simple main course salad is perfect for lunch or as a light supper option. Plums or peaches would be a delicious substitute for the apricots.

Yield: 4 servings

2 (6-ounce) skinless, boneless chicken breast halves

1 tablespoon minced fresh parsley

2 teaspoons minced fresh tarragon

½ teaspoon salt, divided

¼ teaspoon freshly ground black pepper

Cooking spray

3 tablespoons olive oil

4 teaspoons white wine vinegar

Dash of freshly ground black pepper

4 cups baby arugula

4 cups gourmet salad greens

3 apricots (about 8 ounces), pitted and thinly sliced

⅓ cup thinly vertically sliced red onion

1. Prepare grill to medium-high heat.

2. Place chicken between 2 sheets of heavy-duty plastic wrap; pound each piece to ½-inch thickness using a meat mallet or small heavy skillet. Sprinkle chicken with parsley, tarragon, ¼ teaspoon salt, and ¼ teaspoon pepper.

3. Place chicken on grill rack coated with cooking spray; grill 4 minutes on each side or until done. Transfer to a plate; cool to room temperature.

4. Combine oil, vinegar, remaining ¼ teaspoon salt, and dash of pepper in a small bowl, stirring with a whisk.

5. Combine arugula, greens, apricots, and onion in a large bowl. Pour vinaigrette over arugula mixture; toss well to coat. Place about 2 cups arugula mixture on each of 4 plates. Cut chicken breast halves crosswise into thin slices; top each serving evenly with chicken. Serve immediately.

CALORIES 243; FAT 12.9g (sat 2.1g, mono 8.3g, poly 1.7g); PROTEIN 22.2g; CARB 10.1g; FIBER 2.9g; CHOL 54mg; IRON 2.1mg; SODIUM 364mg; CALC 86mg

WINE TIP

In this salad, arugula's peppery bite is nicely balanced by fragrant herbs, sweet apricots, and grilled chicken. A pinot gris from Oregon is a great wine to serve with a complexly flavored salad like this. It has a fresh, clean feel and a creamy, fruity flavor.

Hearts of Romaine Caesar Salad with Grilled Chicken

Coddling the egg makes it creamy but does not heat it to 160°, the temperature required to kill bacteria. Use a pasteurized whole egg if you have safety concerns.

Yield: 4 servings

1 large egg

½ teaspoon freshly ground black pepper

¼ teaspoon kosher salt

2 canned anchovy fillets

2 garlic cloves, peeled

1 tablespoon fresh lemon juice

1 tablespoon extra-virgin olive oil

1 tablespoon water

1⅓ cups plain croutons

2 heads hearts of romaine lettuce, leaves separated (about 14 ounces)

3 servings Lemon-Grilled Chicken Breasts (recipe on page 35), thinly sliced

¼ cup (1 ounce) grated Parmigiano-Reggiano cheese

1. Place egg in a small bowl or coffee mug; cover with boiling water. Let stand 1 minute. Rinse egg with cold water; break egg into a small bowl.

2. Place pepper and next 3 ingredients in a mini food processor; process until minced. Add egg and juice; process 1 minute or until thick. Gradually add oil and 1 tablespoon water, processing until blended.

3. Combine croutons, lettuce, Lemon-Grilled Chicken Breasts, and egg mixture in a large bowl; toss gently. Divide salad evenly among 4 plates. Sprinkle each serving with 1 tablespoon cheese.

CALORIES 261; FAT 10.1g (sat 2.8g, mono 5.2g, poly 1.3g); PROTEIN 29.3g; CARB 12.5g; FIBER 1.8g; CHOL 115mg; IRON 2.9mg; SODIUM 561mg; CALC 165mg

Mediterranean Chicken Salad Pitas

Add honeydew melon and cantaloupe slices on the side to complete your meal.

Yield: 6 servings (serving size: 2 stuffed pita halves)

1 cup plain whole-milk Greek yogurt

2 tablespoons lemon juice

½ teaspoon ground cumin

¼ teaspoon crushed red pepper

3 cups chopped cooked chicken

1 cup chopped red bell pepper (about 1 large)

½ cup chopped pitted green olives (about 20 small)

½ cup diced red onion

¼ cup chopped fresh cilantro

1 (15-ounce) can no-salt-added chickpeas (garbanzo beans), rinsed and drained

6 (6-inch) whole-wheat pitas, cut in half

12 Bibb lettuce leaves

6 (⅛-inch-thick) slices tomato, cut in half

1. Combine first 4 ingredients in a small bowl; set aside. Combine chicken and next 5 ingredients in a large bowl. Add yogurt mixture to chicken mixture; toss gently to coat. Line each pita half with 1 lettuce leaf and 1 tomato piece; add ½ cup chicken mixture to each pita half.

CALORIES 404; FAT 10.2g (sat 3.8g, mono 4g, poly 1.5g); PROTEIN 33.6g; CARB 46.4g; FIBER 6g; CHOL 66mg; IRON 3.4mg; SODIUM 575mg; CALC 110mg

INGREDIENT TIP

Greek yogurt has a thick, rich consistency similar to sour cream. It gives the pita filling a creamy texture.

Mozzarella Chicken Sandwich

This sandwich provides two grain servings from the ciabatta, a little more than two servings of meat from the chicken, and half a dairy serving from the cheese. Serve with orange wedges and baked chips.

Yield: 4 servings (serving size: 1 sandwich)

¼ cup (about 2 ounces) sun-dried tomato pesto

2 tablespoons fat-free mayonnaise

¾ pound skinless, boneless chicken breasts

¼ teaspoon pepper

⅛ teaspoon salt

1 teaspoon olive oil

1 (8-ounce) loaf ciabatta

12 large fresh basil leaves

¾ cup (3 ounces) shredded part-skim mozzarella cheese

½ cup sliced bottled roasted red bell peppers

1 large tomato, thinly sliced

1. Combine pesto and mayonnaise in a small bowl, stirring to blend.
2. Sprinkle chicken with pepper and salt. Heat oil in a large nonstick skillet over medium-high heat. Add chicken, and cook 3 minutes on each side or until done. Remove chicken to a cutting board, and cool slightly. Cut chicken lengthwise into thin slices.
3. Preheat broiler.
4. Cut ciabatta in half horizontally. Place bread, cut sides up, on a baking sheet. Broil 3 minutes or until lightly browned. Remove bread from pan. Spread pesto mixture evenly over cut sides of bread. Arrange chicken slices evenly over bottom half. Top chicken evenly with basil leaves, and sprinkle cheese over top. Place bottom half on baking sheet, and broil 2 minutes or until cheese melts. Arrange bell pepper and tomato over cheese, and cover with top half of bread. Cut into 4 equal pieces.

CALORIES 394; FAT 13.4g (sat 3.9g, mono 7.4g, poly 1.1g); PROTEIN 31.3g; CARB 37.3g; FIBER 2g; CHOL 63mg; IRON 2.8mg; SODIUM 796mg; CALC 187mg

Honey-Chipotle Barbecue Chicken Sandwiches

This recipe yields slow-cooked barbecue flavor in less than an hour. Broil the sandwiches just before serving.

Yield: 4 sandwiches (serving size: 1 sandwich)

½ cup water

1 teaspoon ground cumin

4 garlic cloves, thinly sliced

1 pound skinless, boneless chicken breasts

1 (7-ounce) can chipotle chiles in adobo sauce

1 tablespoon canola oil

1 tablespoon minced garlic

1 teaspoon ground cumin

½ cup canned tomato puree

¼ cup cider vinegar

3 tablespoons honey

1 tablespoon Worcestershire sauce

¼ teaspoon salt

4 (1½-ounce) sandwich rolls

2 ounces Monterey Jack cheese, thinly sliced

4 (⅛-inch-thick) slices red onion

1. Combine water, 1 teaspoon cumin, 4 sliced garlic cloves, and chicken in a large saucepan. Cover and bring to a boil over medium-high heat. Reduce heat to medium-low; cook 10 minutes or until chicken is done. Drain, and place chicken on a cutting board. Cut chicken across grain into thin slices; keep warm.

2. Remove 2 tablespoons adobo sauce from can; set aside. Remove 2 chipotle chiles from can; finely chop and set aside. Reserve remaining chiles and adobo sauce for another use.

3. Heat oil in a large nonstick skillet over medium-high heat. Add 1 tablespoon minced garlic; sauté 3 minutes or until just beginning to brown. Add 1 teaspoon cumin; sauté 1 minute. Stir in tomato puree; cook 4 minutes or until mixture thickens to a pastelike consistency, stirring constantly. Stir in reserved 2 tablespoons adobo sauce, 2 chopped chipotle chiles, vinegar, honey, Worcestershire, and ¼ teaspoon salt. Add sliced chicken to sauce; simmer for 3 minutes or until thoroughly heated.

4. Preheat broiler.

5. Split rolls in half; arrange in a single layer, cut sides up, on a baking sheet. Broil 1 minute or until lightly toasted. Remove top halves of rolls from baking sheet. Divide chicken mixture evenly among bottom halves of rolls, and top chicken mixture evenly with cheese. Broil chicken-topped rolls 2 minutes or until cheese melts. Remove from oven; top with onion and top roll halves. Serve immediately.

CALORIES 424; FAT 11.8g (sat 3.9g, mono 4.7g, poly 1.9g); PROTEIN 34.5g; CARB 45.1g; FIBER 2.6g; CHOL 78mg; IRON 3.6mg; SODIUM 765mg; CALC 211mg

Rosemary Chicken Salad Sandwiches

Although this seems like your typical chicken and mayonnaise mixture, crunchy smoked almonds, fresh rosemary, green onions, and a little Dijon mustard make this anything but ordinary. Add a lettuce leaf to each sandwich, if desired.

Yield: 5 servings (serving size: 1 sandwich)

3 cups chopped roasted skinless, boneless chicken breast (about ¾ pound)

⅓ cup chopped green onions

¼ cup chopped smoked almonds

¼ cup plain fat-free yogurt

¼ cup light mayonnaise

1 teaspoon chopped fresh rosemary

1 teaspoon Dijon mustard

⅛ teaspoon salt

⅛ teaspoon freshly ground black pepper

10 slices whole-grain bread

1. Combine first 9 ingredients, stirring well. Spread about ⅔ cup chicken mixture over each of 5 bread slices, and top with remaining bread slices. Cut sandwiches diagonally in half.

CALORIES 360; FAT 11.6g (sat 2.1g, mono 3.5g, poly 1.8g); PROTEIN 33.6g; CARB 29.9g; FIBER 4.4g; CHOL 76mg; IRON 2.9mg; SODIUM 529mg; CALC 104mg

Skillet Chicken Souvlaki

Prepare a family-friendly Mediterranean-style dish that's sure to please even the pickiest eater. The quick-cooking chicken and simple homemade yogurt sauce make this a perfect dish for a busy weeknight. Serve with a simple side salad.

Yield: 4 servings (serving size: 1 cup chicken mixture, ¼ cup sauce, 1 pita, and about ¼ cup tomato slices)

1 tablespoon olive oil, divided

1 pound skinless, boneless chicken breast, thinly sliced

½ teaspoon salt

¼ teaspoon freshly ground black pepper

1½ cups vertically sliced onion (about 1 medium)

1 cup thinly sliced green bell pepper (about 1)

2 teaspoons minced garlic

½ teaspoon dried oregano

½ cup grated English cucumber

¼ cup 2% Greek yogurt

¼ cup reduced-fat sour cream

1 tablespoon chopped fresh flat-leaf parsley

½ teaspoon grated lemon rind

1 teaspoon fresh lemon juice

⅛ teaspoon salt

4 (6-inch) whole wheat soft pitas, cut in half and warmed

2 plum tomatoes, thinly sliced

1. Heat 2 teaspoons oil in a large nonstick skillet over medium-high heat. Sprinkle chicken with ½ teaspoon salt and black pepper. Add chicken to pan; sauté 5 minutes or until done. Remove from pan.

2. Add 1 teaspoon oil to pan. Add onion and bell pepper; sauté 3 minutes. Add chicken, garlic, and oregano; cook 30 seconds.

3. Combine cucumber and next 6 ingredients. Serve chicken mixture with yogurt sauce, warmed pita, and tomato slices.

CALORIES 361; FAT 7.4g (sat 2.3g, mono 3.3g, poly 0.8g); PROTEIN 35.1g; CARB 39g; FIBER 4.7g; CHOL 72mg; IRON 3.1mg; SODIUM 589mg; CALC 105mg

QUICK TIP

To quickly vertically slice an onion, start at the end opposite the root. Slice the top off the onion, leaving the root intact. Remove the papery skin, and slice the onion vertically. Continue cutting the onion vertically into thin slices.

BBQ Chicken Pizza

Online reviews raved about the contrast of flavors provided by tangy tomato chutney, savory chicken, and sharp cheddar cheese. If you can't find tomato chutney, make your own (see note below), or use store-bought barbecue sauce.

Yield: 6 servings (serving size: 1 wedge)

1 (10-ounce) Italian cheese-flavored thin pizza crust (such as Boboli)

¾ cup tomato chutney

2 cups chopped roasted skinless, boneless chicken breast (about 2 breasts)

⅔ cup diced plum tomato

¾ cup (3 ounces) shredded extra-sharp white cheddar cheese

⅓ cup chopped green onions

1. Preheat oven to 450°.

2. Place crust on a baking sheet. Bake at 450° for 3 minutes. Remove from oven; spread chutney over crust, leaving a ½-inch border.

3. Top chutney with chicken. Sprinkle diced tomato, cheese, and green onions evenly over chicken. Bake at 450° for 9 minutes or until cheese melts. Cut pizza into 6 wedges.

Note: If you can't find tomato chutney, make your own. Combine 2 cups diced plum tomato, 3 tablespoons brown sugar, 3 tablespoons cider vinegar, ⅛ teaspoon Jamaican jerk seasoning, and 1 minced garlic clove in a small saucepan; bring to a boil. Reduce heat to medium; cook 20 minutes or until thickened.

CALORIES 300; FAT 8.5g (sat 3.9g, mono 2.9g, poly 1g); PROTEIN 21.3g; CARB 35.2g; FIBER 1.2g; CHOL 48mg; IRON 1.7mg; SODIUM 622mg; CALC 247mg

QUICK TIP

We've used a Boboli crust here to speed up the preparation time. It's a great alternative to making and baking your own crust.

Ratatouille Pizza with Chicken

The addition of chicken to a quick ratatouille makes a great-tasting and satisfying pizza when put on a crust. Serve with a green salad for a light weekday supper.

Yield: 6 servings (serving size: 1 wedge)

1 teaspoon olive oil

1 Japanese eggplant, halved lengthwise and cut into (¼-inch-thick) slices

1 red bell pepper, cut into ¼-inch strips

½ small red onion, thinly sliced

1 cup sliced mushrooms

¾ teaspoon dried Italian seasoning

¼ teaspoon salt

4 garlic cloves, minced

1 (10-ounce) Italian cheese-flavored thin pizza crust (such as Boboli)

1 cup chopped skinless, boneless rotisserie chicken breast

1 cup (4 ounces) preshredded reduced-fat pizza-blend cheese

3 plum tomatoes, cut into (¼-inch-thick) slices

Cooking spray

3 tablespoons finely chopped fresh flat-leaf parsley

1. Preheat oven to 375°.

2. Heat a large nonstick skillet over medium-high heat. Add oil to pan. Add eggplant, bell pepper, and onion; sauté 3 minutes or until eggplant begins to soften. Reduce heat to medium. Add mushrooms; cook 3 minutes, stirring frequently. Add Italian seasoning, salt, and garlic; cook 1 minute, stirring constantly. Remove from heat.

3. Place crust on a baking sheet. Spread vegetable mixture evenly over crust, leaving a ½-inch border. Arrange chicken over vegetable mixture; sprinkle evenly with cheese. Arrange tomatoes over cheese, and lightly coat with cooking spray. Bake at 375° for 25 minutes or until cheese is bubbly and tomatoes are softened. Sprinkle with parsley. Cut pizza into 6 wedges.

CALORIES 249; FAT 8.3g (sat 3.9g, mono 2g, poly 0.8g); PROTEIN 18.1g; CARB 26.3g; FIBER 1.8g; CHOL 33mg; IRON 2mg; SODIUM 409mg; CALC 273mg

pasta
tonight!

cooking
class

In this Cooking Class, you'll find answers to the most frequently asked questions about pasta and must-have information on selecting, preparing, and serving it—as well as recipes for essential sauces and our top suggestions for using bottled sauces when you're in a pinch. There's no magic required, just loving attention.

Purchasing Pasta

Once pasta is incorporated into a recipe, the different brands all taste about the same, so don't pay more for a fancy name, domestic or imported. What does matter is choosing the right noodle for your dish and cooking it properly.

Dried and Fresh Pasta

Dried pasta is a mixture of water and semolina. In factories, the mix is made into a paste that's turned into different shapes when it's passed through dies, or large metal discs filled with holes. The pasta is then dried and packaged. When cooked, dried pasta has a nutty wheat flavor and pleasant chewy bite. The *Cooking Light* Test Kitchen mostly use dried pasta in recipes. Fresh pasta is made with regular soft wheat flour, or a combination of other flours, and eggs, giving it a rich flavor and silky texture. It's perishable, so it's generally pricier than dried. Fresh pasta cooks quickly, 2 to 3 minutes on average, making it a handy substitution when you're short on time.

Essential Tips for Cooking Pasta

Cooking pasta is fairly simple, and most packages give directions. Here are some additional recommendations from our staff.

• Put the water on to boil before beginning the rest of the recipe.

• Fill a large pot, such as a Dutch oven or stockpot, with enough water so the pasta can move freely while cooking. (Too little water may cause uneven cooking; too much might overflow.) For 8 ounces of dried pasta, you'll need to use a 4-quart pot.

• Cover the pot, and bring the water to a full rolling boil over high heat.

• It's not necessary to add oil or salt to the cooking water. Sauce won't adhere as well to the pasta's surface when it's cooked with oil. Salt does make pasta taste better on its own, but when it's tossed with a flavorful sauce, there's no need to add extra sodium.

• Add the pasta, and stir with a pasta fork. When the water returns to a rolling boil, start the timer. Stir often. If you use fresh pasta, remember that it cooks more quickly than dried.

• Always cook pasta uncovered over high heat.

• Start testing for doneness a few minutes before the indicated cooking time.

• Set a large colander in the sink so the water drains quickly.

• Do not rinse cooked pasta unless the recipe specifically calls for you to do so. Rinsing washes away some of the starch, making it less sticky. Less starch is ideal for pasta salads that benefit from less stickiness once chilled. But that starch helps the sauce adhere to warm or freshly cooked pasta.

• Return the pasta to the warm cooking pot or add to the skillet with the sauce; toss immediately with large tongs or a pasta fork.

• Pasta can be tricky to serve because it has a tendency to slip and slide. The best serving utensil, especially for longer pasta, is a metal or wooden pasta fork or tongs. For short pasta, a large slotted spoon works fine.

Perfect Pasta

Perfectly cooked pasta has a firm, tender consistency, called *al dente,* Italian for "to the tooth." When testing for doneness, remove a piece of pasta from the water, and bite into it. It should offer resistance to the bite but have no trace of brittleness. If an undercooked piece of pasta is cut in half, a white dot or line is clearly visible in the center. Al dente pasta has only a speck of white remaining, meaning the pasta has absorbed just enough water to hydrate it. Cook pasta slightly less than al dente if you're going to cook it for additional time with the sauce.

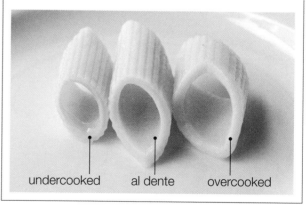

undercooked   al dente   overcooked

Amounts of Dry and Cooked Pasta

Use this guide to help you determine either how much pasta you'll need or how much you'll get. Approximate cooking times are also included.

Type	Dry Measure (8 ounces)	Cooked Volume	Cooking Time
Acini de pepe (small balls similar to orzo)	1¼ cups	3 cups	5 minutes
Alphabets	2 cups	4 cups	5 minutes
Capellini or angel hair	8 ounces	3½ cups	5 minutes
Cavatappi	3 cups	5 cups	8 minutes
Conchiglie rigate (seashell pasta)	3 cups	4 cups	14 minutes
Egg noodles, medium	4 cups	5 cups	5 minutes
Egg noodles, wide	4½ cups	5 cups	5 minutes
Elbow macaroni	2 cups	4 cups	5 minutes
Farfalle (bow tie pasta)	3 cups	4 cups	11 minutes
Fettuccine	8 ounces	4 cups	10 minutes
Fusilli (short twisted spaghetti)	3 cups	4 cups	10 minutes
Gemelli	2 cups	4 cups	10 minutes
Linguine	8 ounces	4 cups	10 minutes
Orecchiette ("little ears" pasta)	2½ cups	4 cups	11 minutes
Orzo (rice-shaped pasta)	1¼ cups	2½ cups	6 minutes
Penne or mostaccioli (tube-shaped pasta)	2 cups	4 cups	10 minutes
Penne rigate	2 cups	4 cups	10 minutes
Perciatelli	8 ounces	4 cups	11 minutes
Radiatore (short coiled pasta)	3 cups	4½ cups	10 minutes
Rigatoni	4 cups	4 cups	10 minutes
Rotini (corkscrew pasta)	2 cups	4 cups	8 minutes
Small seashell pasta	3 cups	4 cups	10 minutes
Spaghetti	8 ounces	3½ cups	10 minutes
Vermicelli	8 ounces	4 cups	5 minutes
Ziti (short tube-shaped pasta)	3 cups	4 cups	10 minutes

Pasta Shapes

Many varieties of pasta are interchangeable if similar in shape and size (see below). There are also specially shaped pastas, such as lasagna (also available in "no-boil" form) and manicotti, that are used in baked dishes. Ravioli and tortellini are filled with meat, cheese, and other ingredients. Ridged pastas will have "rigati" or "rigate" added to their names.

Long Thin Shapes	**Long Wide Shapes**	**Twisted and Curved Shapes**	**Tubular Shapes**	**Pastinas (small pastas)**
• Angel hair	• Pappardelle	• Cavatappi	• Ditalini	• Couscous
• Fettuccine (small ribbons)		• Elbow macaroni (gomiti)	• Mezzani	• Orzo (rice-shaped pasta)
• Linguine		• Farfalle (bow tie)	• Mostaccioli	• Pennette
• Spaghetti		• Fusilli (short twisted spaghetti)	• Penne	• Tubetti
• Spaghettini		• Orecchiette ("little ears")	• Rigatoni	
• Vermicelli		• Radiatore	• Ziti	
		• Rotelle (wheels)		
		• Rotini (corkscrews)		
		• Seashell macaroni		

Orecchiette

Fusilli

Orzo

World of Pasta

Often when we think of pasta, we think of Italian pasta, made from a durum wheat flour, called semolina, and water. Pastas from other cultures, with different tastes, textures, and ingredients, open up a whole new world of possibilities.

Asia

Cellophane noodles: Also called bean threads, these translucent dried noodles are made from the starch of mung beans, potatoes, or green peas.

Chinese egg noodles: These noodles are usually made from a dough of wheat flour, eggs, and salt. If they don't contain eggs, they can be labeled "imitation" or "egg-flavored."

Chinese wheat-flour noodles: These noodles are made with flour and water. Many stores offer a wide variety of "flavored" noodles (shrimp, crab, and chicken), and they can be round or flat.

Rice sticks: The most popular of all Asian noodles, rice sticks are made from rice flour and water. Although any type of rice-flour noodle can be called rice sticks, we use this term for flat rice noodles, which are sold mainly in three forms. Thin flat rice sticks are most often used in soups and some stir-fried dishes. Medium-thick rice sticks (called *pho* in Vietnamese) are all-purpose and can be used in soups, stir-fries, and salads (a slightly wider Thai version is called *jantaboon*). The widest rice sticks (*sha he fen* in Chinese) are used in meat, seafood, and vegetable stir-fries.

Soba: Soba noodles from Japan are made with a combination of buckwheat flour, wheat flour, and water. This is one of the few Asian noodles for which there is no substitute.

Somen: The most delicate of noodles, somen are made with wheat flour, a dash of oil, and water. They're served cold with a dipping sauce or hot in soups. The closest substitution would be a very fine pasta, such as capellini or vermicelli.

North Africa

Couscous: Regarded by many as a grain, couscous is actually a pasta made from semolina (durum wheat) flour and salted water. In Tunisia, Algeria, and Morocco, where it's a national favorite, couscous ranges in size from fine- to medium-grained. Another variety, Israeli couscous, is larger.

Cellophane noodles

Soba noodles

Israeli couscous

Homemade Fettuccine

1¼ cups plus 1 tablespoon all-purpose flour, divided
½ teaspoon salt
2 large eggs, lightly beaten

1. Weigh or lightly spoon flour into dry measuring cups; level with a knife. Combine 1 cup flour and salt. Make a well in center of mixture. Add eggs; stir with a fork to gradually incorporate flour into a dough.
2. Turn dough out onto a lightly floured surface; shape into a ball. Knead until smooth and elastic; add enough of remaining flour, 1 tablespoon at a time, to prevent dough from sticking to hands. Wrap in plastic wrap; let rest 10 minutes.
3. Divide dough into 4 equal portions. Working with 1 portion at a time (cover remaining dough with plastic wrap to keep from drying), pass through smooth rollers of pasta machine on widest setting. Continue moving width gauge to narrower settings; pass dough through rollers at each setting, dusting lightly with flour if needed to prevent sticking.
4. Roll dough to about ¹⁄₁₆ inch. Pass through fettuccine cutting rollers of machine. Hang on a wooden drying rack (dry no longer than 30 minutes). Repeat procedure with remaining dough.
5. Bring 3 quarts water to a rolling boil. Add pasta; cook 2 to 4 minutes or until al dente. Drain; serve immediately.
Yield: 6 servings (serving size: ½ cup).

CALORIES 125; FAT 1.9g (sat 0.6g, mono 0.7g, poly 0.3g); PROTEIN 4.9g; CARB 21.2g; FIBER 0.7g; CHOL 71mg; IRON 1.5mg; SODIUM 217mg; CALC 12mg

Essential Techniques for Making Pasta

A simple mixture of flour, salt, and eggs creates a versatile paste that can be shaped, cut, and cooked in a variety of ways. Here, we show you how to make fettuccine. (To make dough in a food processor: Place flour and salt in processor; pulse 3 times or until combined. With processor on, slowly add eggs through food chute; process until dough forms a ball. Follow the essential techniques starting with Step 4.)

How to make the dough:

1. Make a well in center of flour mixture, and add eggs.
2. Stir eggs with a fork to gradually incorporate flour and form a dough.
3. Turn dough out onto a lightly floured surface; shape into a ball.
4. Knead until smooth and elastic (about 10 to 15 minutes).
5. Wrap dough in plastic wrap; let rest 10 minutes.

How to make the noodles:

6. Pass dough through smooth rollers of pasta machine, beginning on widest setting.
7. Pass dough through cutting rollers of machine.
8. Hang pasta on a wooden drying rack.

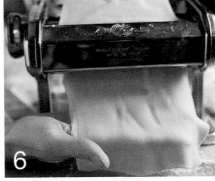

The Essential Sauces

It's almost impossible to think of pasta without thinking of sauce. And though there are some wonderful convenience products on the market (see opposite page), sometimes nothing can compare to homemade.

We've included homemade versions of classic Alfredo, arrabbiata, clam, marinara, mushroom, and pesto sauces in the The Extras chapter (pages 390-399), but here are two more sauces that no pasta lover should be without.

Quick-and-Easy Tomato Sauce

Use this sauce anywhere you might use a store-bought sauce, such as on pasta, in lasagna, or over polenta. Chop the tomatoes in the can with kitchen shears.

1 tablespoon olive oil

1½ cups chopped onion

1 cup chopped green bell pepper

1 teaspoon dried oregano

4 garlic cloves, minced

½ cup dry red wine

1 teaspoon dried basil

½ teaspoon salt

¼ teaspoon black pepper

2 (28-ounce) cans whole plum tomatoes, undrained and chopped

1 (6-ounce) can tomato paste

2 bay leaves

1. Heat oil in a large saucepan over medium-high heat. Add onion, bell pepper, oregano, and garlic; cook 5 minutes or until vegetables are tender, stirring occasionally.
2. Add wine and remaining ingredients, and bring to a boil. Reduce heat, and simmer 30 minutes. Discard bay leaves. Yield: 8 cups (serving size: 1 cup).

CALORIES 93; FAT 2.4g (sat 0.4g, mono 1.4g, poly 0.5g); PROTEIN 3.3g; CARB 17.1g; FIBER 3.3g; CHOL 0mg; IRON 2.4mg; SODIUM 487mg; CALC 77mg

Spaghetti Aglio e Olio

In Italian, *aglio e olio* (AH-lyoh ay OH-lyoh) means "garlic and oil." Add some crushed red pepper flakes for a spicier version.

2 tablespoons extra-virgin olive oil

¼ teaspoon dried oregano

4 large garlic cloves, minced

4 quarts water

8 ounces uncooked spaghetti

½ cup fat-free, lower-sodium chicken broth

2 tablespoons minced fresh parsley

1. Combine olive oil, oregano, and minced garlic in a small microwave-safe bowl. Cover bowl with wax paper, and microwave at HIGH 1 minute.
2. Bring 4 quarts water to a boil in a large stockpot. Add spaghetti; return to a boil. Cook, uncovered, 10 minutes or until al dente, stirring occasionally. Drain. Return to pot. Stir in garlic mixture and broth. Cook over medium heat 4 minutes or until broth is absorbed, stirring constantly. Stir in parsley. Yield: 4 servings (serving size: 1 cup).

CALORIES 278; FAT 7.7g (sat 1g, mono 5.1g, poly 1g); PROTEIN 7.9g; CARB 43.7g; FIBER 1.5g; CHOL 0mg; IRON 2.4mg; SODIUM 66mg; CALC 20mg

How to Sauce Pasta

When saucing pasta, think of the sauce as a seasoning or dressing that you toss with the pasta, much like a salad and dressing, until each piece of pasta is moist. The idea is to impart well-flavored seasoning to each bite of the finished dish.

Long shapes are generally most compatible with smoother sauces that coat them all over (think of the perfect marriage of fettuccine and Alfredo sauce). Short shapes work well with chunky sauces that can be caught in the nooks and crannies of the pasta.

Store-Bought Pasta Sauce

Supermarket shelves are groaning with jarred pasta sauces. And if you are in a rush, sometimes only a jarred sauce will do. After tasting 11 of them, we concluded that the sauce you pick really does matter. Quality differs tremendously among brands.

Among tomato-basil sauces, we found startling variations in consistency (from watery to pasty) and flavor (from basil-free to far-too-much funny-tasting basil). One sauce tasted like a pot of overcooked onions. But there are very good tomato-basil sauces available, and these are our favorites.

Our Top Pick: Rao's Homemade Tomato Basil Marinara Sauce with Basil

Get it: $9 (24-ounce bottle), available at many large supermarkets and gourmet grocery stores

Testers said: $9 for a jar of tomato sauce? Consider, though: Half a jar can feed four people for a dollar and change per diner. Rao's struck tasters as very fresh tasting, a balanced mix of fruity olive oil, tomato, and basil. This will work in a recipe—such as lasagna—in which you want homemade flavor without the time investment.

Very Good: Bove's Basil Pasta Sauce

Get it: $5 (26-ounce bottle), available at many supermarkets

Testers said: Some raters thought Bove's captured the essence of homemade tomato sauce. It was the only sauce that contained Parmesan cheese, and the cheesy flavor and herby notes gave this sauce a pizzeria quality. Great for pizzas, calzones, or meatball subs.

Good: Emeril's All Natural Tomato & Basil Pasta Sauce

Get it: $5 (25-ounce bottle), available at supermarkets

Testers said: Most testers noted sweetness and a subtle basil taste. This sauce also received high marks for its tomato flavor and texture, which one rater said was "smooth but not too acidic." Use this sauce in dishes where you can cut its sweetness with fat or spice. Try it in lasagnas or cheese-stuffed shells, in fiery shrimp *fra diavolo,* or with hot Italian sausage.

Great Value: Classico Tomato & Basil Pasta Sauce

Get it: $3 (24-ounce bottle), available at supermarkets

Testers said: Basil makes a minor appearance in this choice, but many welcomed the garlicky flavor in a slightly thinner tomato-based sauce. Adding a little fresh basil at home yields a balanced option that could work on pizzas or in baked pastas or vegetable soups.

Farfalle with Creamy Wild Mushroom Sauce

This recipe scored high in our Test Kitchen for its rich flavor and ultra-creamy texture. The exotic mushroom blend, a combination of shiitake, cremini, and oyster mushrooms, is sold in 8-ounce packages. If unavailable, you can use all cremini mushrooms.

Yield: 8 servings (serving size: 1¼ cups)

1 pound uncooked farfalle (bow tie pasta)

1 tablespoon butter

12 ounces presliced exotic mushroom blend

½ cup chopped onion

⅓ cup finely chopped shallots

1 tablespoon minced garlic

1½ teaspoons salt, divided

¼ teaspoon freshly ground black pepper

¼ cup dry white wine

⅔ cup whipping cream

½ cup (2 ounces) grated fresh Parmigiano-Reggiano cheese

2 tablespoons chopped fresh parsley

Minced fresh parsley (optional)

1. Cook pasta according to package directions, omitting salt and fat; drain.

2. Melt butter in a large nonstick skillet over medium-high heat. Add mushrooms, onion, shallots, garlic, 1 teaspoon salt, and pepper; cook 12 minutes or until liquid evaporates and mushrooms are tender, stirring occasionally. Add wine; cook 2 minutes or until liquid evaporates, stirring occasionally. Remove from heat.

3. Add cooked pasta, whipping cream, cheese, and 2 tablespoons parsley, tossing gently to coat. Stir in remaining ½ teaspoon salt. Garnish with minced fresh parsley, if desired. Serve immediately.

CALORIES 336; FAT 11.4g (sat 6.9g, mono 3.1g, poly 0.4g); PROTEIN 12.1g; CARB 47.5g; FIBER 2.3g; CHOL 36mg; IRON 2.3mg; SODIUM 577mg; CALC 124mg

INGREDIENT TIP

Bow tie pasta is also known as farfalle pasta. Three cups (or 8 ounces) will yield about 4 cups of cooked pasta. Bow tie pasta, on average, takes about 11 minutes to cook.

Fettuccine Alfredo

A rich, smooth sauce easily coats the long strands of fettuccine. The two ingredients are a perfect match. Use a spoon to help swirl the noodles neatly onto your fork.

Yield: 6 servings (serving size: 1½ cups)

1 pound uncooked fettuccine

1 tablespoon butter

1¼ cups half-and-half

¾ cup (3 ounces) grated fresh Parmesan cheese

½ teaspoon salt

¼ teaspoon black pepper

1. Cook pasta according to package directions, omitting salt and fat.
2. Melt butter in a large skillet over medium heat. Add half-and-half, cheese, salt, and pepper; cook 1 minute, stirring constantly. Reduce heat; add pasta, tossing gently to coat.

CALORIES 427; FAT 14.6g (sat 7.8g, mono 4.2g, poly 1.3g); PROTEIN 17.2g; CARB 56.5g; FIBER 2.1g; CHOL 105mg; IRON 3.6mg; SODIUM 479mg; CALC 245mg

NUTRITION TIP

We lowered the fat in this classic pasta dish by about 10 grams per serving by using half-and-half instead of whipping cream and decreasing the amount of butter and cheese ever so slightly.

Pasta Primavera

Fresh and flavorful, this dish is chock full of vegetables and makes a lovely entrée for spring. A combination of equal parts milk and cream, half-and-half creates a silky, full-bodied sauce.

Yield: 4 servings (serving size: 2 cups pasta mixture, 1 tablespoon basil, and 1 tablespoon cheese)

2 cups green beans, trimmed and halved crosswise

2 cups broccoli florets

½ cup (1-inch) sliced asparagus (about 2 ounces)

6 ounces uncooked fettuccine

1 tablespoon olive oil

1 cup chopped onion

2 teaspoons minced fresh garlic

⅛ teaspoon crushed red pepper

½ cup fresh or frozen green peas

1 cup grape tomatoes, halved

⅔ cup half-and-half

1 teaspoon cornstarch

¾ teaspoon salt

¼ cup chopped fresh basil

¼ cup (1 ounce) shaved Parmigiano-Reggiano cheese

1. Cook green beans in boiling water 1 minute. Add broccoli and asparagus; cook 2 minutes or until vegetables are crisp-tender. Remove vegetables from pan with a slotted spoon; place in a large bowl. Return water to a boil. Add pasta; cook 10 minutes or until al dente. Drain and add to vegetable mixture.

2. Heat oil in a large nonstick skillet over medium-high heat. Add 1 cup onion, and sauté 2 minutes. Add garlic and red pepper; sauté 3 minutes or until onion begins to brown.

3. Add peas, and sauté 1 minute. Add tomatoes; sauté 2 minutes. Combine half-and-half and cornstarch, stirring with a whisk. Reduce heat to medium. Add half-and-half mixture and salt to pan; cook 1 minute or until sauce thickens, stirring constantly. Pour sauce over pasta mixture; toss gently to coat. Sprinkle with basil and cheese. Serve immediately.

CALORIES 338; FAT 10.8g (sat 4.7g, mono 4.4g, poly 0.8g); PROTEIN 13.7g; CARB 49.6g; FIBER 7.1g; CHOL 20mg; IRON 2.9mg; SODIUM 607mg; CALC 205mg

WINE NOTE

Because this is a cream-based pasta primavera, consider serving it with a pinot blanc.

Ragù alla Bolognese with Fettuccine

Ragùs are rich and flavorful meat sauces that begin with a *soffrito*—minced aromatic vegetables sautéed in oil. Wine is often added and reduced. *Ragùs* are typical rustic fare in neighborhood trattorias in Italy. This recipe is adapted from the classic *ragùs* of Italy's Emilia-Romagna region.

Yield: 8 servings (serving size: 1½ cups)

1 tablespoon olive oil

1 cup finely chopped onion

1 cup finely chopped celery

½ cup finely chopped carrot

5 ounces ground veal

5 ounces ground pork

5 ounces ground round

1 cup dry white wine

½ teaspoon salt

½ teaspoon black pepper

¼ teaspoon ground nutmeg

1 bay leaf

1 (14-ounce) can fat-free, lower-sodium chicken broth

1 (10¾-ounce) can tomato puree

1 cup whole milk

2 tablespoons minced fresh flat-leaf parsley

2 (9-ounce) packages fresh fettuccine, cooked and drained

2 tablespoons grated fresh Parmesan cheese

Parsley sprigs (optional)

1. Heat oil in a large Dutch oven over medium heat. Add onion, celery, and carrot; cover and cook 8 minutes, stirring occasionally. Remove onion mixture from pan.

2. Add veal, pork, and beef to pan; cook over medium heat until browned, stirring to crumble. Add wine, salt, pepper, nutmeg, and bay leaf; bring to a boil. Cook 5 minutes. Add onion mixture, broth, and tomato puree; bring to a simmer. Cook 1 hour, stirring occasionally.

3. Stir in milk and minced parsley; bring to a boil. Reduce heat, and simmer 40 minutes.

4. Discard bay leaf. Add pasta, and toss to coat. Sprinkle evenly with cheese. Garnish with parsley sprigs, if desired.

CALORIES 369; FAT 11.8g (sat 4.2g, mono 4.8g, poly 1.4g); PROTEIN 21.4g; CARB 44g; FIBER 4.2g; CHOL 87mg; IRON 3.7mg; SODIUM 546mg; CALC 117mg

WINE NOTE

The best all-around choice when a recipe calls for dry white wine is a quality American sauvignon blanc. Wine contributes flavors to the final dish, so don't be tempted to use a low-quality wine.

Creamy Four-Cheese Macaroni

The combination of fontina, Parmesan, cheddar, and processed cheese packs a flavor punch. Fresh Parmesan and a good extra-sharp cheddar are essential.

Yield: 8 servings (serving size: 1 cup)

1.5 ounces all-purpose flour (about ⅓ cup)

2⅔ cups 1% low-fat milk

¾ cup (3 ounces) shredded fontina cheese or Swiss cheese

½ cup (2 ounces) grated fresh Parmesan cheese

½ cup (2 ounces) shredded extra-sharp cheddar cheese

3 ounces light processed cheese, cubed

6 cups cooked elbow macaroni (about 3 cups uncooked)

¼ teaspoon salt

Cooking spray

⅓ cup crushed onion Melba toasts (about 12 pieces)

1 tablespoon reduced-calorie butter, softened

1. Preheat oven to 375°.

2. Weigh or lightly spoon flour into a dry measuring cup, and level with a knife. Place flour in a large saucepan. Gradually add milk, stirring with a whisk until blended. Cook over medium heat 8 minutes or until thick, stirring constantly. Add cheeses; cook 3 minutes or until cheeses melt, stirring frequently. Remove from heat; stir in macaroni and salt.

3. Spoon mixture into a 2-quart casserole coated with cooking spray. Combine crushed toasts and butter in a small bowl; stir until well blended. Sprinkle over macaroni mixture. Bake at 375° for 30 minutes or until bubbly.

CALORIES 350; FAT 11.2g (sat 6.3g, mono 2.9g, poly 0.9g); PROTEIN 18g; CARB 42.4g; FIBER 2.1g; CHOL 32mg; IRON 1.9mg; SODIUM 497mg; CALC 306mg

FLAVOR TIP

Often found on top of soups and salads or as an accompaniment to dips and spreads, Melba toast adds flavor

without adding many calories or fat. The crispiness of the toasts is a wonderful contrast to the creamy cheese and tender noodles.

Beef, Cheese, and Noodle Bake

This family-friendly casserole is a great way to incorporate more vegetables into your kids' food. For creamiest results, do not overbake.

Yield: 8 servings (serving size: about 1 cup)

1 (8-ounce) package small elbow macaroni

Cooking spray

1 cup prechopped onion

1 cup preshredded carrot

2 teaspoons bottled minced garlic

1 pound lean ground sirloin

1 cup tomato sauce

1 teaspoon kosher salt, divided

½ teaspoon freshly ground black pepper

1 cup fat-free milk

2 tablespoons all-purpose flour

⅛ teaspoon ground nutmeg

1½ cups (6 ounces) reduced-fat shredded sharp cheddar cheese, divided

1. Preheat oven to 350°.

2. Cook pasta according to package directions, omitting salt and fat; drain. Lightly coat pasta with cooking spray.

3. Heat a Dutch oven over medium-high heat. Coat pan with cooking spray. Add onion and carrot, and sauté 4 minutes. Add garlic; sauté 1 minute. Add beef; cook 5 minutes or until browned, stirring to crumble. Add tomato sauce, ½ teaspoon salt, and pepper. Cook 2 minutes or until most of liquid evaporates.

4. Add pasta to beef mixture in pan, stirring to combine. Spoon pasta mixture into an 11 x 7–inch baking dish coated with cooking spray.

5. Place milk, flour, nutmeg, and remaining ½ teaspoon salt in a medium saucepan; stir with a whisk until blended. Cook over medium heat 2 minutes or until thick, stirring constantly with a whisk. Add 1 cup cheese, stirring until smooth. Pour cheese mixture over pasta mixture; stir. Top evenly with remaining ½ cup cheese. Bake at 350° for 20 minutes or until lightly browned. Let stand 5 minutes before serving.

CALORIES 283; FAT 7.7g (sat 4.2g, mono 2.4g, poly 0.7g); PROTEIN 22.3g; CARB 30.1g; FIBER 2.1g; CHOL 46mg; IRON 3.1mg; SODIUM 622mg; CALC 209mg

NUTRITION TIP

With more than 200 milligrams of calcium per serving, this dish is a good source of the bone-building mineral.

Linguine with Clam Sauce

Because this dish is so fresh and simple, you will absolutely want to use fresh clams. Use the larger amount of red pepper for a zestier dish.

Yield: 6 servings (serving size: 1⅓ cups pasta mixture and 6 clams)

¼ cup olive oil, divided

2 garlic cloves, minced

⅓ cup clam juice

¼ cup chopped fresh flat-leaf parsley

½ to ¾ teaspoon crushed red pepper

½ teaspoon salt

¼ teaspoon freshly ground black pepper

3 dozen littleneck clams

8 cups hot cooked linguine (about 1 pound uncooked pasta)

1. Heat 2 tablespoons oil in a large skillet over medium heat. Add garlic; cook 3 minutes or until golden, stirring frequently. Stir in clam juice and next 5 ingredients. Cover and cook 10 minutes or until clams open. Discard any unopened shells.

2. Place pasta in a large bowl. Add remaining 2 tablespoons oil; toss well to coat. Add clam mixture to pasta; toss well.

CALORIES 398; FAT 10.6g (sat 1.6g, mono 6.7g, poly 0.9g); PROTEIN 17.4g; CARB 58.4g; FIBER 2.6g; CHOL 19mg; IRON 10.3mg; SODIUM 258mg; CALC 46mg

INGREDIENT TIP

Cleaning clams is quick and easy. Scrub them with a stiff brush under cold

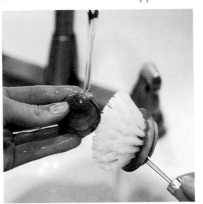

running water to remove sand and dirt.

Italian Sausage Puttanesca

Puttanesca (poot-tah-NEHS-kah) sauce is a spicy mélange of tomatoes, onions, capers, olives, anchovies, and garlic. Add mixed greens and fresh bread to complete the meal.

Yield: 6 servings

8 ounces uncooked penne (tube-shaped pasta)

Cooking spray

8 ounces hot turkey Italian sausage

1 cup chopped onion

1 cup chopped green bell pepper

3 garlic cloves, minced

½ cup halved pitted kalamata olives

2 tablespoons tomato paste

1 tablespoon capers, drained

1 teaspoon anchovy paste

2 (14.5-ounce) cans no-salt-added whole tomatoes, undrained and chopped

½ cup (2 ounces) finely shredded Parmesan cheese

1. Preheat oven to 400°.

2. Cook pasta according to package directions, omitting salt and fat. Drain well.

3. Heat a Dutch oven over medium-high heat. Coat pan with cooking spray. Remove casings from sausage. Add sausage, onion, bell pepper, and garlic to pan; sauté 8 minutes, stirring to crumble sausage.

4. Add olives, tomato paste, capers, anchovy paste, and tomatoes to pan; bring to a boil. Reduce heat, and simmer 5 minutes. Remove from heat. Add pasta, tossing well to combine. Spoon pasta mixture into an 11 x 7–inch baking dish coated with cooking spray; sprinkle evenly with cheese. Bake at 400° for 15 minutes or until cheese melts and begins to brown.

CALORIES 321; FAT 10.6g (sat 3.1g, mono 4.6g, poly 1.6g); PROTEIN 14.8g; CARB 41.8g; FIBER 4g; CHOL 28mg; IRON 3.1mg; SODIUM 649mg; CALC 152mg

FLAVOR TIP

For a little less heat, use sweet turkey Italian sausage instead of hot.

Marinara Sauce over Rotini

If you don't have rotini, try another pasta—just about any pasta will do, even spaghetti. Top with Parmesan cheese for an extra-special treat.

Yield: 4 servings (serving size: 1 cup pasta and ¾ cup sauce)

1 teaspoon olive oil

½ cup chopped onion

2 garlic cloves, minced

2 tablespoons chopped fresh or 2 teaspoons dried basil

2 tablespoons chopped fresh or 2 teaspoons dried parsley

1 teaspoon sugar

½ teaspoon dried oregano

¼ teaspoon salt

¼ teaspoon black pepper

1 (28-ounce) can diced tomatoes, undrained

1 tablespoon capers

4 cups hot cooked rotini (about 4 cups uncooked corkscrew pasta)

1. Heat oil in a medium saucepan over medium heat. Add onion and garlic, and sauté 2 minutes. Add basil and next 6 ingredients; bring to a boil.

2. Reduce heat, and simmer 15 minutes, stirring occasionally. Stir in capers. Serve over pasta.

CALORIES 277; FAT 2.5g (sat 0.4g, mono 1g, poly 0.7g); PROTEIN 9.7g; CARB 54.7g; FIBER 3.3g; CHOL 0mg; IRON 3.7mg; SODIUM 531mg; CALC 77mg

QUICK TIP

If you don't have any fresh herbs or garlic on hand and don't have time to swing by the supermarket, dried herbs and bottled minced garlic make good stand-ins.

Salmon, Asparagus, and Orzo Salad with Lemon-Dill Vinaigrette

This savory salad is quick, easy, and loaded with flavorful ingredients such as crisp-tender asparagus, perfectly cooked salmon, red onion, and a refreshing lemon juice–based vinaigrette. It received our highest Test Kitchen rating.

Yield: 6 servings (serving size: about 1¼ cups)

6 cups water

1 pound asparagus, trimmed and cut into 3-inch pieces

1 cup uncooked orzo (rice-shaped pasta)

1 (1¼-pound) skinless salmon fillet

¼ teaspoon salt

¼ teaspoon freshly ground black pepper

Cooking spray

¼ cup thinly sliced red onion

⅓ cup Lemon-Dill Vinaigrette

1. Preheat broiler.

2. Bring 6 cups water to a boil in a large saucepan. Add asparagus; cook 3 minutes or until crisp-tender. Remove asparagus from water with tongs or a slotted spoon, reserving water in pan. Plunge asparagus into ice water; drain and set aside.

3. Return reserved water to a boil. Add orzo, and cook according to package directions, omitting salt and fat.

4. While orzo cooks, sprinkle fillet evenly with salt and pepper. Place fish on a foil-lined broiler pan coated with cooking spray. Broil 5 minutes or until desired degree of doneness. Using 2 forks, break fish into large chunks. Combine fish, orzo, asparagus, onion, and Lemon-Dill Vinaigrette in a large bowl; toss gently to coat.

CALORIES 310; FAT 11g (sat 3.2g, mono 4.7g, poly 2g); PROTEIN 26g; CARB 24.6g; FIBER 2.2g; CHOL 56mg; IRON 1.4mg; SODIUM 333mg; CALC 67mg

Lemon-Dill Vinaigrette

Yield: ⅓ cup (serving size: about 1 tablespoon)

⅓ cup (1.3 ounces) crumbled feta cheese

1 tablespoon chopped fresh dill

3 tablespoons fresh lemon juice

2 teaspoons extra-virgin olive oil

¼ teaspoon salt

¼ teaspoon freshly ground black pepper

1. Combine all ingredients in a small bowl, stirring well with a whisk.

CALORIES 43; FAT 4g (sat 1.7g, mono 1.8g, poly 0.2g); PROTEIN 1.4g; CARB 1.2g; FIBER 0.1g; CHOL 8mg; IRON 0.1mg; SODIUM 214mg; CALC 48mg

Easy Penne and Tuna Salad

Instead of cleaning out the fridge to put dinner together, toss pasta with quality tuna; its richness and flavor will carry the salad, which is embellished with simple flavorings. Serve with a torn baguette.

Yield: 4 servings (serving size: 2 cups)

1 large red bell pepper

4 quarts water

2¼ teaspoons salt, divided

6 ounces uncooked penne pasta

2 cups coarsely chopped arugula

¼ cup thinly sliced shallots

2 tablespoons red wine vinegar

1 tablespoon capers, drained

1 tablespoon extra-virgin olive oil

1 (7.8-ounce) jar premium tuna packed in oil, drained and flaked

Freshly ground black pepper (optional)

1. Preheat broiler.

2. Cut bell pepper in half lengthwise; discard seeds and membranes. Place pepper halves, skin sides up, on a foil-lined baking sheet; flatten with hand. Broil 15 minutes or until blackened. Place in a zip-top plastic bag; seal. Let stand 15 minutes. Peel and chop.

3. Bring 4 quarts water and 2 teaspoons salt to a boil in a large saucepan. Cook pasta according to package directions, omitting additional salt and fat. Drain and rinse with cold water; drain well.

4. Combine bell pepper, pasta, remaining ¼ teaspoon salt, arugula, and remaining ingredients in a large bowl; toss well. Garnish with freshly ground black pepper, if desired.

CALORIES 310; FAT 8.8g (sat 1.4g, mono 4.3g, poly 2.3g); PROTEIN 21.4g; CARB 36.3g; FIBER 2.5g; CHOL 17mg; IRON 2.2mg; SODIUM 556mg; CALC 34mg

Tex-Mex Pasta Salad

This kid-friendly recipe is a takeoff on macaroni and cheese; it makes a large batch that holds well for two or three days. Serve with pickled jalapeño slices for grownups who like spicy food.

Yield: 12 servings (serving size: about 1⅓ cups)

1 pound uncooked radiatore (short coiled pasta)

2 teaspoons olive oil

3 garlic cloves, minced

1½ pounds ground turkey

⅔ cup water

1 (1.25-ounce) package 40%-less-sodium taco seasoning

2 cups (8 ounces) preshredded reduced-fat Mexican blend cheese

2 cups chopped seeded tomato

1 cup chopped bell pepper

½ cup chopped fresh cilantro

½ cup chopped green onions

½ cup sliced ripe olives

1 (15.5-ounce) can black beans, rinsed and drained

2 tablespoons fresh lime juice

½ teaspoon salt

¼ teaspoon ground cumin

1 (8-ounce) container reduced-fat sour cream

Salsa (optional)

1. Cook pasta according to package directions, omitting salt and fat. Drain and rinse with cold water. Drain; set aside.

2. Heat oil in a large nonstick skillet over medium-high heat. Add garlic; sauté 1 minute.

3. Add turkey; cook until browned, stirring to crumble. Stir in ⅔ cup water and taco seasoning; bring to a boil. Reduce heat, and simmer 4 minutes or until liquid almost evaporates and turkey is done, stirring frequently. Remove from heat; cool slightly.

4. Combine pasta, turkey mixture, reduced-fat cheese, and next 6 ingredients in a large bowl.

5. Combine lime juice, salt, cumin, and sour cream, stirring until well blended. Pour over pasta mixture; toss gently to coat. Serve with salsa, if desired.

CALORIES 344; FAT 11.4g (sat 5.3g, mono 4.1g, poly 1.4g); PROTEIN 23.4g; CARB 38.5g; FIBER 3.6g; CHOL 51mg; IRON 2.9mg; SODIUM 632mg; CALC 193mg

NUTRITION TIP

Rinsing canned beans gets rid of the thick liquid in the can and reduces the sodium by 40%.

Seashell Salad with Buttermilk-Chive Dressing

While this creamy salad is delicious when served immediately, it is equally good the next day. The flavors meld beautifully overnight. (Pictured on page 86.)

Yield: 4 servings (serving size: about 1¼ cups salad and 1 tablespoon prosciutto)

8 ounces uncooked seashell pasta

1 cup frozen green peas

¼ cup organic canola mayonnaise

¼ cup fat-free buttermilk

1 tablespoon minced fresh chives

1 teaspoon chopped fresh thyme

½ teaspoon salt

½ teaspoon freshly ground black pepper

2 garlic cloves, minced

2 cups loosely packed baby arugula

1 teaspoon olive oil

2 ounces finely chopped prosciutto (about ½ cup)

1. Cook pasta according to package directions. Add peas to pasta during last 2 minutes of cooking. Drain and rinse with cold water; drain well.

2. While pasta cooks, combine mayonnaise and next 6 ingredients in a large bowl. Add pasta mixture and arugula; toss to coat.

3. Heat oil in a skillet over medium-high heat. Add prosciutto; sauté 2 minutes. Drain on paper towels. Sprinkle prosciutto over salad.

CALORIES 373; FAT 14.9g (sat 1.4g, mono 4.4g, poly 7.5g); PROTEIN 13.6g; CARB 45.7g; FIBER 3.6g; CHOL 18mg; IRON 2.8mg; SODIUM 677mg; CALC 50mg

Mac and Cheese with Roasted Tomatoes

The breadcrumb and Parmesan mixture forms a gratin-style topping that adds a light crunchiness.

Yield: 10 servings (serving size: about 1 cup)

Cooking spray

8 plum tomatoes, cut into ¼-inch-thick slices (about 2 pounds)

1 tablespoon olive oil

1 tablespoon minced fresh thyme

¾ teaspoon salt, divided

4 garlic cloves, thinly sliced

1 pound uncooked multigrain whole-wheat elbow macaroni

2.25 ounces all-purpose flour (about ½ cup)

5 cups 1% low-fat milk

1½ cups (6 ounces) shredded extra-sharp white cheddar cheese

1 cup (4 ounces) shredded fontina cheese

½ teaspoon black pepper

½ cup (2 ounces) grated fresh Parmesan cheese

⅓ cup dry breadcrumbs

½ teaspoon paprika

1. Preheat oven to 400°.

2. Cover a baking sheet with foil, and coat foil with cooking spray. Arrange tomato slices in a single layer on baking sheet. Drizzle oil over tomatoes. Sprinkle with thyme, ¼ teaspoon salt, and garlic. Bake at 400° for 35 minutes or until tomatoes start to dry out.

3. Cook pasta according to package directions, omitting salt and fat. Drain well.

4. Weigh or lightly spoon flour into a dry measuring cup; level with a knife. Place flour in a large Dutch oven; gradually add milk, stirring with a whisk until blended. Cook over medium heat 8 minutes or until thick and bubbly, stirring constantly with a whisk. Add cheddar, fontina, remaining ½ teaspoon salt, and pepper, stirring until cheese melts. Remove from heat. Stir in tomatoes and pasta. Spoon into a 13 x 9–inch baking dish coated with cooking spray. Combine grated Parmesan cheese, breadcrumbs, and paprika; sprinkle over pasta mixture. Bake at 400° for 25 minutes or until bubbly.

CALORIES 411; FAT 14g (sat 6.9g, mono 2.9g, poly 0.9g); PROTEIN 22.8g; CARB 49.9g; FIBER 4.7g; CHOL 39mg; IRON 2.5mg; SODIUM 638mg; CALC 414mg

MAKE-AHEAD TIP

Bake this dish the night before, and reheat single servings in the microwave the next day.

Make-Ahead Cheese-and-Hamburger Casserole

The penne doesn't have to be cooked beforehand because it absorbs the liquid when refrigerated overnight. If you want to make it the same day, cook the pasta before combining it with the rest of the ingredients. For convenience, use precrumbled feta and preshredded mozzarella.

Yield: 8 servings

1 pound ground round

1 cup chopped onion

3 garlic cloves, crushed

1 (8-ounce) package presliced mushrooms

6 tablespoons tomato paste

1 teaspoon sugar

1 teaspoon dried thyme

1 teaspoon dried oregano

¼ teaspoon pepper

1 (28-ounce) can whole tomatoes, undrained and chopped

1.5 ounces all-purpose flour (about ⅓ cup)

2½ cups 2% reduced-fat milk

1 cup (4 ounces) crumbled feta cheese

¾ cup (3 ounces) shredded part-skim mozzarella cheese

4 cups uncooked penne (tube-shaped pasta)

1 tablespoon chopped fresh parsley (optional)

1. Combine first 3 ingredients in a large nonstick skillet; cook over medium-high heat until browned, stirring to crumble. Add mushrooms; cook 5 minutes or until tender. Add tomato paste and next 5 ingredients; stir well. Bring to a boil; reduce heat, and simmer, uncovered, 20 minutes. Set aside.

2. Weigh or lightly spoon flour into a dry measuring cup; level with a knife. Place flour in a medium saucepan. Gradually add milk, stirring with a whisk until blended. Place over medium heat; cook 10 minutes or until thick, stirring constantly. Stir in cheeses; cook 3 minutes or until cheeses melt, stirring constantly. Reserve ½ cup cheese sauce. Pour remaining cheese sauce, beef mixture, and pasta into a 13 x 9–inch baking dish, and stir gently. Drizzle reserved cheese sauce over pasta mixture. Cover and refrigerate 24 hours.

3. Preheat oven to 350°.

4. Bake at 350°, covered, 1 hour and 10 minutes or until thoroughly heated and pasta is tender; sprinkle with parsley, if desired.

CALORIES 412; FAT 10.8g (sat 5.5g, mono 3.2g, poly 0.9g); PROTEIN 27.5g; CARB 51.1g; FIBER 3.2g; CHOL 60mg; IRON 4.9mg; SODIUM 448mg; CALC 286mg

Bow Tie Pasta with Roasted Red Bell Peppers and Cream Sauce

Roasted red peppers and a cream sauce deliver rich flavor in this quick and easy recipe. Balsamic vinegar helps balance the natural sweetness of the red bell peppers.

Yield: 6 servings

1 pound uncooked farfalle (bow tie pasta)

2 teaspoons extra-virgin olive oil

½ cup finely chopped onion

1 (12-ounce) bottle roasted red bell peppers, drained and coarsely chopped

2 teaspoons balsamic vinegar

1 cup half-and-half

1 tablespoon tomato paste

⅛ teaspoon ground red pepper

1 cup (4 ounces) freshly grated Parmigiano-Reggiano cheese, divided

Thinly sliced fresh basil (optional)

1. Cook pasta according to package directions, omitting salt and fat.

2. Heat oil in a large skillet over medium heat. Add onion, and cook 8 minutes or until tender, stirring frequently. Add bell peppers; cook 2 minutes or until thoroughly heated. Increase heat to medium-high. Stir in vinegar; cook 1 minute or until liquid evaporates. Remove from heat; cool 5 minutes.

3. Place bell pepper mixture in a blender; process until smooth. Return bell pepper mixture to pan; cook over low heat until warm. Combine half-and-half and tomato paste in a small bowl, stirring with a whisk. Stir tomato mixture into bell pepper mixture, stirring with a whisk until well combined. Stir in ground red pepper.

4. Combine pasta and bell pepper mixture in a large bowl. Add ½ cup cheese, tossing to coat. Spoon 1⅓ cups pasta into each of 6 bowls; top each with about 1½ tablespoons cheese. Garnish with basil, if desired.

CALORIES 424; FAT 10.7g (sat 5.6g, mono 3.7g, poly 0.5g); PROTEIN 17.6g; CARB 62.9g; FIBER 3g; CHOL 32mg; IRON 2.9mg; SODIUM 383mg; CALC 222mg

Aunt Liz's Chicken Spaghetti Casserole

This chicken spaghetti casserole is low in calories. The recipe makes two casseroles, so enjoy one for dinner and freeze the other for later. To prepare the frozen casserole, cover and bake for 55 minutes at 350°; uncover and bake an additional 10 minutes or until hot and bubbly.

Yield: 2 casseroles, 4 servings each (serving size: about 1 cup)

2 cups chopped cooked chicken breast

2 cups uncooked spaghetti, broken into 2-inch pieces (about 7 ounces)

1 cup (¼-inch-thick) sliced celery

1 cup chopped red bell pepper

1 cup chopped onion

1 cup fat-free, lower-sodium chicken broth

½ teaspoon salt

¼ teaspoon freshly ground black pepper

2 (10.75-ounce) cans condensed 30% reduced-sodium 98% fat-free cream of mushroom soup, undiluted

Cooking spray

1 cup (4 ounces) shredded cheddar cheese, divided

1. Preheat oven to 350°.
2. Combine first 5 ingredients in a large bowl. Combine broth, salt, pepper, and soup in a medium bowl, stirring with a whisk. Add soup mixture to chicken mixture; toss. Divide mixture evenly between 2 (8-inch) square or 2-quart baking dishes coated with cooking spray. Sprinkle ½ cup cheese over each casserole. Cover with foil coated with cooking spray. Bake at 350° for 35 minutes. Uncover and bake an additional 10 minutes.

CALORIES 261; FAT 7.8g (sat 3.9g, mono 2.2g, poly 1.1g); PROTEIN 19g; CARB 28g; FIBER 2.1g; CHOL 47mg; IRON 1.8mg; SODIUM 652mg; CALC 134mg

QUICK TIP

Purchase prechopped onion from your grocer's produce section to save the time you would spend chopping your own.

Special Occasion Lasagna

Serve this company-worthy lasagna with a tossed green or Caesar salad and breadsticks to round out the meal.

Yield: 8 servings

1 (8-ounce) package uncooked lasagna noodles (about 9 noodles)

1⅓ cups (6 ounces) fat-free cottage cheese

¾ cup (6 ounces) ⅓-less-fat cream cheese, softened

⅔ cup (6 ounces) part-skim ricotta cheese

¼ cup (1 ounce) grated fresh Parmesan cheese

2 tablespoons minced fresh chives

1 teaspoon Dijon mustard

½ teaspoon salt

½ teaspoon dry mustard

½ teaspoon freshly ground black pepper

4 garlic cloves, minced

2 large egg whites, lightly beaten

1 large egg, lightly beaten

1 (26-ounce) jar fat-free pasta sauce, divided

Cooking spray

¼ cup (1 ounce) shredded part-skim mozzarella cheese

1. Preheat oven to 350°.
2. Cook noodles according to package directions, omitting salt and fat.
3. Combine cottage cheese, cream cheese, and ricotta cheese in a large bowl; stir to blend well. Stir in Parmesan and next 8 ingredients.
4. Spread ½ cup pasta sauce in bottom of a 13 x 9–inch baking dish coated with cooking spray. Arrange 3 noodles over pasta sauce; top with half of cheese mixture and one-third of remaining pasta sauce. Repeat layers once, ending with noodles. Spread remaining pasta sauce over noodles.
5. Bake at 350° for 20 minutes. Sprinkle with mozzarella; bake an additional 20 minutes or until cheese is melted. Remove from oven; let stand 10 minutes before serving.

CALORIES 284; FAT 8.8g (sat 5.2g, mono 2.5g, poly 0.4g); PROTEIN 15.7g; CARB 34.2g; FIBER 3.3g; CHOL 53mg; IRON 0.9mg; SODIUM 657mg; CALC 179mg

MAKE-AHEAD TIP

You can make this dish ahead—just cover it, and refrigerate or freeze it after you've spread the final layer of marinara sauce.

Pumpkin Ravioli with Gorgonzola Sauce

For a new way to enjoy pumpkin in season, try these pumpkin ravioli with a rich yet mellow Gorgonzola sauce. The ravioli will float when they are perfectly cooked. Pour a chilled chardonnay to round out your meal.

Yield: 6 servings

1¼ cups canned pumpkin

2 tablespoons dry breadcrumbs

2 tablespoons grated fresh Parmesan cheese

½ teaspoon salt

½ teaspoon minced fresh sage

¼ teaspoon freshly ground black pepper

⅛ teaspoon ground nutmeg

30 round wonton wrappers

1 tablespoon cornstarch

Cooking spray

1 cup fat-free milk

1 tablespoon all-purpose flour

1½ tablespoons butter

½ cup (2 ounces) crumbled Gorgonzola cheese

3 tablespoons chopped hazelnuts, toasted

Sage sprigs (optional)

1. Spoon pumpkin onto several layers of heavy-duty paper towels, and spread to ½-inch thickness. Cover with additional paper towels; let stand 5 minutes. Scrape into a medium bowl using a rubber spatula. Stir in breadcrumbs, Parmesan, salt, minced sage, pepper, and nutmeg.

2. Working with 1 wonton wrapper at a time (cover remaining wrappers with a damp towel to keep from drying), spoon 2 teaspoons pumpkin mixture into center of wrapper. Brush edges of wrapper with water and fold in half, pressing edges firmly with fingers to form a half-moon. Place on a large baking sheet sprinkled with cornstarch. Repeat procedure with remaining wonton wrappers and pumpkin mixture.

3. Fill a large Dutch oven with water; bring to a simmer. Add half of ravioli to pan (cover remaining ravioli with a damp towel to keep from drying). Cook 4 minutes or until done (do not boil), stirring gently. Remove ravioli with a slotted spoon; lightly coat with cooking spray, and keep warm. Repeat procedure with remaining ravioli.

4. Combine milk and flour in a saucepan, stirring with a whisk. Bring to a boil; cook 1 minute or until thick, stirring constantly. Remove from heat. Add butter, stirring until butter melts. Gently stir in Gorgonzola.

5. Place 5 ravioli in each of 6 shallow bowls, and drizzle each serving with 3 tablespoons Gorgonzola mixture. Sprinkle each serving with 1½ teaspoons hazelnuts. Garnish with sage sprigs, if desired. Serve immediately.

CALORIES 250; FAT 9.1g (sat 4.5g, mono 2.7g, poly 0.7g); PROTEIN 9.5g; CARB 33g; FIBER 3.1g; CHOL 22mg; IRON 2.4mg; SODIUM 636mg; CALC 162mg

MAKE-AHEAD TIP

You can assemble the ravioli a day ahead, cover with plastic wrap, and refrigerate.

Hamburger Stroganoff

Add a tossed green salad and sautéed red and green bell pepper strips for a satisfying family-friendly meal.

Yield: 6 servings (serving size: about ½ cup stroganoff, ⅔ cup pasta, and 1½ teaspoons parsley)

8 ounces uncooked medium egg noodles

1 teaspoon olive oil

1 pound ground beef, extra lean

1 cup prechopped onion

1 teaspoon bottled minced garlic

1 (8-ounce) package presliced cremini mushrooms

2 tablespoons all-purpose flour

1 cup fat-free, lower-sodium beef broth

1¼ teaspoons kosher salt

⅛ teaspoon black pepper

¾ cup reduced-fat sour cream

1 tablespoon dry sherry

3 tablespoons chopped fresh parsley

1. Cook pasta according to package directions, omitting salt and fat. Drain and rinse under cold water; drain.

2. Heat oil in a large nonstick skillet over medium-high heat. Add beef to pan; cook 4 minutes or until browned, stirring to crumble. Add onion, garlic, and mushrooms to pan; cook 4 minutes or until most of liquid evaporates, stirring frequently. Sprinkle with flour; cook 1 minute, stirring constantly. Stir in broth; bring to a boil. Reduce heat, and simmer 1 minute or until slightly thick. Stir in salt and pepper.

3. Remove from heat. Stir in sour cream and sherry. Serve over pasta. Sprinkle with parsley.

CALORIES 322; FAT 9.8g (sat 4.4g, mono 3.5g, poly 1.1g); PROTEIN 23.9g; CARB 35.1g; FIBER 2.1g; CHOL 82mg; IRON 3.2mg; SODIUM 541mg; CALC 70mg

Roasted Tomato–Beef Goulash with Caraway

Sheryl Chomak of Beaverton, Oregon, says that Hungarian goulash was a family favorite when she was growing up. Here's an updated version of her mom's recipe with fresh vegetables. Replacing plain tomato sauce with roasted diced tomatoes improves the taste and texture of the gravy.

Yield: 8 servings (serving size: ½ cup goulash and ½ cup noodles)

2 pounds bottom round roast, trimmed and cut into 1-inch pieces

1 teaspoon kosher salt, divided

½ teaspoon freshly ground black pepper

2 teaspoons canola oil

2 tablespoons paprika, divided

1 to 2 teaspoons caraway seeds

1¼ cups coarsely chopped onion (about 1 large)

½ cup finely chopped celery

½ cup finely chopped carrot

1 tablespoon minced garlic

1 (14.5-ounce) can fire-roasted diced tomatoes, undrained

4 cups cooked medium egg noodles (about 2½ cups uncooked pasta)

Chopped fresh parsley (optional)

1. Sprinkle beef with ½ teaspoon salt and pepper.

2. Heat oil in a large Dutch oven over medium-high heat. Add beef to pan; cook 3 minutes or until browned on all sides. Add 1 tablespoon paprika and caraway seeds. Reduce heat to medium, and cook 2 minutes, stirring constantly. Stir in remaining ½ teaspoon salt, remaining 1 tablespoon paprika, onion, celery, carrot, and garlic; cook 5 minutes, stirring occasionally. Add tomatoes; bring to a boil. Cover, reduce heat, and simmer 1½ hours or until beef is tender. Serve over noodles. Garnish with parsley, if desired.

CALORIES 299; FAT 8.5g (sat 2.3g, mono 3.6g, poly 1.2g); PROTEIN 27.2g; CARB 27.6g; FIBER 2.9g; CHOL 91mg; IRON 4.5mg; SODIUM 403mg; CALC 41mg

Osso Buco with Gremolata

Inexpensive veal shanks become a succulent meal in the slow cooker. Even if you aren't an anchovy lover, don't omit the anchovy paste—it adds immeasurably to the flavor. Use the remaining broth mixture in soups and stews.

Yield: 8 servings (serving size: 3 ounces veal, 1 cup pasta, ½ cup broth mixture, and 1 tablespoon gremolata)

Osso Buco:

3 ounces all-purpose flour (about ⅔ cup)

¾ teaspoon freshly ground black pepper, divided

½ teaspoon kosher salt, divided

6 veal shanks, trimmed (about 5 pounds)

2 teaspoons butter

2 teaspoons olive oil

2 cups coarsely chopped red onion

1½ cups chopped celery

6 garlic cloves, minced

4 cups beef broth

2 cups dry white wine

1 tablespoon chopped fresh rosemary

1 tablespoon anchovy paste

Gremolata:

½ cup chopped fresh flat-leaf parsley

1 tablespoon grated lemon rind

2 garlic cloves, minced

Remaining Ingredient:

8 cups hot cooked pappardelle pasta (about 1 pound uncooked wide ribbon pasta)

1. To prepare osso buco, combine flour, ¼ teaspoon pepper, and ¼ teaspoon salt in a shallow dish. Dredge veal in flour mixture.

2. Heat 1 teaspoon butter and 1 teaspoon oil in a large skillet over medium heat. Add half of veal; cook 6 minutes, browning on both sides. Place browned veal in a large electric slow cooker. Repeat procedure with remaining butter, oil, and veal.

3. Add onion and celery to pan; sauté 5 minutes over medium-high heat or until tender. Add 6 garlic cloves to pan; sauté 1 minute. Stir in broth, wine, rosemary, and anchovy paste, scraping pan to loosen browned bits. Bring to a boil; cook 4 minutes. Pour over veal.

4. Cover and cook on LOW 9 hours or until done. Sprinkle veal with remaining ½ teaspoon pepper and remaining ¼ teaspoon salt. Remove veal from cooker; cool slightly.

5. To prepare gremolata, combine parsley, lemon rind, and 2 garlic cloves. Place 1 cup pasta in each of 8 pasta bowls. Top each serving with ⅔ cup veal and ½ cup broth mixture. Reserve remaining broth mixture for another use. Sprinkle each serving with 1 tablespoon gremolata.

CALORIES 443; FAT 12.2g (sat 4.1g, mono 4.9g, poly 1.1g); PROTEIN 54.9g; CARB 15.9g; FIBER 1.8g; CHOL 200mg; IRON 3.3mg; SODIUM 485mg; CALC 94mg

Steak Tips with Peppered Mushroom Gravy

Briefly cooking the gravy with thyme sprigs saves the time of stripping the tiny leaves from the stem but still gives you the herb's woodsy flavor.

Yield: 4 servings (serving size: about ¾ cup beef mixture and ⅔ cup noodles)

2 cups uncooked egg noodles

Cooking spray

1 pound top sirloin steak, cut into ¾-inch pieces

1 tablespoon butter

2 tablespoons finely chopped shallots

1 (8-ounce) package presliced baby bella mushrooms

1 teaspoon minced garlic

1 tablespoon lower-sodium soy sauce

3 tablespoons all-purpose flour

1½ cups fat-free, lower-sodium beef broth

½ teaspoon black pepper

¼ teaspoon salt

3 fresh thyme sprigs

1 teaspoon fresh thyme leaves (optional)

1. Cook noodles according to package directions, omitting salt and fat; drain.

2. While noodles cook, heat a large nonstick skillet over medium-high heat. Coat pan with cooking spray. Add steak; sauté 5 minutes, browning on all sides. Remove from pan; cover.

3. Melt butter in pan over medium-high heat. Add shallots and mushrooms; sauté 4 minutes. Add garlic; sauté 30 seconds. Stir in soy sauce. Sprinkle flour over mushroom mixture; cook 1 minute, stirring constantly. Gradually add broth, stirring constantly. Add pepper, salt, and thyme sprigs. Bring to a boil; cook 2 minutes or until thick. Return beef to pan; cook 1 minute or until thoroughly heated. Discard thyme sprigs. Garnish with thyme leaves, if desired.

CALORIES 344; FAT 12.5g (sat 5.3g, mono 4.2g, poly 1.2g); PROTEIN 27.3g; CARB 28.7g; FIBER 1.7g; CHOL 95mg; IRON 4.3mg; SODIUM 538mg; CALC 28mg

Chili Mac

This kid-friendly classic is a staple for school nights, and you can substitute whatever small pasta or cheese you have on hand. For additional convenience, use frozen chopped onion and chopped green bell pepper. Leftovers are even better the next day.

Yield: 8 servings (serving size: 1 cup beef mixture and 2 tablespoons cheese)

1 pound ground round

½ cup chopped onion

½ cup chopped green bell pepper

3 garlic cloves, minced

2 cups cooked elbow macaroni (about 4 ounces uncooked)

½ cup water

1 tablespoon chili powder

1 teaspoon ground cumin

¼ teaspoon black pepper

1 (14.5-ounce) can whole tomatoes, undrained and chopped

1 (15-ounce) can kidney beans, drained

1 (8¾-ounce) can whole-kernel corn, drained

1 (8-ounce) can tomato sauce

1 (6-ounce) can tomato paste

1 cup (4 ounces) shredded sharp cheddar cheese

1. Cook first 4 ingredients in a large Dutch oven over medium-high heat until browned, stirring to crumble beef. Drain well; wipe drippings from pan with paper towels. Return beef mixture to pan; stir in macaroni and next 9 ingredients. Bring to a boil; cover, reduce heat, and simmer 20 minutes, stirring occasionally. Spoon into 8 serving dishes; top with cheese.

CALORIES 295; FAT 9.2g (sat 4.4g, mono 3g, poly 0.8g); PROTEIN 22.6g; CARB 32.5g; FIBER 4.2g; CHOL 50mg; IRON 4.3mg; SODIUM 529mg; CALC 151mg

QUICK TIP

Why use two pans when you can use one? A quick wipe with a paper towel removes any grease from the cooked beef, and your pan is good to go for the remainder of the recipe.

Sirloin Steak and Pasta Salad

A salt-free garlic-pepper blend seasons juicy steak. We recommend using sirloin, but flank steak works great, too.

Yield: 4 servings (serving size: about 1½ cups)

3 quarts water

2 cups uncooked penne or mostaccioli (tube-shaped pasta)

¼ pound green beans, trimmed

1 (¾-pound) boneless sirloin steak, trimmed

1 tablespoon salt-free garlic-pepper blend

1½ cups thinly sliced red onion

1½ cups thinly sliced red bell pepper

¼ cup chopped fresh basil

3 tablespoons Dijon mustard

2 tablespoons balsamic vinegar

1 teaspoon extra-virgin olive oil

1 teaspoon bottled minced garlic

¼ teaspoon salt

¼ teaspoon black pepper

¼ cup (1 ounce) crumbled blue cheese

1. Preheat broiler.

2. While broiler preheats, bring 3 quarts water to a boil in a large Dutch oven. Add pasta; cook 5½ minutes. Add beans, and cook 3 minutes or until pasta is done. Drain and rinse with cold water. Drain well.

3. Sprinkle steak with garlic-pepper blend. Place on a broiler pan; broil 3 inches from heat 10 minutes or until desired degree of doneness, turning after 5 minutes. Let stand 5 minutes. Cut steak diagonally across grain into thin slices.

4. Combine onion and next 8 ingredients in a large bowl. Add pasta mixture and beef slices; toss well to coat. Sprinkle with cheese.

CALORIES 437; FAT 11.8g (sat 4.3g, mono 4.5g, poly 0.8g); PROTEIN 29.4g; CARB 54.4g; FIBER 4.4g; CHOL 54mg; IRON 4.5mg; SODIUM 582mg; CALC 100mg

FLAVOR TIP

Dijon mustard is common as a sandwich spread, but it also works wonders in

sauces and vinaigrettes, as in this pasta salad recipe. It not only adds flavor but also helps bind the ingredients.

Rice Noodles with Sesame-Ginger Flank Steak

You'll love this combination of flank steak, crisp vegetables, and rice noodles coated in a fragrant Chinese-style sauce.

Yield: 6 servings (serving size: 1⅓ cups)

⅓ cup rice vinegar

3 tablespoons lower-sodium soy sauce

1 tablespoon hoisin sauce

2 teaspoons cornstarch

1½ teaspoons sugar

2 teaspoons grated peeled fresh ginger

¼ teaspoon salt

3 garlic cloves, minced

2 teaspoons dark sesame oil

1 (1-pound) flank steak, trimmed and cut into ¼-inch strips

1½ cups shredded carrot

1½ cups sugar snap peas, trimmed

1 cup (¼-inch) sliced red bell pepper strips

½ cup fresh bean sprouts

4 cups hot cooked rice noodles (about 8 ounces uncooked noodles)

½ cup chopped green onions

1 tablespoon sesame seeds, toasted

1. Combine first 8 ingredients, stirring until sugar dissolves.

2. Heat a large nonstick skillet over medium-high heat. Add 1 teaspoon oil to pan. Add half of steak; sauté 4 minutes or until browned. Remove steak from pan. Repeat procedure with remaining oil and steak. Add vinegar mixture, carrot, peas, bell pepper, and sprouts to pan; cook 3 minutes, stirring frequently. Return steak to pan. Add noodles; cook 1 minute, stirring constantly. Sprinkle with onions and sesame seeds.

CALORIES 369; FAT 10.4g (sat 3.7g, mono 4g, poly 1.4g); PROTEIN 24.3g; CARB 42.9g; FIBER 4.4g; CHOL 51mg; IRON 3.1mg; SODIUM 542mg; CALC 63mg

QUICK TIP

To save time, look for presliced vegetables in the produce section of your supermarket.

Whole-Wheat Pasta with Sausage, Leeks, and Fontina

Whole-wheat pasta makes this hearty. The flavors meld and provide just enough of each element in every bite to keep you wanting more.

Yield: 6 servings (serving size: 1⅔ cups)

6 quarts water

2½ teaspoons salt, divided

1 pound uncooked whole-wheat penne or rigatoni

1 tablespoon olive oil

1 (4-ounce) link sweet Italian sausage

2 cups chopped leek

4 cups shredded Savoy cabbage (about 9½ ounces)

1 cup fat-free, lower-sodium chicken broth

¼ teaspoon freshly ground black pepper

½ cup (2 ounces) shredded fontina cheese

1. Bring 6 quarts water and 2 teaspoons salt to a boil in a large stockpot. Stir in pasta; partially cover, and return to a boil, stirring frequently. Cook 8 minutes or until pasta is almost al dente, stirring occasionally. Drain.

2. While pasta cooks, heat olive oil in a Dutch oven over medium-high heat. Remove casing from sausage. Add sausage to Dutch oven; cook 2 minutes or until lightly browned, stirring to crumble. Add leek; cook 2 minutes or until leek is soft, stirring frequently. Add cabbage; cook 2 minutes or until cabbage wilts, stirring frequently. Add remaining ½ teaspoon salt, broth, and pepper; bring to a boil. Reduce heat, and simmer 15 minutes or until vegetables are very tender.

3. Add pasta to Dutch oven, tossing well to coat; bring to a boil. Reduce heat, and cook 1 minute, stirring constantly, or until pasta is al dente. Remove from heat; stir in cheese. Serve immediately.

CALORIES 385; FAT 8.9g (sat 3.2g, mono 3.8g, poly 1.2g); PROTEIN 17.3g; CARB 64.3g; FIBER 8.3g; CHOL 18mg; IRON 3.8mg; SODIUM 658mg; CALC 119mg

Baked Rigatoni with Beef

Slightly undercook the pasta for this classic hamburger casserole because it cooks again in the oven.

Yield: 8 servings (serving size: 1 cup)

4 cups Tomato Sauce

1 pound ground round

4 cups cooked rigatoni (about 2½ cups uncooked pasta)

1½ cups (6 ounces) shredded part-skim mozzarella cheese, divided

Cooking spray

¼ cup (1 ounce) grated fresh Parmesan cheese

1. Prepare Tomato Sauce.

2. Preheat oven to 350°.

3. Cook beef in a large nonstick skillet over medium-high heat until browned; stir to crumble. Drain well. Combine beef, rigatoni, Tomato Sauce, and 1 cup mozzarella in an 11 x 7–inch baking dish coated with cooking spray. Top with ½ cup mozzarella and Parmesan. Bake at 350° for 20 minutes or until thoroughly heated.

CALORIES 305; FAT 9.6g (sat 4.3g, mono 3.5g, poly 0.7g); PROTEIN 24g; CARB 30.5g; FIBER 2.3g; CHOL 50mg; IRON 3.5mg; SODIUM 438mg; CALC 232mg

Tomato Sauce

This sauce will freeze well for up to three months. Place it in an airtight container or zip-top plastic bag and freeze.

Yield: 8 cups (serving size: 1 cup)

1 tablespoon olive oil

1½ cups chopped onion

1 cup chopped green bell pepper

1 teaspoon dried oregano

4 garlic cloves, minced

½ cup dry red wine

1 teaspoon dried basil

½ teaspoon salt

¼ teaspoon black pepper

2 (28-ounce) cans whole plum tomatoes, undrained and chopped

1 (6-ounce) can tomato paste

2 bay leaves

1. Heat oil in a large saucepan over medium-high heat. Add onion, bell pepper, oregano, and garlic; cook 5 minutes or until vegetables are tender, stirring occasionally.

2. Add wine and remaining ingredients, and bring to a boil. Reduce heat, and simmer 30 minutes. Remove bay leaves.

CALORIES 93; FAT 2.4g (sat 0.4g,mono 1.4g,poly 0.5g); PROTEIN 3.3g; CARB 17.1g; FIBER 3.3g; CHOL 0mg; IRON 2.4mg; SODIUM 487mg; CALC 77mg

Bucatini with Eggplant and Roasted Peppers

Eggplant and capers add a delectable flavor to this summery pasta sauce. If you can't find bucatini (long, hollow pasta), you can use linguine or spaghetti.

Yield: 6 servings (serving size: 1⅔ cups pasta mixture and 2 tablespoons cheese)

2 large yellow bell peppers

1 small eggplant, peeled and cut into ½-inch cubes (about ¾ pound)

1 cup water

2 tablespoons extra-virgin olive oil, divided

2 tablespoons minced fresh oregano

2 tablespoons capers

2 garlic cloves, minced

½ teaspoon salt

¼ teaspoon freshly ground black pepper

6 plum tomatoes, seeded and chopped

12 ounces uncooked bucatini or linguine

¾ cup (3 ounces) grated ricotta salata or Romano cheese

1. Preheat broiler.

2. Cut bell peppers in half lengthwise, and discard seeds and membranes. Place pepper halves, skin sides up, on a foil-lined baking sheet; flatten with hand. Broil 10 minutes or until peppers are blackened. Place in a zip-top plastic bag, and seal. Let stand 15 minutes.

3. Peel and cut bell peppers into strips. Reduce oven temperature to 425°.

4. Arrange eggplant cubes in a single layer in a 2-quart baking dish. Pour 1 cup water over eggplant. Bake at 425° for 35 minutes or until eggplant is tender, adding more water as needed.

5. Heat 1 tablespoon oil in a large nonstick skillet over medium-high heat. Add oregano, capers, and garlic; sauté 1 minute. Stir in eggplant, bell pepper strips, salt, black pepper, and tomatoes. Cover, reduce heat, and simmer 15 minutes, stirring occasionally.

6. Cook pasta according to package directions, omitting salt and fat. Drain in a colander over a bowl, reserving ½ cup cooking liquid.

7. Combine pasta, eggplant mixture, and remaining 1 tablespoon oil in a large bowl, tossing to coat. Add reserved cooking liquid, if necessary, to coat pasta. Sprinkle with cheese.

CALORIES 336; FAT 9.7g (sat 3.2g, mono 4.6g, poly 1g); PROTEIN 12.9g; CARB 50.3g; FIBER 5.7g; CHOL 15mg; IRON 2.8mg; SODIUM 461mg; CALC 182mg

MAKE-AHEAD TIP

Prepare the sauce up to two days in advance, and then reheat gently over medium-low heat while you cook the pasta.

Spaghetti with Meat Sauce

Forget spaghetti with marinara. Real meat lovers want a meat sauce with their spaghetti, and this recipe delivers. Be sure to use a good red wine for great flavor. Serve with a side salad and breadsticks.

Yield: 6 servings (serving size: about 1 cup pasta and ⅔ cup sauce)

12 ounces uncooked spaghetti

¾ pound ground sirloin

1 cup chopped onion

1½ teaspoons bottled minced garlic

¾ cup dry red wine

1 (26-ounce) jar low-fat spaghetti sauce

⅔ cup 2% reduced-fat milk

½ teaspoon salt

¼ teaspoon black pepper

1. Cook pasta according to package directions, omitting salt and fat.

2. While pasta cooks, heat a large nonstick skillet over medium-high heat. Add beef; cook until browned, stirring to crumble. Drain beef, and set aside.

3. Add onion and garlic to pan; sauté 3 minutes. Add wine; cook 3 minutes or until liquid almost evaporates.

4. Stir in beef and spaghetti sauce; bring to a boil. Reduce heat, and simmer 5 minutes, stirring occasionally. Stir in milk, salt, and pepper; cook 3 minutes, stirring occasionally. Serve sauce over pasta.

CALORIES 401; FAT 6.9g (sat 1.8g, mono 2.9g, poly 1.1g); PROTEIN 22.8g; CARB 60.1g; FIBER 4.9g; CHOL 37mg; IRON 4.7mg; SODIUM 544mg; CALC 77mg

Gorgonzola-Walnut Fettuccine with Toasted Breadcrumbs

Toasted walnuts and crumbled Gorgonzola cheese enhance this easy weeknight recipe.

Yield: 4 servings (serving size: 1½ cups)

1 slice day-old hearty white bread, torn

1 tablespoon olive oil

4 garlic cloves, minced

8 ounces uncooked fettuccine

¼ cup chopped fresh parsley

¼ cup (1 ounce) crumbled Gorgonzola cheese

3 tablespoons chopped walnuts, toasted

2 teaspoons fresh lemon juice

½ teaspoon salt

¼ teaspoon freshly ground black pepper

1. Preheat oven to 250°.

2. Place bread in a food processor; pulse 10 times or until coarse crumbs measure ⅔ cup. Place breadcrumbs on a baking sheet. Bake at 250° for 30 minutes or until dry.

3. Heat olive oil in a large nonstick skillet over medium heat. Add minced garlic, and cook 30 seconds, stirring constantly. Remove garlic mixture from heat, and let stand 5 minutes. Return pan to heat. Stir in breadcrumbs; cook 6 minutes or until lightly browned, stirring mixture frequently.

4. Cook fettuccine according to package directions, omitting salt and fat; drain. Place fettuccine in a large bowl. Add breadcrumb mixture, parsley, Gorgonzola, walnuts, lemon juice, salt, and black pepper; toss gently to combine. Serve immediately.

CALORIES 327; FAT 10.4g (sat 2.5g, mono 3g, poly 3g); PROTEIN 11.1g; CARB 49.5g; FIBER 2.9g; CHOL 6.3mg; IRON 2.5mg; SODIUM 444mg; CALC 70mg

Italian Vegetable Pie

Even meat eaters are going to love this easy weeknight dish. Although vegetarian, it has a really meaty flavor.

Yield: 8 servings

2 teaspoons olive oil

1 cup chopped green bell pepper

1 cup chopped onion

1 cup chopped mushrooms

1 (12.3-ounce) package firm tofu, drained and crumbled

3 garlic cloves, minced

3 tablespoons tomato paste

1 teaspoon dried Italian seasoning

1 teaspoon fennel seeds

¼ teaspoon crushed red pepper

1 (25.5-ounce) jar fat-free marinara sauce

6 cooked lasagna noodles, cut in half crosswise

Cooking spray

1½ cups (6 ounces) shredded part-skim mozzarella cheese

¼ cup grated Parmesan cheese

1. Preheat oven to 375°.

2. Heat oil in a large nonstick skillet over medium-high heat. Add bell pepper, chopped onion, mushrooms, tofu, and garlic; sauté 3 minutes or until vegetables are tender. Stir in tomato paste, Italian seasoning, fennel seeds, crushed red pepper, and marinara sauce; bring to a boil. Reduce heat; simmer 10 minutes.

3. Arrange noodles spokelike in bottom of an 8-inch round baking dish coated with cooking spray. Spread 3 cups tomato mixture over noodles. Fold ends of noodles over tomato mixture, and top with remaining tomato mixture and cheeses. Bake at 375° for 20 minutes.

CALORIES 307; FAT 10.4g (sat 4.4g, mono 3g, poly 2.1g); PROTEIN 19.7g; CARB 33.8g; FIBER 4.8g; CHOL 20mg; IRON 6.7mg; SODIUM 444mg; CALC 340mg

INGREDIENT TIP

When a recipe calls for a small amount of tomato paste, it's convenient to use paste from a tube rather than a can. However, if you prefer canned, consider

this: Spoon remaining paste by the tablespoon onto a baking sheet and freeze. Store frozen chunks in a freezer bag.

Pasta with Sun-Dried Tomato Pesto and Feta Cheese

This is a spring-inspired dish that can be served year-round. The oil in the sun-dried tomatoes gives the almond-spiced pesto a rich consistency.

Yield: 4 servings (serving size: 1 cup)

1 (9-ounce) package refrigerated fresh linguine

¾ cup oil-packed sun-dried tomato halves, drained

¼ cup loosely packed basil leaves

2 tablespoons slivered almonds

2 tablespoons preshredded fresh Parmesan cheese

1 tablespoon bottled minced garlic

½ teaspoon salt

¼ teaspoon black pepper

½ cup (2 ounces) crumbled feta cheese

1. Cook pasta according to package directions, omitting salt and fat. Drain through a sieve over a bowl, reserving 1 cup cooking liquid. Return pasta to pan.

2. While pasta cooks, place tomatoes and next 6 ingredients in a food processor; process until finely chopped.

3. Combine tomato mixture and reserved 1 cup cooking liquid, stirring with a whisk.

4. Add tomato mixture to pasta; toss well to coat. Sprinkle with feta.

CALORIES 300; FAT 9.9g (sat 3.3g, mono 3.9g, poly 1.6g); PROTEIN 12.3g; CARB 42g; FIBER 4.3g; CHOL 61mg; IRON 3.1mg; SODIUM 570mg; CALC 141mg

QUICK TIP

Bottled minced garlic is a convenient, quick way to get all the flavor of garlic without all the fuss.

Pasta with Asparagus and Mushrooms

If you're looking for a simple, light meal, this is it. It's super easy, and the mushrooms smell sublime while they're cooking.

Yield: 4 servings

¼ cup chopped fresh parsley

2 teaspoons chopped fresh basil

2 garlic cloves, minced

4 teaspoons butter

⅓ cup diced shallots

6 cups sliced cremini mushrooms

½ teaspoon salt

½ cup dry white wine

8 ounces uncooked pappardelle (wide ribbon pasta) or fettuccine

2 cups (2-inch) sliced asparagus (1 pound)

½ cup (2 ounces) grated fresh Parmesan cheese, divided

¼ teaspoon freshly ground black pepper

1. Combine first 3 ingredients, and set aside.

2. Melt butter in a large nonstick skillet over medium-high heat. Add shallots; sauté 1 minute. Add mushrooms and salt; sauté 5 minutes. Stir in wine; cook 1 minute. Reduce heat to low. Add 2 tablespoons parsley mixture; sauté 2 minutes. Keep warm.

3. Bring water to a boil in a large Dutch oven. Add pasta; cook 6½ minutes. Add asparagus; cook 1½ minutes or until asparagus is crisp-tender. Drain pasta mixture in a colander over a bowl, reserving ½ cup cooking liquid. Combine reserved cooking liquid, pasta mixture, mushroom mixture, and ¼ cup cheese. Arrange 2 cups pasta mixture on each of 4 plates. Sprinkle evenly with remaining parsley mixture, remaining ¼ cup cheese, and ¼ teaspoon pepper.

CALORIES 357; FAT 9g (sat 5g, mono 2.3g, poly 0.9g); PROTEIN 16.7g; CARB 54.2g; FIBER 4.4g; CHOL 20mg; IRON 4.8mg; SODIUM 575mg; CALC 215mg

FLAVOR TIP

For an extra-tasty touch, drizzle a few drops of truffle oil over the dish.

Fava Beans with Pesto and Cavatappi

Pasta is a dry ingredient that becomes water-rich when cooked. This vegetarian main dish shows off fava beans.

Yield: 8 servings (serving size: about 1¼ cups pasta and 1 tablespoon cheese)

2 pounds unshelled fava beans
(about 3 cups shelled)

1 cup fresh basil leaves
(about 1 ounce)

¼ cup chopped fresh mint

2 tablespoons fresh lemon juice

1 teaspoon salt

¼ teaspoon freshly ground
black pepper

1 garlic clove, minced

3 tablespoons extra-virgin olive oil

1 pound uncooked cavatappi pasta

½ cup grape tomatoes, halved

½ cup (2 ounces) grated fresh
Parmesan cheese

1. Remove beans from pods; discard pods. Cook beans in boiling water 1 minute. Drain and rinse with cold water; drain. Remove outer skins from beans; discard skins.

2. Combine basil and next 5 ingredients in a food processor; process until smooth. With processor on, slowly pour oil through food chute, and process until well blended.

3. Cook pasta according to package directions, omitting salt and fat; drain. Combine pasta and basil mixture in a large bowl, tossing to coat. Add beans and tomatoes, tossing to combine. Sprinkle with Parmesan cheese.

CALORIES 335; FAT 8.9g (sat 1.9g, mono 4.7g, poly 1.5g); PROTEIN 17.3g; CARB 51.9g; FIBER 2.7g; CHOL 46mg; IRON 4.1mg; SODIUM 411mg; CALC 116mg

INGREDIENT TIP

If you can't find fava beans, substitute fresh lima beans or even thawed frozen edamame.

Roasted Vegetable Pasta

This aromatic, colorful, delicious pasta will please your senses of smell, sight, and taste. You'll hardly be able to wait to sit down and eat!

Yield: 4 servings (serving size: 1½ cups pasta and 1 tablespoon cheese)

3 cups (8 ounces) uncooked farfalle (bow tie pasta)

2 cups Roasted Vegetables

1 cup frozen petite green peas, thawed

¼ cup chopped fresh parsley

¼ cup (1½ ounces) thinly shaved fresh Parmesan cheese

1. Cook pasta according to package directions, omitting salt and fat. Drain and keep warm.

2. Combine pasta, Roasted Vegetables, and peas in a large bowl. Top with parsley and cheese.

CALORIES 338; FAT 6g (sat 1.8g, mono 2.5g, poly 0.7g); PROTEIN 14.3g; CARB 54.9g; FIBER 5.5g; CHOL 5mg; IRON 3mg; SODIUM 485mg; CALC 106mg

Roasted Vegetables

Yield: 2 cups (serving size: ½ cup)

1 (8-ounce) package baby portobello mushrooms, halved

2 cups grape or cherry tomatoes

1 red onion, sliced

1 tablespoon olive oil

½ teaspoon salt

¼ teaspoon freshly ground black pepper

¼ cup dry white wine

1. Preheat oven to 475°.

2. Combine first 6 ingredients in a bowl; toss well to coat. Arrange mushroom mixture in a single layer on a jelly-roll pan.

3. Bake at 475° for 15 minutes; turn vegetables over. Drizzle wine evenly over vegetables; bake an additional 7 minutes or until vegetables are tender and lightly browned.

CALORIES 84; FAT 3.9g (sat 0.6g, mono 2.5g, poly 0.7g); PROTEIN 2.4g; CARB 9.3g; FIBER 2.2g; CHOL 0mg; IRON 0.8mg; SODIUM 302mg; CALC 15mg

Asian Noodle, Tofu, and Vegetable Stir-Fry

Stir-fries feel so easy and undemanding. This one is even more so because it has cellophane noodles right in it, making it a one-dish meal. Soaked dried mushrooms add flavor to the stock.

Yield: 4 servings (serving size: 2 cups)

2 ounces uncooked bean threads (cellophane noodles)

½ ounce dried wood ear mushrooms (about 6)

1 cup boiling water

2 teaspoons peanut oil or vegetable oil

1 cup coarsely chopped onion

1 tablespoon minced seeded jalapeño pepper

2 teaspoons minced peeled fresh ginger

2 garlic cloves, minced

3 cups (¼-inch) diagonally sliced carrot (about 1 pound)

¼ teaspoon salt

7 cups (1-inch) sliced bok choy

2 tablespoons lower-sodium soy sauce

1 (12.3-ounce) package reduced-fat firm tofu, cubed

3 tablespoons water

2 teaspoons cornstarch

1 teaspoon dark sesame oil or chili oil

1. Place noodles in a large bowl; cover with warm water. Let stand 20 minutes. Drain; set aside.
2. Combine mushrooms and 1 cup boiling water in a bowl; let stand 20 minutes. Strain through a sieve into a bowl, reserving mushroom liquid. Cut mushrooms into strips.
3. Heat peanut oil in a wok or nonstick Dutch oven over medium-high heat. Add onion, jalapeño, ginger, and garlic; stir-fry 1 minute. Add mushrooms, carrot, and salt; stir-fry 2 minutes. Stir in ¼ cup reserved mushroom liquid; cover and cook 3 minutes or until carrots are crisp-tender and liquid evaporates.
4. Add bok choy; stir-fry 1 minute. Stir in noodles, remaining mushroom liquid, soy sauce, and tofu; cook 2 minutes.
5. Combine 3 tablespoons water and cornstarch; pour into pan. Bring to a boil; cook 2 minutes or until slightly thick. Drizzle with sesame oil.

CALORIES 195; FAT 6.4g (sat 1g, mono 1.9g, poly 2.8g); PROTEIN 10.3g; CARB 27.4g; FIBER 6.1g; CHOL 0mg; IRON 2.6mg; SODIUM 539mg; CALC 206mg

Vegetarian Bolognese with Whole-Wheat Penne

The Parmigiano-Reggiano rind simmers with the sauce, infusing it with deep, savory umami taste.

Yield: 6 servings

¼ cup dried porcini mushrooms (about ¼ ounce)

1 tablespoon olive oil

1½ cups finely chopped onion

½ cup finely chopped carrot

½ cup finely chopped celery

1 (8-ounce) package cremini mushrooms, finely chopped

½ cup dry red wine

¼ cup warm water

½ teaspoon salt

½ teaspoon freshly ground black pepper

1 (28-ounce) can organic crushed tomatoes with basil, undrained

1 (2-inch) piece Parmigiano-Reggiano cheese rind

12 ounces uncooked whole-wheat penne (tube-shaped pasta)

½ cup (2 ounces) shaved Parmigiano-Reggiano cheese

1. Place dried mushrooms in a spice or coffee grinder; process until finely ground.

2. Heat oil in a large saucepan over medium-high heat. Add onion, carrot, celery, and cremini mushrooms; sauté 10 minutes. Add wine; simmer 2 minutes or until liquid almost evaporates. Add ¼ cup warm water and next 4 ingredients to onion mixture. Stir in ground porcini. Cover, reduce heat, and simmer 40 minutes. Keep warm. Remove rind; discard.

3. Cook pasta according to package directions, omitting salt and fat. Place 1 cup pasta in each of 6 bowls. Top each portion with ¾ cup sauce and about 1 tablespoon cheese.

CALORIES 334; FAT 7.2g (sat 2.1g, mono 2.5g, poly 1.9g); PROTEIN 14.8g; CARB 57.7g; FIBER 9.7g; CHOL 9mg; IRON 3.3mg; SODIUM 542mg; CALC 156mg

Greek-Style Scampi

This quick, filling weeknight meal relies on easy-to-find ingredients. To round out the menu, add a spinach-mushroom salad.

Yield: 4 servings

6 ounces uncooked angel hair pasta

1 teaspoon olive oil

½ cup chopped green bell pepper

2 teaspoons bottled minced garlic

1 (14.5-ounce) can diced tomatoes with basil, garlic, and oregano, undrained

⅛ teaspoon black pepper

1 pound peeled and deveined medium shrimp

⅛ teaspoon ground red pepper

6 tablespoons (about 1½ ounces) crumbled feta cheese

1. Cook pasta according to package directions, omitting salt and fat. Drain and keep warm.

2. Heat oil in a large nonstick skillet over medium-high heat. Add green bell pepper to pan; sauté 1 minute. Add garlic and tomatoes; cook 1 minute. Add black pepper and shrimp; cover and cook 3 minutes or until shrimp reach desired degree of doneness. Stir in red pepper; remove from heat. Place 1 cup pasta on each of 4 plates. Top each serving with 1 cup shrimp mixture and 1½ tablespoons cheese.

CALORIES 379; FAT 8.5g (sat 3g, mono 2.8g, poly 1.7g); PROTEIN 31.7g; CARB 43.3g; FIBER 2.6g; CHOL 185mg; IRON 4.1mg; SODIUM 139mg; CALC 656mg

QUICK TIP

Prechopped bell pepper is now widely available in the produce section of most supermarkets and is a definite time-saver.

Spicy Malaysian-Style Stir-Fried Noodles

This popular Southeast Asian street fare is known as *mee goreng* (fried noodles). Look for the sweet bean sauce and noodles (which are sometimes frozen) at Asian markets; substitute dried linguine for lo mein. You can always use less chile paste to make a milder version.

Yield: 6 servings (serving size: 1⅔ cups)

1 (14-ounce) package water-packed extra-firm tofu, drained

1 (1-pound) package fresh Chinese lo mein egg noodles

2 tablespoons dark sesame oil

4 garlic cloves, minced

¼ teaspoon salt

4 heads baby bok choy, trimmed and cut crosswise into 2-inch-thick strips

1 tablespoon sugar

3 tablespoons sambal oelek (ground fresh chile paste)

2 tablespoons fresh lime juice

2 tablespoons sweet bean sauce

2 tablespoons lower-sodium soy sauce

1. Line a plate with a triple layer of paper towels; top with tofu. Place a triple layer of paper towels on top of tofu; top with another plate. Let stand 20 minutes. Cut tofu into ½-inch cubes.

2. Cook noodles in a large pan of boiling water 3 minutes or until desired degree of doneness; drain in a colander over a bowl, reserving 1 cup cooking liquid. Wipe pan with paper towels. Heat oil in pan over medium heat. Add garlic to pan; cook 30 seconds, stirring constantly. Add salt and bok choy; cook 30 seconds, stirring frequently. Stir in ½ cup reserved cooking liquid; bring to a boil. Reduce heat, and cook 4 minutes.

3. Combine sugar and next 4 ingredients, stirring until combined. Add noodles, remaining ½ cup cooking liquid, and sugar mixture to pan; toss to combine. Cook 30 seconds or until thoroughly heated, tossing to coat. Add tofu; toss to combine. Serve immediately.

CALORIES 359; FAT 9.5g (sat 1.4g, mono 2.6g, poly 4.2g); PROTEIN 15.1g; CARB 53g; FIBER 2.1g; CHOL 17mg; IRON 3.4mg; SODIUM 617mg; CALC 65mg

Noodle-Vegetable Toss

Rice noodles make this a hearty dish that doesn't leave you feeling overly full.

Yield: 3 servings (serving size: 1⅓ cups)

6 cups water

6 ounces uncooked linguine-style rice noodles

1 tablespoon sugar

2 tablespoons water

1 tablespoon fish sauce

1 tablespoon fresh lime juice

2 cups packaged tricolor slaw mix

1 cup grated English cucumber

1 cup fresh bean sprouts

1 cup fresh cilantro leaves

½ cup chopped unsalted, dry-roasted peanuts

1. Bring 6 cups water to a boil in a large saucepan. Remove from heat; add rice noodles. Let soak 3 minutes or until tender. Drain.
2. While noodles soak, combine sugar and next 3 ingredients in a small bowl, stirring well with a whisk.
3. Combine noodles, slaw mix, and next 3 ingredients in a large bowl. Toss with sugar mixture. Sprinkle with peanuts. Serve immediately.

CALORIES 388; FAT 12g (sat 1.7g, mono 6g, poly 3.9g); PROTEIN 10.7g; CARB 61g; FIBER 3.8g; CHOL 0mg; IRON 2mg; SODIUM 397mg; CALC 49mg

INGREDIENT TIP

English, or seedless, cucumbers are usually twice the size of regular cucumbers and contain fewer seeds and less water. They're also milder in flavor than regular cucumbers.

Five-Spice Pork Lo Mein

Cutting the cooked noodles makes them easier to combine with the other ingredients, and easier to serve, too.

Yield: 6 servings (serving size: 1⅓ cups)

8 ounces uncooked Chinese-style noodles

1 tablespoon grated peeled fresh ginger

2 teaspoons five-spice powder

1 (¾-pound) pork tenderloin, trimmed and cut into thin strips

½ teaspoon salt, divided

2 tablespoons toasted peanut oil

¼ cup water

¼ cup hoisin sauce

½ cup chopped green onions

1. Cook noodles according to package directions, omitting salt and fat; drain. Place in a large bowl. Snip noodles several times with kitchen scissors.

2. Combine ginger, five-spice powder, and pork in a medium bowl; add ¼ teaspoon salt, tossing to coat. Heat oil in a large nonstick skillet over medium-high heat. Add pork mixture; sauté 2 minutes or until browned. Stir in remaining ¼ teaspoon salt, ¼ cup water, and hoisin sauce; cook 2 minutes or until pork reaches desired degree of doneness. Add pork mixture and green onions to noodles; toss well to combine.

CALORIES 273; FAT 8.9g (sat 1.9g, mono 3.6g, poly 2g); PROTEIN 16.3g; CARB 34.8g; FIBER 5.7g; CHOL 38mg; IRON 2.8mg; SODIUM 399mg; CALC 31mg

INGREDIENT TIP

Chinese five-spice powder is a common spice blend that can be found in most supermarkets. It is a mixture of five assertive components: cinnamon, cloves, fennel seed, star anise, and Szechuan peppercorns.

Cambodian Summer Rolls

The fresh herbs, sweet shrimp, slight spicy heat, and crisp lettuce offer well-balanced taste and texture.

Yield: 12 servings (serving size: 1 roll and about 1½ tablespoons sauce)

Rolls:

6 cups water

1 pound medium shrimp

6 ounces uncooked rice noodles

12 (8-inch) round sheets rice paper

¼ cup hoisin sauce

3 cups shredded red leaf lettuce

¼ cup thinly sliced fresh basil

¼ cup thinly sliced fresh mint

Dipping Sauce:

⅓ cup lower-sodium soy sauce

¼ cup water

2 tablespoons sugar

2 tablespoons chopped fresh cilantro

2 tablespoons fresh lime juice

1 teaspoon minced peeled fresh ginger

1 teaspoon sambal oelek (ground fresh chile paste)

1 garlic clove, minced

1. To prepare rolls, bring 6 cups water to a boil in a large saucepan. Add shrimp; cook 3 minutes or until desired degree of doneness. Drain and rinse with cold water. Peel shrimp; chill.

2. Place rice noodles in a large bowl; cover with boiling water. Let stand 8 minutes; drain.

3. Add cold water to a large, shallow dish to a depth of 1 inch. Place 1 rice paper sheet in water. Let stand 2 minutes or until soft. Place rice paper sheet on a flat surface.

4. Spread 1 teaspoon hoisin sauce in center of sheet; top with 2 to 3 shrimp, ¼ cup lettuce, about ¼ cup rice noodles, 1 teaspoon basil, and 1 teaspoon mint. Fold sides of sheet over filling, roll up jelly-roll fashion, and gently press seam to seal. Place roll, seam side down, on a serving platter; cover to keep from drying. Repeat procedure with remaining rice paper, hoisin sauce, shrimp, lettuce, rice noodles, basil, and mint.

5. To prepare dipping sauce, combine soy sauce and next 7 ingredients in a small bowl; stir with a whisk.

CALORIES 140; FAT 0.8g (sat 0.1g, mono 0.1g, poly 0.3g); PROTEIN 9g; CARB 23.5g; FIBER 0.7g; CHOL 47mg; IRON 1.3mg; SODIUM 385mg; CALC 32mg

Peanut Chicken Soba Salad

You'll only need about 15 minutes to cook the chicken and noodles for this Asian salad. If you're short on time, substitute rotisserie chicken or leftover cooked chicken, and purchase preshredded carrots from your supermarket's produce section.

Yield: 4 servings (serving size: 1 cup salad and 1 teaspoon peanuts)

2 cups water

2 (6-ounce) skinless, boneless chicken breast halves

4 black peppercorns

1 bay leaf

2 tablespoons roasted peanut oil

1 tablespoon rice vinegar

2 teaspoons lower-sodium soy sauce

1 teaspoon honey

1 teaspoon chili garlic sauce

½ teaspoon salt

2 cups cooked soba (about 4 ounces uncooked buckwheat noodles)

1 cup grated carrot

½ cup thinly sliced green onions

¼ cup minced red onion

¼ cup chopped fresh basil

4 teaspoons chopped unsalted, dry-roasted peanuts

Lime wedges (optional)

1. Combine first 4 ingredients in a medium saucepan; bring to a boil. Cover, remove from heat, and let stand 15 minutes or until chicken reaches desired degree of doneness. Remove chicken from pan, and discard peppercorns, bay leaf, and cooking liquid. Shred chicken; place in a large bowl.

2. Combine oil and next 5 ingredients, stirring with a whisk. Pour over chicken; let stand 5 minutes. Add soba noodles and next 4 ingredients to chicken mixture, and toss well. Sprinkle with peanuts. Garnish with lime wedges, if desired.

CALORIES 256; FAT 9.5g (sat 1.7g, mono 4.2g, poly 2.9g); PROTEIN 23.9g; CARB 19.5g; FIBER 2.5g; CHOL 49mg; IRON 1.3mg; SODIUM 538mg; CALC 30mg

Beef-Broccoli Lo Mein

Serve this quick-and-easy noodle dish with store-bought egg rolls and fortune cookies.

Yield: 6 servings (serving size: 1⅓ cups)

4 cups hot cooked spaghetti (about 8 ounces uncooked pasta)

1 teaspoon dark sesame oil

1 tablespoon peanut oil

1 tablespoon minced peeled fresh ginger

4 garlic cloves, minced

3 cups chopped broccoli

1½ cups vertically sliced onion

1 (1-pound) flank steak, trimmed and cut across grain into long, thin strips

3 tablespoons lower-sodium soy sauce

2 tablespoons brown sugar

1 tablespoon oyster sauce

1 tablespoon sambal oelek (ground fresh chile paste)

1. Combine pasta and sesame oil, tossing well to coat.

2. While pasta cooks, heat peanut oil in a large nonstick skillet over medium-high heat. Add ginger and garlic; sauté 30 seconds. Add broccoli and onion; sauté 3 minutes. Add steak, and sauté 5 minutes or until desired degree of doneness. Add pasta mixture, soy sauce, and remaining ingredients; cook 1 minute or until lo mein is thoroughly heated, stirring constantly.

CALORIES 327; FAT 9.3g (sat 3g, mono 3.6g, poly 1.6g); PROTEIN 21.7g; CARB 39.1g; FIBER 2.9g; CHOL 36mg; IRON 3.6mg; SODIUM 382mg; CALC 47mg

QUICK TIP

For convenience, instead of buying broccoli and spending time cutting and separating the florets, purchase broccoli florets from your grocer's produce section.

soups
& stews
tonight!

cooking class

Soup is the true melting pot of all the world's best ingredients. And at *Cooking Light*, we've found that soup can be one of the best introductions to the genius and chemistry of cooking.

All About Soup

Soup is basic. Its techniques are classic. And by blending time-honored skills such as sautéing, caramelizing, deglazing, and thickening, you can have a meal on the table without feeling overwhelmed or intimidated. Just remember, it all starts with the stock or broth.

Stocks: The key to a great soup is a homemade stock. The slow simmering of meats, vegetables, herbs, and spices produces a flavorful liquid—the foundation for soup. Making homemade stock creates an intense natural flavor while keeping the amount of sodium low.

Broths: A broth is basically made from the same ingredients as a stock. However, broth is cooked in less time, isn't as intensely flavored, and often contains more sodium. Broths may be used in place of stock when you are short on time.

Commercial Products: Homemade stocks and broths are superior to commercial products, but they're not always practical. In those cases, we suggest using commercial products.

Stock Versus Broth Nutritional Comparisons

Here's how homemade and commercial stocks and broths compare nutritionally:

Ingredient (1 cup)	Calories	Fat	Sodium
Homemade beef stock	8	0.3g	9mg
Regular commercial beef stock	15	1g	890mg
Fat-free, lower-sodium beef broth	15	1g	440mg
Homemade white chicken stock	28	0.8g	18mg
Regular commercial chicken stock	10	0.5g	960mg
*Fat-free, lower-sodium chicken broth	15	0g	570mg
Homemade vegetable stock	8	0.1g	2mg
*Lower-sodium organic vegetable broth	15	0g	570mg

Cooking Light Test Kitchen prefers to use Swanson's Natural Goodness Chicken Broth and Emeril's All Natural Organic Vegetable Stock in recipes.

Essential Techniques for Making Stocks

Master the art of making stocks with this step-by-step guide.

White Chicken Stock

White stock is best to use when you need a mild flavor that won't overpower delicate ingredients, and it's also good to keep in the freezer for other recipes. Its light color suits risotto, mashed potatoes, and cream soups. White stock is prepared entirely on the stovetop.

Yield: 10 cups (serving size: 1 cup)

½ teaspoon black peppercorns

10 parsley sprigs

8 thyme sprigs

3 celery stalks, cut into 2-inch-thick pieces

3 bay leaves

2 medium onions, peeled and quartered

2 carrots, cut into 2-inch-thick pieces

2 garlic cloves, crushed

6 pounds chicken pieces

16 cups cold water

1. Place first 8 ingredients in an 8-quart stockpot; add chicken and water. Bring mixture to a boil over medium heat. Reduce heat, and simmer, uncovered, 3 hours, skimming surface occasionally to remove foam. Strain stock through a fine sieve into a large bowl. Reserve chicken for another use; discard remaining solids. Cool stock to room temperature, then cover and chill stock 8 hours. Skim solidified fat from surface of stock; discard fat. Refrigerate stock in an airtight container for up to 1 week, or freeze for up to 3 months.

CALORIES 28; FAT 0.8g (sat 0.2g, mono 0.3g, poly 0.2g); PROTEIN 4.7g; CARB 0.4g; FIBER 0.1g; CHOL 15mg; IRON 0.3mg; SODIUM 18mg; CALC 4mg

How to Make White Chicken Stock

1. Prepare the ingredients. Peel and quarter the onions. Rinse, peel, and trim the carrots and celery. This will result in a cleaner, less-cloudy stock and will help infuse the stock with the flavor of the vegetables. Add herbs and spices.

2. Start with cold water. Add only enough cold water to barely cover the ingredients in the pot. Too much water will dilute the stock's flavor. Be sure the water is cold. Pouring hot water over chicken or meat will release specks of protein that will make the stock cloudy. Don't add salt. The stock will concentrate during cooking, so it doesn't need salt. Instead, add salt to the final soup recipe so that you can control the amount of sodium.

3. Simmer and skim. As soon as the water in the stockpot comes to a boil, reduce the heat to a simmer. Simmering means the liquid is not quite boiling, but there should be noticeable small bubbles that continually rise to the surface. You will also notice gray foam, impurities, rising to the surface of the stock. Gently remove and discard this foam with a spoon, ladle, or skimmer. If you don't remove the foam, it will eventually reincorporate into the stock, making it cloudy and affecting the taste. Continue to allow the stock to simmer for several hours to develop a rich flavor.

4. Strain. Place a fine sieve over a large bowl or pot in the sink. Start by straining the stock in batches, transferring it from the pot to the sieve with a ladle until the stockpot is light enough to lift.

5. Remove the fat. Cool the stock to room temperature, then return the strained stock to the stockpot or divide it among smaller containers and place it in the refrigerator. As the stock chills, the fat will solidify on top, making it easy to remove with a large spoon.

6. Reduce. Once the fat is removed, the stock is ready to use. However, it's a good idea to reduce all of it right away to concentrate the flavors and save on storage space. Bring the stock to a simmer again, and let it reduce by half the volume.

7. Store. Cool up to 4 quarts of stock in a stockpot in the refrigerator. Reduced stock takes on the consistency of gelatin after it has chilled, making it easy to handle. Just keep it in a tub, and spoon it out as needed. Stock will keep in the refrigerator up to a week and in the freezer up to three months. Just pour the stock into airtight containers, filling them three-fourths full to allow room for the liquid to expand as it freezes. Freeze smaller amounts in ice-cube trays; then remove the cubes from the trays, and store them in zip-top freezer bags.

No Time to Chill

Chilling the stock overnight makes degreasing a cinch because the fat solidifies on top. But it's also fine to proceed with a recipe right after making the stock. Our Test Kitchen's favorite methods involve either a zip-top plastic bag or a fat separator cup. The cup is made of inexpensive plastic or glass and has a spout at the base. When you pour out the stock, the fat floating on the top stays behind. The zip-top bag works similarly. Pour stock into a bag and seal; and let stand 10 minutes (fat will rise to the top). Carefully snip off 1 bottom corner of the bag. Drain stock into a container, stopping before the fat layer reaches the opening; discard the fat.

How to Make Brown Chicken Stock

Brown stock has deeper flavor than white stock, and the procedure involves caramelizing chicken and vegetables in the oven for half the cooking time, and then putting them in a stockpot to simmer during the second half of cooking.

1. Roasting the vegetables and chicken until browned creates a deep, rich, caramelized flavor.

2. The browned bits from the pan add even more flavor. Deglaze the pan by adding water and scraping up the flavorful bits.

3. Simmer the stock ingredients for 1½ hours. Then strain through a fine sieve.

4. Skim the fat from the stock after the stock has chilled for 8 hours or overnight.

Brown Chicken Stock

Use a pan large enough to roast the chicken and all the vegetables. If the pan is too small, the chicken won't brown properly.

Yield: 10 cups (serving size: 1 cup)

¼ pound fennel stalks, cut into 2-inch-thick pieces

3 carrots, cut into 2-inch-thick pieces

1 celery stalk, cut into 2-inch-thick pieces

1 medium onion, peeled and quartered

6 pounds chicken pieces

½ teaspoon black peppercorns

6 parsley sprigs

5 thyme sprigs

2 bay leaves

16 cups cold water, divided

1. Preheat oven to 400°.
2. Arrange first 4 ingredients in bottom of a broiler or roasting pan; top with chicken. Bake at 400° for 1½ hours; turn chicken once every 30 minutes (chicken and vegetables should be very brown).
3. Place peppercorns, parsley, thyme, and bay leaves in an 8-quart stockpot. Remove vegetables and chicken from broiler pan; place in stockpot. Discard drippings from broiler pan, leaving browned bits. Place broiler pan on stovetop; add 4 cups water. Bring to a boil over medium-high heat. Reduce heat; simmer 10 minutes, scraping pan to loosen browned bits.
4. Pour contents of pan into stockpot. Add remaining 12 cups water; bring to a boil over medium-high heat. Reduce heat; simmer, uncovered, 1½ hours, skimming surface occasionally to remove foam.
5. Strain stock through a fine sieve into a large bowl. Reserve chicken for another use; discard remaining solids. Cool stock to room temperature. Cover and chill stock 8 hours. Skim solidified fat from surface of stock; discard fat. Refrigerate stock in an airtight container for up to 1 week, or freeze for up to 3 months.

CALORIES 31; FAT 1.1g (sat 0.3g, mono 0.4g, poly 0.2g); PROTEIN 4.7g; CARB 0.4g; FIBER 0.1g; CHOL 15mg; IRON 0.3mg; SODIUM 19mg; CALC 4mg

Vegetable Stock

This all-purpose vegetable stock has woodsy undertones. Improvise with a variety of vegetables, but avoid bitter ones such as eggplant or dark greens, which can compete with the flavors of the finished dish.

Yield: 6 cups (serving size: 1 cup)

12 cups cold water

1 (8-ounce) package mushrooms, sliced

1 cup chopped onion

¾ cup chopped carrot

½ cup coarsely chopped celery

½ cup chopped parsnip

2 bay leaves

2 thyme sprigs

1 whole garlic head, halved

1. Combine all ingredients in a stockpot; bring to a boil. Reduce heat, and simmer, uncovered, until reduced to 6 cups (about 1 hour). Strain stock through a fine sieve into a large bowl; discard solids. Cool stock to room temperature. Refrigerate stock in an airtight container for up to 1 week, or freeze for up to 3 months.

CALORIES 8; FAT 0.1g (sat 0g, mono 0g, poly 0.1g); PROTEIN 0.3g; CARB 1.7g; FIBER 0.3g; CHOL 0mg; IRON 0.1mg; SODIUM 2mg; CALC 7mg

Beef Stock

Beef stock (made from beef and veal bones) is the basis of many classic European sauces. It makes quick, light, deeply flavored pan sauces. Find oxtails at a butcher shop.

Yield: 10 cups (serving size: 1 cup)

3½ pounds meaty beef bones (such as oxtail)

3 cups coarsely chopped celery

1½ cups chopped carrot (about ¾ pound)

2 tablespoons tomato paste

3 medium onions, peeled and halved (about 1½ pounds)

20 cups cold water

1. Preheat oven to 400°.

2. Arrange bones in an even layer in a shallow roasting pan. Bake at 400° for 45 minutes or until browned.

3. Transfer bones to an 8-quart stockpot. Add celery, carrot, tomato paste, and onions to pot; stir well to combine. Pour cold water over mixture; bring mixture to a simmer. Reduce heat, and simmer, uncovered, 5 hours, skimming surface occasionally to remove foam.

4. Strain stock through a fine sieve into a large bowl; discard solids. Cool stock to room temperature. Cover and chill stock 8 to 24 hours. Skim solidified fat from surface; discard. Refrigerate stock in an airtight container for up to 1 week, or freeze for up to 3 months.

CALORIES 8; FAT 0.3g (sat 0.1g, mono 0.1g, poly 0g); PROTEIN 0.7g; CARB 0.7g; FIBER 0.1g; CHOL 2mg; IRON 0.1mg; SODIUM 9mg; CALC 4mg

Arrange the bones in an even layer in a shallow roasting pan. Bake at 400° for 45 minutes or until browned.

Reduce heat, and simmer, uncovered, 5 hours, skimming the surface occasionally to remove the foam.

Shellfish Stock

Next time you cook lobster, save the shells to prepare this stock. You can also make the stock with an equivalent quantity of crab shells, or use a combination of crab and lobster shells. For a less expensive option, use shrimp shells. Straining the stock twice makes for a clean-tasting, smooth final product.

Yield: 10 cups (serving size: 1 cup)

2½ pounds lobster shells (about 4 small lobsters)

2 cups coarsely chopped celery

2 cups coarsely chopped fennel bulb

1 cup coarsely chopped carrot

2 tablespoons no-salt-added tomato paste

2 medium onions, peeled and halved (about 1 pound)

5 quarts water

1. Preheat oven to 450°.
2. Arrange shells in an even layer in a shallow roasting pan. Bake at 450° for 30 minutes or until toasted.
3. Transfer shells to an 8-quart stockpot. Add celery, fennel, carrot, tomato paste, and onions to pot; stir well to combine. Pour water over vegetable mixture; bring to a boil. Reduce heat, and simmer, uncovered, 4 hours, skimming surface occasionally to remove foam.
4. Strain stock through a sieve into a large bowl; discard solids. Strain again through a paper towel-lined sieve. Cool stock to room temperature. Cover and chill stock. Refrigerate stock in an airtight container for up to 2 days, or freeze for up to 3 months.

CALORIES 9; FAT 0.1g (sat 0.0g, mono 0.0g, poly 0.0g); PROTEIN 1.3g; CARB 0.8g; FIBER 0.2g; CHOL 4mg; IRON 0.1mg; SODIUM 35mg; CALC 15mg

Corn Stock

This is a great way to use leftover corn cobs (cut the kernels off first, and use them in a soup or salad). Corn stock adds a fresh, sweet taste to corn or seafood chowders, tortilla soup or other Mexican-flavored soups, and vegetable soups. This version takes a shortcut by using canned vegetable broth as a base.

Yield: 10 cups (serving size: 1 cup)

Cooking spray

1 small unpeeled onion, sliced

2 garlic cloves, minced

3 scraped corn cobs

8 (14½-ounce) cans vegetable broth

1. Coat a large Dutch oven with cooking spray, and place over medium-high heat until hot. Add onion and garlic; sauté 5 minutes.
2. Add corn cobs and broth; bring to a boil. Reduce heat, and simmer, uncovered, 1 hour. Remove from heat; cover and let stand 30 minutes. Strain mixture through a sieve into a large bowl; discard solids. Cool stock to room temperature. Cover and chill stock. Refrigerate stock in an airtight container for up to 2 days, or freeze for up to 3 months.

CALORIES 22; FAT 0.1g (sat 0g, mono 0g, poly 0g); PROTEIN 0.2g; CARB 5.4g; FIBER 0.2g; CHOL 0mg; IRON 0mg; SODIUM 316mg; CALC 2.8mg

Essential Techniques for Making Soups

Use these cooking tips and techniques as a quick reference when making soup.

1. Sauté. Sautéing vegetables fills the kitchen with a wonderful aroma. Slowly cook a combination of vegetables (such as onions, garlic, carrots, and celery) plus herbs and spices in a small amount of fat (butter, oil, or even bacon drippings for a salty, smoky flavor) until the vegetables are tender. It's a good idea to pay close attention and to stir constantly with a wooden spoon to keep the food from burning. The goal is to cook the vegetables until they're tender. If the vegetables burn, they may add a bitter, undesirable flavor to the soup. It's much better to start over at this point in the recipe rather than to compromise the flavor of the whole pot of soup.

2. Caramelize and brown. Vegetables contain natural sugars. As vegetables slowly cook, these sugars are released and begin to turn the vegetables brown, or caramelize them. This is different from scorching or burning. As the vegetables brown, they begin to release rich flavors. It's the blending of these flavors that's the foundation of soups. Soup and stew recipes that call for beef, pork, or game often direct you to brown the meat before continuing with the recipe. Cook the meat in small batches so that it gets a nice brown color on all sides. This browning process contributes deep flavor to the soup. Don't rush and try to cook all of the meat at one time. If you do, the meat will steam rather than brown, and you won't have the rich flavor or brown color that is so important to the overall taste and appearance of the soup.

3. Deglaze. It's important not to leave any concentrated flavor in the bottom of a skillet or pan. Add a small amount of liquid—stock, broth, water, wine, or a combination—to loosen the browned bits of caramelized food. These browned bits contribute greatly to the flavor of the soup. Besides that, leaving the browned bits on the bottom of the pan may cause the soup or stew to stick, which will cause burning.

4. Simmer. Once you have the flavor base for the soup, it's time to add the remaining ingredients. Begin with those that have to cook the longest, such as beans, rice, potatoes, and the remaining liquid. Cover the pot, and cook over low heat until done. Stir the soup occasionally to make sure that nothing sticks to the bottom of the pan.

5. Thicken. Some soups have a clear, thin broth. Others, such as chowders and cream soups, are thick and creamy. To reduce the fat but maintain the flavor and texture of a cream soup, combine a small amount of cream, evaporated fat-free milk, or reduced-fat milk with flour, and stir this mixture into the soup near the end of cooking time. Remember to bring the soup back to a boil, reduce the heat, and cook, stirring occasionally, at least 10 to 15 minutes or until thick. Otherwise, the soup may taste like flour and be too thin. For bean, lentil, or vegetable soups, remove about 1 cup of the soup near the end of the cooking time. Puree it in a blender or mash it with a fork or potato masher, and stir it back into the soup.

Deglaze

Simmer

Thicken

Freezing Soups & Stews

1. Chill. To keep food safe, cool freshly cooked dishes quickly before freezing. Putting foods that are still warm in the freezer can raise the temperature, causing surrounding frozen items to partially thaw and refreeze, which can alter the taste and texture of some foods. Place food in a shallow, wide container and refrigerate, uncovered, until cool. To chill soup or stew even faster, pour it into a metal bowl and set in an ice bath—a larger bowl filled halfway with ice water. Stir occasionally. For stews, braises, or other semi-liquid dishes with some fat content, chill completely, and then skim the fat from the top before freezing. Fat spoils over time in the freezer and shortens a dish's frozen shelf life.

2. Store. Avoid freezer burn by using moisture-proof zip-top plastic bags and wrap. Remove the air from bags before sealing. Store soups and stews in freezer bags, which can be placed flat and freeze quickly. Store foods in small servings, no more than 1 quart, to help them freeze quickly. This also allows you to defrost only what you need. Use a permanent marker to label each container with the name of the dish, volume or weight if you've measured it, and the date you put it in the freezer.

3. Freeze quickly. The quicker food freezes, the better its quality once thawed. Do not crowd the freezer—arrange containers in a single layer in the freezer to allow enough room for air to circulate around them so food will freeze rapidly. Food frozen slowly forms large ice crystals that may turn the food mushy. Most cooked dishes will keep for two to three months in the freezer. Use a freezer thermometer to ensure that your unit remains at 0° or below.

4. Defrost. You can defrost food in the microwave but allowing enough time for it to defrost in the refrigerator (roughly 5 hours per pound) is better. To avoid the risk of contamination, never defrost food at room temperature.

10 Ways to Dress Up Soup with Style

1. For casual meals, serve soup right from the pot. For formal entertaining, use soup tureens.

2. Use your imagination when choosing individual serving bowls. Deep bowls and mugs are good for chunky soups. Wide-rimmed, shallow bowls are ideal for smooth, creamy soups or for clear broth soups where the broth itself creates its own beauty.

3. Consider nontraditional serving dishes such as a cup and saucer for a first-course soup.

4. To keep the soup from cooling too quickly, rinse the serving bowls with hot water just before ladling. For chilled soups, place the empty bowls in the refrigerator about 30 minutes before filling.

5. Use simple garnishes, such as lemon or lime wedges or grated, shredded, or shaved cheeses. Sometimes the ingredients used in the recipe can be used to garnish the soup as well as to enhance flavor and texture.

6. If the soup calls for fresh herbs, set aside a few extra sprigs before beginning. Use the sprigs later as a garnish, or chop a little extra to scatter over the soup before serving.

7. For creamy or pureed soups, garnish with whole, thinly sliced, or chopped vegetables.

8. A dollop of reduced-fat sour cream or yogurt can tame the heat and add the finishing touch to a bowl of spicy soup. Or it can be swirled into a creamy soup for a decorative presentation.

9. Sprinkle soup with homemade or store-bought croutons or fresh tortillas cut into strips. Or simply lay a breadstick across the rim of the soup bowl.

10. Mound rice or pasta in the center of a bowl (or even off-center), and ladle the soup around it, taking care not to completely cover the rice or pasta.

Creamy Sweet Potato Soup

Just a bit of Dijon mustard and nutmeg pair beautifully to enhance the rich flavor of sweet potatoes.

Yield: 4 servings (serving size: ¾ cup soup)

2 cups (¼-inch) cubed peeled sweet potato

1½ cups thinly sliced leek (about 1 medium)

1¼ cups fat-free, lower-sodium chicken broth, divided

⅔ cup evaporated fat-free milk

1½ teaspoons Dijon mustard

Dash of white pepper

Dash of ground nutmeg

Chopped leek (optional)

1. Combine sweet potato, sliced leek, and ¼ cup broth in a 1½-quart casserole; stir well. Cover, and microwave at HIGH 10 minutes, stirring after 5 minutes. Place sweet potato mixture in a blender or food processor; process until smooth. Add 1 cup broth, evaporated milk, and remaining ingredients except chopped leek; process 30 seconds or until blended. Garnish with chopped leek, if desired. Serve warm.

CALORIES 118; FAT 0.2g (sat 0.1g, mono 0g, poly 0.1g); PROTEIN 6g; CARB 23.7g; FIBER 2.6g; CHOL 2mg; IRON 1.2mg; SODIUM 315mg; CALC 163mg

FLAVOR TIP

Use freshly grated nutmeg to get the most of its warm, slightly sweet flavor and great aroma. Buy whole nutmeg, and use a Microplane® or another fine spice grater. A little goes a long way!

Creamy Pumpkin Soup

Yield: 5 servings (serving size: 1 cup soup)

2 teaspoons butter

1 cup chopped onion

¾ teaspoon dried rubbed sage

½ teaspoon curry powder

¼ teaspoon ground nutmeg

3 tablespoons all-purpose flour

3 (10½-ounce) cans fat-free, lower-sodium chicken broth

1 tablespoon tomato paste

¼ teaspoon salt

3 cups cubed peeled fresh pumpkin (1 pound)

1 cup chopped peeled McIntosh or other sweet cooking apple

½ cup evaporated fat-free milk

Sage sprigs (optional)

1. Melt butter in a Dutch oven over medium heat. Add onion; sauté 3 minutes. Add sage, curry powder, and nutmeg; cook 30 seconds. Stir in flour; cook 30 seconds. Add broth, tomato paste, and salt, stirring well with a whisk. Stir in pumpkin and apple; bring to a boil. Cover, reduce heat, and simmer 25 minutes or until pumpkin and apple are tender, stirring occasionally. Remove from heat; cool slightly.

2. Place mixture in a blender or food processor; process until smooth. Return mixture to Dutch oven; add evaporated milk. Cook until thoroughly heated. Garnish with sage sprigs, if desired.

CALORIES 133; FAT 3g (sat 1.4g, mono 0.9g, poly 0.3g); PROTEIN 7.5g; CARB 21.8g; FIBER 1.7g; CHOL 5mg; IRON 1.7mg; SODIUM 240mg; CALC 114mg

INGREDIENT TIP

If you can't find McIntosh apples, try sweet cooking apples like Macoun or Empire.

Hot and Sour Soup with Shrimp

Fresh lemon juice lends a tangy, sour flavor to this soup. Add more juice, if you like.

Yield: 4 servings (serving size: 1¾ cups soup)

3 cups fat-free, lower-sodium chicken broth

½ cup presliced mushrooms

2 teaspoons lower-sodium soy sauce

1 (8-ounce) can sliced bamboo shoots, drained

2½ tablespoons fresh lemon juice

1 teaspoon white pepper

1½ pounds medium shrimp, peeled and deveined

1½ cups reduced-fat firm tofu (about 8 ounces), drained and cut into 1-inch cubes

1 tablespoon cornstarch

2 tablespoons water

1 large egg white, beaten

¼ teaspoon chili oil

2 tablespoons chopped green onions

1. Combine first 4 ingredients in a large saucepan; bring to a boil. Reduce heat, and simmer 5 minutes. Add juice, pepper, shrimp, and tofu to pan; bring to a boil. Cook 2 minutes or until shrimp are almost done. Combine cornstarch and water in a small bowl, stirring until smooth. Add cornstarch mixture to pan; cook 1 minute, stirring constantly with a whisk. Slowly drizzle egg white into pan, stirring constantly. Remove from heat; stir in chili oil and onions.

CALORIES 241; FAT 5.5g (sat 0.6g, mono 0.5g, poly 1.2g); PROTEIN 37.4g; CARB 9.4g; FIBER 2.8g; CHOL 204mg; IRON 4.8mg; SODIUM 600mg; CALC 114mg

Quick Chicken Noodle Soup

Heat the broth mixture in the microwave to jump-start the cooking. Meanwhile, sauté the aromatic ingredients in your soup pot to get this dish under way.

Yield: 6 servings (serving size: about 1 cup soup)

2 cups water

1 (32-ounce) carton fat-free, lower-sodium chicken broth

1 tablespoon olive oil

½ cup prechopped onion

½ cup prechopped celery

½ teaspoon salt

½ teaspoon freshly ground black pepper

1 medium carrot, chopped

6 ounces fusilli pasta

2½ cups shredded skinless, boneless rotisserie chicken breast

2 tablespoons chopped fresh flat-leaf parsley

1. Combine 2 cups water and chicken broth in a microwave-safe dish, and microwave at HIGH 5 minutes.

2. While broth mixture heats, heat a large saucepan over medium-high heat. Add oil to pan; swirl to coat. Add onion, celery, salt, pepper, and carrot; sauté 3 minutes or until almost tender, stirring frequently. Add hot broth mixture and pasta; bring to a boil. Reduce heat; simmer 7 minutes or until pasta is almost al dente. Stir in chicken; cook 1 minute or until thoroughly heated. Stir in parsley.

CALORIES 237; FAT 4.8g (sat 1g, mono 2.4g, poly 0.9g); PROTEIN 22.9g; CARB 23.9g; FIBER 1.7g; CHOL 50mg; IRON 1.8mg; SODIUM 589mg; CALC 28mg

INGREDIENT TIP

Though we like the shape of fusilli for this soup, you can also make it with

other pasta, such as wide egg noodles or even rice-shaped orzo.

Chicken, Sausage, and Rice Soup

Make a meal of this comforting soup by adding crackers or warm bread.

Yield: 4 servings (serving size: 1½ cups soup)

4 ounces hot turkey Italian sausage

Cooking spray

2 (2½-ounce) skinless, boneless chicken thighs, cut into ½-inch pieces

1½ cups frozen chopped onion

2 thyme sprigs

⅓ cup chopped celery

⅓ cup chopped carrot

2 (14½-ounce) cans fat-free, lower-sodium chicken broth

1 (3½-ounce) bag boil-in-bag brown rice

1 tablespoon chopped fresh parsley

⅛ teaspoon salt

⅛ teaspoon black pepper

1. Remove casings from sausage. Heat a large saucepan over high heat. Coat pan with cooking spray. Add sausage and chicken to pan; cook 2 minutes, stirring to crumble sausage. Add onion and thyme; cook 2 minutes, stirring occasionally. Add celery, carrot, and broth; bring to a boil.

2. Remove rice from bag; stir into broth mixture. Cover, reduce heat to medium, and cook 7 minutes or until rice is tender. Discard thyme sprigs. Stir in parsley, salt, and pepper.

CALORIES 219; FAT 5.2g (sat 1.3g, mono 1.6g, poly 1.2g); PROTEIN 17.2g; CARB 26.5g; FIBER 3.9g; CHOL 53mg; IRON 1.6mg; SODIUM 623mg; CALC 38mg

NUTRITION TIP

Chicken thighs and other dark-meat pieces have more iron than white meat.

They stay tender better than chicken breasts, and they have more flavor, too.

Pasta e Fagioli

Yield: 6 servings (serving size: 1 cup soup)

1 tablespoon olive oil

6 ounces hot turkey Italian sausage

1½ tablespoons bottled minced garlic

1 cup water

1 (16-ounce) can fat-free, lower-sodium chicken broth

1 (8-ounce) can no-salt-added tomato sauce

1 cup uncooked small seashell pasta (about 4 ounces)

½ cup (2 ounces) grated Romano cheese, divided

1½ teaspoons dried oregano

⅛ teaspoon salt

¼ teaspoon white pepper

2 (15-ounce) cans no-salt-added cannellini or other white beans, drained

Minced fresh parsley (optional)

Crushed red pepper (optional)

1. Heat oil in a large saucepan over medium-high heat. Add sausage and garlic; sauté 2 minutes or until browned, stirring to crumble. Add water, broth, and tomato sauce; bring to a boil. Stir in pasta, ¼ cup cheese, oregano, salt, pepper, and beans; bring to a boil. Cover, reduce heat, and simmer 8 minutes or until pasta is done. Let stand 5 minutes; sprinkle with remaining ¼ cup cheese. Garnish each serving with parsley and red pepper, if desired.

CALORIES 254; FAT 9.2g (sat 2.2g, mono 1.7g, poly 0.4g); PROTEIN 15g; CARB 27.1g; FIBER 6g; CHOL 23mg; IRON 3.4mg; SODIUM 570mg; CALC 173mg

Quick Avgolemono, Orzo, and Chicken Soup

Avgolemono (ahv-goh-LEH-moh-noh) is a tangy Greek soup that combines chicken broth, eggs, and lemon juice. Traditional versions include rice; our interpretation uses orzo. Serve with pita chips.

Yield: 4 servings (serving size: 2 cups soup)

5 cups fat-free, lower-sodium chicken broth

1 cup water

1 teaspoon finely chopped fresh dill

½ cup uncooked orzo (rice-shaped pasta)

4 large eggs

⅓ cup fresh lemon juice

1 cup shredded carrot

¼ teaspoon black pepper

8 ounces skinless, boneless chicken breast, cut into bite-sized pieces

Chopped fresh dill (optional)

1. Bring broth, 1 cup water, and dill to a boil in a large saucepan. Add orzo. Reduce heat, and simmer 5 minutes or until orzo is slightly tender. Remove from heat.

2. Place eggs and juice in a blender; process until smooth. Remove 1 cup broth from pan with a ladle, making sure to leave out orzo. With blender on, slowly add broth; process until smooth.

3. Add carrot, pepper, and chicken to pan. Bring to a simmer over medium-low heat, and cook 5 minutes or until chicken and orzo are done. Reduce heat to low. Slowly stir in egg mixture; cook 30 seconds, stirring constantly (do not boil). Garnish with dill, if desired.

CALORIES 222; FAT 6.2g (sat 1.9g, mono 2.2g, poly 0.9g); PROTEIN 24.7g; CARB 16.3g; FIBER 2.5g; CHOL 244mg; IRON 2.5mg; SODIUM 611mg; CALC 65mg

Chipotle Turkey and Corn Soup

Stacking the turkey cutlets and then thinly slicing them will save you some time during preparation. Chipotle chiles come canned in adobo sauce; use that for the adobo sauce called for in this recipe.

Yield: 4 servings (serving size: 1½ cups soup and 2 tablespoons chips)

1 tablespoon canola oil

1 pound turkey cutlets, cut into thin strips

2 teaspoons adobo sauce

1 to 2 teaspoons chopped canned chipotle chiles in adobo sauce

2 (14-ounce) cans fat-free, lower-sodium chicken broth

1 (14¾-ounce) can cream-style corn

¼ cup chopped fresh cilantro, divided

½ cup crushed tortilla chips (about 1½ ounces)

4 lime wedges

1. Heat oil in a large saucepan over medium-high heat. Add turkey; cook 3 minutes or until browned, stirring occasionally. Stir in adobo sauce, chiles, broth, and corn; bring to a boil. Reduce heat to medium-low; simmer 5 minutes. Stir in 3 tablespoons cilantro. Divide soup evenly among 4 bowls; sprinkle evenly with remaining cilantro and crushed chips. Serve with lime wedges.

CALORIES 303; FAT 7.6g (sat 0.6g, mono 2.9g, poly 2.3g); PROTEIN 32.2g; CARB 27.4g; FIBER 2.8g; CHOL 45mg; IRON 2.4mg; SODIUM 561mg; CALC 23mg

INGREDIENT TIP

You can freeze leftover canned chipotle chiles in the adobo sauce. Package the chiles individually with a little sauce in small plastic freezer bags. Use them in salsas, with pork, or in Mexican-inspired scrambled eggs.

Turkey Soup Provençal

The secret ingredient in this aromatic soup is herbes de Provence. Complete the meal with slices of French bread.

Yield: 4 servings (serving size: 1¼ cups soup)

1 pound ground turkey breast

½ teaspoon dried herbes de Provence, crushed

1 (15-ounce) can no-salt-added cannellini or other white beans, drained and rinsed

1 (14.5-ounce) can fat-free, lower-sodium chicken broth

1 (14.5-ounce) can diced tomatoes with garlic and onion, undrained

4 cups chopped fresh spinach

1. Cook turkey in a large saucepan over medium-high heat until browned, stirring to crumble.

2. Add herbes de Provence, beans, broth, and tomatoes to pan; bring to a boil. Reduce heat, and simmer 5 minutes. Stir in spinach; simmer 5 minutes or until spinach wilts.

CALORIES 271; FAT 10.2g (sat 2.6g, mono 3.6g, poly 2.3g); PROTEIN 26.6g; CARB 17.4g; FIBER 4.7g; CHOL 90mg; IRON 4.7mg; SODIUM 641mg; CALC 92mg

Tequila Pork Chile Verde

An upscale Mexican meal, this surprisingly easy stew combines crispy cornmeal-and-ancho chile–crusted pork tenderloin, tart tomatillos, green chiles, jalapeños, and broth. As it simmers, the flavors mellow until it's time for the final touch: a splash of tequila. Serve with black beans.

Yield: 4 servings (serving size: 1¼ cups stew)

2 teaspoons canola oil

3 tablespoons yellow cornmeal

1 tablespoon ancho chile powder

1 pound pork tenderloin, trimmed and cut into ¾-inch pieces

2 cups coarsely chopped fresh tomatillos (about 12 ounces)

1 (14-ounce) can fat-free, lower-sodium chicken broth

1 (4.5-ounce) can chopped mild green chiles, drained

1 jalapeño pepper, seeded and finely chopped

½ cup thinly sliced green onions

¼ cup chopped fresh cilantro

2 tablespoons tequila

¼ teaspoon salt

1. Heat oil in a large nonstick skillet over medium-high heat.

2. Combine cornmeal and chile powder in a medium bowl. Add pork, tossing to coat. Remove pork from bowl, reserving any remaining cornmeal mixture. Add pork to pan; sauté 5 minutes or until browned. Stir in remaining cornmeal mixture; cook 30 seconds, stirring constantly. Stir in tomatillos, broth, green chiles, and jalapeño; bring to a simmer over medium-low heat. Cook 8 minutes or until tomatillos are tender. Stir in onions and remaining ingredients; simmer 1 minute.

CALORIES 245; FAT 7.4g (sat 1.7g, mono 3.3g, poly 1.6g); PROTEIN 26.5g; CARB 14.8g; FIBER 3.4g; CHOL 74mg; IRON 2.7mg; SODIUM 407mg; CALC 30mg

Sausage, Kale, and Bean Soup

Cajun sausage fires a simple five-ingredient soup with smoky spice. Serve with crusty bread.

Yield: 4 servings (serving size: 1¾ cups soup)

2 ounces Cajun smoked sausage, chopped

3 cups fat-free, lower-sodium chicken broth

1 (14.5-ounce) can no-salt-added diced tomatoes, undrained

6 cups coarsely chopped kale (about 8 ounces)

1 (16-ounce) can organic navy beans, drained and rinsed

1. Heat a large saucepan over medium-high heat. Add smoked sausage to pan; cook 2 minutes, stirring occasionally. Add broth and diced tomatoes; bring to a boil over high heat. Stir in kale. Reduce heat, and simmer 4 minutes or until kale is tender. Stir in beans, and cook 1 minute or until soup is thoroughly heated.

CALORIES 171; FAT 4.9g (sat 1.6g, mono 2g, poly 0.7g); PROTEIN 10.2g; CARB 21.9g; FIBER 6.3g; CHOL 10mg; IRON 3.4mg; SODIUM 436mg; CALC 150mg

Garden Minestrone

You'll truly enjoy our version of minestrone—it pairs fresh vegetables with the rich feel and taste of Asiago cheese.

Yield: 8 servings (serving size: 1½ cups soup)

2 teaspoons olive oil

1 cup chopped onion

2 teaspoons chopped fresh oregano

4 garlic cloves, minced

3 cups chopped yellow squash

3 cups chopped zucchini

1 cup chopped carrot

1 cup fresh corn kernels (about 2 ears)

4 cups chopped tomato, divided

3 (14-ounce) cans fat-free, lower-sodium chicken broth, divided

½ cup uncooked ditalini pasta (very short tube-shaped macaroni)

1 (15.5-ounce) can no-salt-added Great Northern beans, rinsed and drained

1 (6-ounce) package fresh baby spinach

¾ teaspoon salt

½ teaspoon freshly ground black pepper

1 cup (4 ounces) grated Asiago cheese

Coarsely ground black pepper (optional)

1. Heat oil in a Dutch oven over medium-high heat. Add onion to pan; sauté 3 minutes or until softened. Add oregano and garlic; sauté 1 minute. Stir in squash, zucchini, carrot, and corn; sauté 5 minutes or until vegetables are tender. Remove from heat.

2. Place 3 cups tomato and 1 can broth in a blender or food processor; process until smooth. Add tomato mixture to pan; return pan to heat. Stir in remaining 1 cup tomato and remaining 2 cans broth; bring mixture to a boil. Reduce heat, and simmer 20 minutes.

3. Add pasta and beans to pan; cook 10 minutes or until pasta is tender, stirring occasionally. Remove from heat. Stir in spinach, salt, and ½ teaspoon pepper. Ladle soup into individual bowls; top with cheese. Garnish with coarsely ground black pepper, if desired.

CALORIES 201; FAT 6.8g (sat 2.9g, mono 1g, poly 0.4g); PROTEIN 10.3g; CARB 27.3g; FIBER 7.6g; CHOL 13mg; IRON 2.4mg; SODIUM 664mg; CALC 187mg

French Onion Soup

Once you try this classic onion soup recipe, you'll never try another. It culminates in a rich-tasting soup with melt-in-your-mouth onions and bubbly cheese on top of toasted croutons.

Yield: 8 servings (serving size: 1 cup soup, 1 ounce bread, and 1 cheese slice)

2 teaspoons olive oil

4 cups thinly vertically sliced Walla Walla or other sweet onion

4 cups thinly vertically sliced red onion

½ teaspoon sugar

½ teaspoon freshly ground black pepper

¼ teaspoon salt

¼ cup dry white wine

8 cups fat-free, lower-sodium beef broth

¼ teaspoon chopped fresh thyme

8 (1-ounce) slices French bread, cut into 1-inch cubes

8 (1-ounce) slices reduced-fat, reduced-sodium Swiss cheese

1. Heat oil in a Dutch oven over medium-high heat. Add onions to pan; sauté 5 minutes or until tender. Stir in sugar, pepper, and ¼ teaspoon salt. Reduce heat to medium; cook 20 minutes, stirring frequently. Increase heat to medium-high, and sauté 5 minutes or until onion is golden brown. Stir in wine, and cook 1 minute. Add broth and thyme; bring to a boil. Cover, reduce heat, and simmer 2 hours.
2. Preheat broiler.
3. Place bread in a single layer on a baking sheet; broil 2 minutes or until toasted, turning after 1 minute.
4. Place 8 ovenproof bowls on a jelly-roll pan. Ladle 1 cup soup into each bowl. Divide bread evenly among bowls; top each serving with 1 cheese slice. Broil 3 minutes or until cheese begins to brown.

CALORIES 290; FAT 9.6g (sat 4.8g, mono 1.9g, poly 0.7g); PROTEIN 16.8g; CARB 33.4g; FIBER 3.1g; CHOL 20mg; IRON 1.6mg; SODIUM 359mg; CALC 317mg

INGREDIENT TIP

When cooked to the point that their natural sugars caramelize, onions darken to a deep golden brown color and take on an interesting sweetness. We prefer to use

yellow onions when caramelizing onions because they aren't too sweet or too pungent. But any type of onion— yellow, white, red, or sweet—works just fine.

Split Pea Soup with Rosemary

For the best flavor, make this soup with the Vegetable Stock on page 167. If you use canned broth instead of the homemade stock, omit the added salt in the recipe.

Yield: 6 servings (serving size: 1 cup soup)

1½ cups green split peas

2 teaspoons olive oil, divided

2 cups chopped onion

1 cup diced carrot

1 bay leaf

1 tablespoon minced garlic cloves, divided (about 3 cloves)

1 tablespoon minced fresh rosemary, divided

1 teaspoon paprika

¼ teaspoon black pepper

1 tablespoon tomato paste

1 tablespoon lower-sodium soy sauce

4 cups water

2 cups Vegetable Stock or 1 (14½-ounce) can organic vegetable broth

1 teaspoon salt

¼ cup chopped fresh parsley

¼ cup reduced-fat sour cream

1. Sort and wash peas; cover with water to 2 inches above peas, and set aside. Heat 1 teaspoon oil in a Dutch oven over medium-high heat. Add onion, carrot, and bay leaf; sauté 5 minutes, stirring frequently. Add 2 teaspoons garlic, 1 teaspoon rosemary, paprika, and pepper; cook 3 minutes. Add tomato paste and soy sauce; cook until liquid evaporates, scraping pan to loosen browned bits.

2. Drain peas. Add peas, 4 cups water, Vegetable Stock, and salt to onion mixture; bring to a boil. Cover, reduce heat to medium-low, and simmer 1 hour, stirring often. Discard bay leaf. Place half of soup in blender or food processor; process until smooth. Pour pureed soup into a large bowl. Repeat procedure with remaining soup.

3. Combine remaining 1 teaspoon oil, remaining 1 teaspoon garlic, remaining 2 teaspoons rosemary, and parsley. Stir parsley mixture into soup. Spoon soup into bowls; top each with sour cream.

CALORIES 233; FAT 3.5g (sat 1.1g, mono 1.6g, poly 0.5g); PROTEIN 13.7g; CARB 38.7g; FIBER 4.8g; CHOL 4mg; IRON 2.9mg; SODIUM 559mg; CALC 65mg

Vichyssoise

This version of the classic cold potato-leek soup is also delicious served warm.

Yield: 5 servings (serving size: 1 cup soup)

1 teaspoon canola oil

3 cups diced leek (about 3 large)

3 cups diced peeled baking potato (about 1¼ pounds)

1 (16-ounce) can fat-free, lower-sodium chicken broth

⅔ cup half-and-half

¼ teaspoon salt

⅛ teaspoon black pepper

1 tablespoon minced fresh chives

1. Heat oil in a large saucepan over medium-low heat. Add leek; cover and cook 10 minutes or until soft. Stir in potato and broth, and bring to a boil. Cover potato mixture, reduce heat, and simmer 15 minutes or until the potato is tender. Place potato mixture in a blender or food processor, and process until smooth. Place potato mixture in a large bowl, and cool to room temperature. Stir in half-and-half, salt, and pepper. Cover and chill. Sprinkle soup with minced chives.

CALORIES 195; FAT 5g (sat 2.5g, mono 0.6g, poly 0.4g); PROTEIN 4.9g; CARB 33.8g; FIBER 3.1g; CHOL 12mg; IRON 1.7mg; SODIUM 291mg; CALC 77mg

INGREDIENT TIP

Leeks often have sand trapped between their layers, so it's important to rinse them well. Cut the root end and the tough green leaves off, then cut the leek in half vertically. Fan the layers out under cold running water to rinse out any dirt and sand.

Loaded Potato Soup

Based on a casual dining classic, this soup has a terrific balance of flavors—a creamy base with crunchy, salty bacon, the intense flavor of cheddar, and a bit of pungent onion.

Yield: 4 servings (serving size: about 1¼ cups soup)

4 (6-ounce) red potatoes

2 teaspoons olive oil

½ cup prechopped onion

1¼ cups fat-free, lower-sodium chicken broth

3 tablespoons all-purpose flour

2 cups 1% low-fat milk, divided

¼ cup reduced-fat sour cream

½ teaspoon salt

¼ teaspoon freshly ground black pepper

3 bacon slices, halved

⅓ cup shredded cheddar cheese

4 teaspoons thinly sliced green onions

1. Pierce potatoes with a fork. Microwave at HIGH 13 minutes or until tender. Cut in half; cool slightly.

2. While potatoes cook, heat oil in a saucepan over medium-high heat. Add onion; sauté 3 minutes. Add broth. Combine flour and ½ cup milk in a bowl; add to pan with remaining 1½ cups milk. Bring to a boil; stir often. Cook 1 minute. Remove from heat; stir in sour cream, salt, and pepper.

3. Arrange bacon on a paper towel on a microwave-safe plate. Cover with a paper towel; microwave at HIGH 4 minutes. Crumble bacon.

4. Discard potato skins. Coarsely mash potatoes into soup. Ladle soup into bowls. Top evenly with cheese, green onions, and bacon.

CALORIES 325; FAT 11.1g (sat 5.2g, mono 4.5g, poly 0.8g); PROTEIN 13.2g; CARB 43.8g; FIBER 3g; CHOL 27mg; IRON 1.3mg; SODIUM 670mg; CALC 261mg

Vatapa

This classic Brazilian dish offers a harmonious balance of tangy, sweet, and spicy flavors. For an authentic touch, sprinkle the soup with chopped peanuts just before serving. Try making this soup with a Brazilian lager or a Mexican beer.

Yield: 6 servings (serving size: about 1⅓ cups soup and ½ cup rice)

Stock:

6 cups water

1 cup chopped onion

¾ cup chopped carrot

1 tablespoon grated peeled fresh ginger

4 garlic cloves, minced

1 pound fish bones

Soup:

Cooking spray

1 cup chopped onion

1 tablespoon brown sugar

1 teaspoon salt

1 tablespoon grated peeled fresh ginger

3 garlic cloves, minced

1 serrano chile, seeded and finely chopped

3 cups chopped seeded peeled tomato

1 (12-ounce) bottle beer

1 (13.5-ounce) can light coconut milk

1 pound grouper or other firm white fish fillets, cut into 1-inch pieces

⅓ cup chopped fresh cilantro

1 tablespoon fresh lime juice

3 cups hot cooked basmati rice

6 lime wedges

1. Combine first 6 ingredients in a large Dutch oven; bring to a boil. Reduce heat, and simmer 30 minutes. Drain stock through a fine sieve into a bowl; discard solids.

2. Wipe pan dry with a paper towel. Heat pan over medium-high heat. Coat pan with cooking spray. Add 1 cup onion, sugar, and salt; sauté 3 minutes. Add 1 tablespoon ginger, 3 garlic cloves, and chile; sauté 30 seconds. Stir in reserved stock, tomato, and beer; bring to a boil. Cook until reduced to 6 cups (about 15 minutes). Stir in coconut milk; bring to a boil. Reduce heat, and simmer 20 minutes, stirring occasionally. Add fish; cook 5 minutes over medium-high heat or until fish flakes easily when tested with a fork or until desired degree of doneness. Stir in cilantro and juice. Serve with rice and lime wedges.

CALORIES 241; FAT 4.5g (sat 3.5g, mono 0.2g, poly 0.4g); PROTEIN 18.4g; CARB 32.1g; FIBER 1.8g; CHOL 28mg; IRON 1.6mg; SODIUM 464mg; CALC 50mg

Canadian Cheese Soup with Pumpernickel Croutons

A cheese soup that is full of flavor, thanks to the contrast of sharp cheddar and pumpernickel.

Yield: 8 servings (serving size: 1 cup soup and ¼ cup croutons)

3 (1-ounce) slices pumpernickel bread, cut into ½-inch cubes

1 onion, peeled and quartered

1 carrot, peeled and quartered

1 celery stalk, quartered

1 teaspoon butter

3.4 ounces all-purpose flour (about ¾ cup)

2 (16-ounce) cans fat-free, lower-sodium chicken broth, divided

3 cups 2% reduced-fat milk

½ teaspoon salt

½ teaspoon paprika

½ teaspoon freshly ground black pepper

1½ cups (6 ounces) shredded reduced-fat sharp cheddar cheese

1. Preheat oven to 375°.

2. Place bread cubes on a jelly-roll pan, and bake at 375° for 15 minutes or until toasted.

3. While croutons bake, place onion, carrot, and celery in a food processor, and pulse until chopped. Melt butter in a large sauce-pan over medium-high heat. Add vegetables; sauté 5 minutes or until tender.

4. Lightly spoon flour into a dry measuring cup; level with a knife. Gradually add 1 can of broth to flour in a medium bowl; stir well with a whisk. Add flour mixture to pan. Stir in remaining 1 can of broth; bring to a boil. Reduce heat to medium, and cook 10 minutes or until thick. Stir in milk, salt, paprika, and pepper; cook 10 minutes. Remove from heat; add cheese, stirring until cheese melts. Ladle soup into bowls, and top with croutons.

CALORIES 203; FAT 6.8g (sat 3.8g, mono 1.9g, poly 0.4g); PROTEIN 13.2g; CARB 21.9g; FIBER 1.8g; CHOL 23mg; IRON 1.1mg; SODIUM 671mg; CALC 318mg

Chipotle Chicken Tortilla Soup

If you like spicy food, you'll love this soup. Purchase corn muffins from your supermarket bakery to round out the meal.

Yield: 4 servings (serving size: 1¼ cups soup and ¼ cup chips)

1 tablespoon canola oil

1½ teaspoons bottled minced garlic

¾ pound chicken breast tenders, cut into bite-sized pieces

1 teaspoon chipotle chile powder

1 teaspoon ground cumin

1 cup water

⅛ teaspoon salt

1 (14-ounce) can fat-free, lower-sodium chicken broth

1 (14.5-ounce) can no-salt-added diced stewed tomatoes, undrained

1 cup crushed baked tortilla chips

¼ cup chopped fresh cilantro

1 lime, cut into 4 wedges

1. Heat oil in a large saucepan over medium-high heat. Add minced garlic and chicken; sauté 2 minutes. Add chile powder and cumin; stir well. Add water, salt, broth, and tomatoes; bring to a boil. Cover, reduce heat, and simmer 5 minutes. Top with tortilla chips and cilantro, and serve with lime wedges.

CALORIES 227; FAT 5.5g (sat 0.6g, mono 2.5g, poly 1.3g); PROTEIN 23.2g; CARB 20.6g; FIBER 3g; CHOL 49mg; IRON 1.8mg; SODIUM 440mg; CALC 60mg

Gramercy Crawfish Gumbo

Traditionally, gumbo starts with a roux–a mixture of flour and fat that cooks slowly until browned. In this recipe, named for a small town in Louisiana, you brown the flour in the oven. This technique provides a deep, nutty flavor without the fat.

Yield: 8 servings (serving size: 1⅓ cups soup and ¾ cup rice)

2.25 ounces all-purpose flour (½ cup)

¼ cup vegetable oil

1 cup finely chopped onion

8 cups water

1½ cups sliced okra pods (about 6 ounces)

¼ cup finely chopped green bell pepper

¼ cup chopped fresh parsley

¼ cup chopped celery leaves

2 to 3 tablespoons Cajun seasoning

1 teaspoon salt

8 garlic cloves, minced

1 (14.5-ounce) can stewed tomatoes, undrained

2 cups cooked crawfish tail meat (about 12 ounces)

1 cup lump crabmeat, shell pieces removed (about ⅓ pound)

1 teaspoon hot sauce

6 cups hot cooked rice

Chopped fresh parsley (optional)

1. Preheat oven to 350°.

2. Weigh or lightly spoon flour into a dry measuring cup; level with a knife. Place flour in a 9-inch pie plate; bake at 350° for 45 minutes or until lightly browned, stirring frequently. Cool on a wire rack.

3. Heat oil in a large Dutch oven over medium-high heat. Add onion; sauté 4 minutes. Stir in browned flour; cook 1 minute, stirring constantly. Gradually stir in water and next 8 ingredients; bring to a boil. Reduce heat; simmer 1 hour.

4. Stir in crawfish, crabmeat, and hot sauce. Bring to a boil; reduce heat, and simmer 25 minutes. Serve gumbo with rice; sprinkle with parsley, if desired.

CALORIES 325; FAT 8.5g (sat 1g, mono 3.3g, poly 3.4g); PROTEIN 15.5g; CARB 46.7g; FIBER 2.4g; CHOL 75mg; IRON 3.5mg; SODIUM 597mg; CALC 93mg

SUBSTITUTION TIP

Instead of using bottled Cajun seasoning, you can make your own All That Jazz Seasoning: Combine ¼ cup garlic powder, ¼ cup onion powder, 2 tablespoons paprika, 1 tablespoon ground red pepper, 1 tablespoon black pepper, 1½ teaspoons celery seeds, 1½ teaspoons chili powder, 1 teaspoon salt, 1 teaspoon lemon pepper, and ½ teaspoon ground nutmeg. Yield: 1 cup.

CALORIES 20; FAT 0.3g (sat 0.1g, mono 0.1g, poly 0.1g); PROTEIN 0.8g; CARB 4.3g; FIBER 1.1g; CHOL 0mg; IRON 0.6mg; SODIUM 177mg; CALC 18mg

Brunswick Stew with Smoked Paprika

This dish is said to have originated in Brunswick County, Virginia, in the 1800s. We spiced it up with a little smoked Spanish paprika (available at gourmet specialty stores and some supermarkets). Use rotisserie chicken to speed up preparation.

Yield: 6 servings (serving size: about 1½ cups soup)

2 cups (¾-inch) cubed Yukon gold potato

2 cups thinly sliced yellow onion

2 cups frozen corn kernels, thawed

1 cup frozen baby lima beans, thawed

½ cup tomato sauce

2 (14-ounce) cans fat-free, lower-sodium chicken broth

2 bacon slices, cut crosswise into ½-inch strips

3 cups shredded cooked chicken breast

½ teaspoon sweet Spanish smoked paprika

½ teaspoon kosher salt

¼ teaspoon ground red pepper

1. Combine first 7 ingredients in a Dutch oven over medium-high heat; bring to a boil. Reduce heat to low; simmer 30 minutes or until potato is tender, stirring occasionally. Stir in chicken, paprika, salt, and pepper; simmer 15 minutes.

CALORIES 308; FAT 7.5g (sat 2.4g, mono 3g, poly 1.4g); PROTEIN 29.4g; CARB 31.6g; FIBER 4.9g; CHOL 65mg; IRON 2.2mg; SODIUM 645mg; CALC 36mg

WINE TIP

A sparkling wine complements the strong, smoky flavors in the stew. It's a delicious combination that could become a regular autumn weeknight treat.

Creamy Wild-Rice Soup with Smoked Turkey

Wild rice is not really a rice: It is a grass that originated in the Great Lakes area. It still counts as a whole grain, though, and offers more protein than most other whole grains and is richer in antioxidants than white rice.

Yield: 8 servings (serving size: 1 cup soup)

2 teaspoons butter

1 cup chopped carrot

1 cup chopped onion

1 cup chopped green onions

1 teaspoon chopped fresh or ¼ teaspoon dried rosemary

¼ teaspoon black pepper

3 garlic cloves, minced

2 (16-ounce) cans fat-free, lower-sodium chicken broth

1½ cups chopped smoked turkey breast (½ pound)

1 cup uncooked wild rice

1.5 ounces all-purpose flour (about ⅓ cup)

2¾ cups 2% reduced-fat milk

2 tablespoons dry sherry

½ teaspoon salt

1. Melt butter in a Dutch oven over medium-high heat. Add carrot and next 5 ingredients. Cook 8 minutes or until browned. Stir in broth, scraping pan to loosen browned bits. Stir in turkey and rice; bring to a boil. Cover, reduce heat, and simmer 1 hour and 15 minutes or until rice is tender.

2. Lightly spoon flour into a dry measuring cup; level with a knife. Combine flour and milk in a small bowl, stirring with a whisk. Add to pan. Cook over medium heat until thick (about 8 minutes), stirring frequently. Stir in sherry and salt.

CALORIES 206; FAT 4.1g (sat 2.3g, mono 0.8g, poly 0.3g); PROTEIN 13g; CARB 30.2g; FIBER 3.1g; CHOL 24mg; IRON 1.2mg; SODIUM 629mg; CALC 132mg

Smoked Ham Soup with White Beans

This high-fiber soup is also great when made with dried cannellini beans. If you have the time, soak the beans overnight instead of using the quick-soak method called for; this will produce creamier beans. Serve with your favorite corn bread recipe, or try the Parmesan-Corn Bread Muffins on page 347.

Yield: 8 servings (serving size: 1¼ cups soup)

1 (16-ounce) package dried navy beans

1 tablespoon olive oil

2 cups chopped yellow onion

4 garlic cloves, minced

8 cups fat-free, lower-sodium chicken broth

4 cups water

2 tablespoons chopped fresh parsley

1 teaspoon chopped fresh thyme

¼ teaspoon salt

¼ teaspoon freshly ground black pepper

2 smoked ham hocks (about 1 pound)

2 bay leaves

1 (14.5-ounce) can petite diced tomatoes, undrained

1. Sort and wash beans; place in a large Dutch oven. Cover with water to 2 inches above beans; bring to a boil. Cook 2 minutes. Remove from heat; cover and let stand 1 hour. Drain.

2. Heat oil in pan over medium heat. Add onion; cook until tender, stirring occasionally. Add garlic, and cook 1 minute, stirring frequently. Add drained beans, broth, and remaining ingredients; bring to a boil. Cover, reduce heat, and simmer 2½ hours or until beans are tender. Discard bay leaves.

3. Remove ham hocks with a slotted spoon, and cool slightly. Remove meat from bones; discard fat, gristle, and bones. Shred meat with 2 forks. Place 1 cup of bean mixture in a blender; process until smooth. Return pureed bean mixture to pan; stir until blended. Stir in meat.

CALORIES 323; FAT 8.4g (sat 2.6g, mono 4g, poly 1.1g); PROTEIN 22g; CARB 40.7g; FIBER 16.2g; CHOL 27mg; IRON 5.6mg; SODIUM 558mg; CALC 137mg

Beef Goulash

Hungary's national dish is a beef stew flavored with paprika and caraway seeds. Browning the meat first yields the most flavorful result. You can also serve it over egg noodles.

Yield: 8 servings (serving size: 1 cup soup)

1½ pounds boneless chuck roast, trimmed and cut into 1-inch pieces

1.1 ounces all-purpose flour (about ¼ cup)

1¼ teaspoons salt, divided

¾ teaspoon freshly ground black pepper, divided

1 tablespoon butter

4 cups chopped onion (about 2 large)

2 garlic cloves, minced

2 tablespoons paprika

1 tablespoon red wine vinegar

1 cup chopped plum tomato (about 3)

½ teaspoon caraway seeds, crushed

2 bay leaves

½ cup water

1 (14-ounce) can fat-free, lower-sodium beef broth

2½ cups cubed peeled Yukon gold or red potato (about 1 pound)

1 tablespoon fresh lemon juice

1. Dredge beef in flour; sprinkle with ½ teaspoon salt and ¼ teaspoon pepper. Melt butter in a Dutch oven over medium-high heat. Add beef; cook 8 minutes, browning on all sides. Remove beef from pan.

2. Add onion and garlic to pan; sauté 10 minutes or until lightly browned. Stir in paprika and vinegar; cook 2 minutes. Return beef to pan. Add tomato, caraway seeds, and bay leaves; cook 3 minutes. Add ½ teaspoon salt, ¼ teaspoon pepper, ½ cup water, and broth; bring to a boil. Cover, reduce heat, and simmer 1 hour and 45 minutes. Add potato; cover and cook 1 hour and 15 minutes or until very tender. Stir in remaining ¼ teaspoon salt, remaining ¼ teaspoon pepper, and juice. Discard bay leaves.

CALORIES 242; FAT 6.1g (sat 2.6g, mono 2.3g, poly 0.4g); Protein 24.2g; Carb 22.4g; Fiber 2.5g; CHOL 47mg; IRON 2.8mg; SODIUM 517mg; CALC 31mg

Curried Turkey Soup

The sweet flavors of apples and coconut balance the bold spices in this soup. You also get a pleasing crunch from chopped peanuts.

Yield: 11 servings (serving size: 1 cup soup and ¼ cup rice)

Soup:

1 tablespoon butter

4 teaspoons curry powder

1 teaspoon minced peeled fresh ginger

2 garlic cloves, minced

4 (16-ounce) cartons fat-free, lower-sodium chicken broth, divided

2 cups chopped onion

1 cup chopped leek

½ cup diced peeled Golden Delicious apple

½ cup diced carrot

½ cup diced celery

3 cups finely shredded cooked turkey

1 tablespoon lemon juice

⅛ teaspoon white pepper

1 (12-ounce) can evaporated fat-free milk

2.25 ounces all-purpose flour (about ½ cup)

Remaining Ingredients:

2¾ cups hot cooked rice

¾ cup diced peeled Golden Delicious apple

⅓ cup chopped dry-roasted peanuts

⅓ cup chopped fresh parsley

⅓ cup flaked sweetened coconut, toasted

1. To make soup, melt butter in a large Dutch oven over low heat. Add curry powder, ginger, and garlic; sauté 2 minutes. Add 2 cans of broth, onion, and next 4 ingredients, and bring to a boil. Reduce heat; simmer 20 minutes or until vegetables are tender.

2. Place half of the vegetable mixture in a food processor, and process until smooth. Spoon into a bowl. Repeat procedure with remaining vegetable mixture. Combine vegetable puree, 1 can of broth, turkey, juice, pepper, and milk in pan, and stir well. Combine remaining 1 can of broth and flour in a bowl. Stir with a whisk; add to vegetable mixture in pan. Bring to a boil; reduce heat, and simmer 10 minutes or until thick, stirring constantly.

3. Spoon ¼ cup rice into each of 11 bowls; top each with 1 cup soup, about 1 tablespoon diced apple, 1½ teaspoons peanuts, 1½ teaspoons parsley, and 1½ teaspoons coconut.

CALORIES 224; FAT 4.5g (sat 1.9g, mono 1.5g, poly 1g); PROTEIN 16.7g; CARB 29g; FIBER 2.9g; CHOL 30mg; IRON 2mg; SODIUM 371mg; CALC 134mg

Harira

During the ninth month of their calendar, Muslims observe the ritual fast of Ramadan. For the entire month, they abstain from eating during the day; in the evening, they take small meals and visit with friends and family. This is a variation of the soup that is traditionally eaten to break the fast at the Ramadan meal.

Yield: 4 servings (serving size: 1¼ cups soup)

1¼ pounds boneless leg of lamb, trimmed and cut into 1-inch cubes

½ teaspoon salt

¼ teaspoon black pepper

1 tablespoon olive oil

1 cup chopped onion

1 tablespoon tomato paste

4 cups water

1 cup drained canned chickpeas (garbanzo beans)

½ teaspoon ground cinnamon

¼ teaspoon ground red pepper

2 cups chopped tomato

½ cup dried small red or brown lentils

½ cup chopped red bell pepper

½ cup hot cooked angel hair pasta (about 1 ounce uncooked pasta)

1 tablespoon minced fresh cilantro

1 tablespoon fresh lemon juice

1. Sprinkle lamb with salt and black pepper. Heat oil in a large Dutch oven over high heat. Add lamb; cook 5 minutes or until browned, stirring occasionally. Add onion; cook 1 minute, stirring frequently. Stir in tomato paste; cook 1 minute, stirring frequently. Stir in water, chickpeas, cinnamon, and ground red pepper. Bring to a boil; reduce heat, and simmer 30 minutes.

2. Stir in tomato, lentils, and bell pepper. Bring to a boil; reduce heat, and simmer 30 minutes or until lentils are tender. Stir in pasta, cilantro, and juice; cook 1 minute or until thoroughly heated.

CALORIES 359; FAT 9.2g (sat 2.1g, mono 4.4g, poly 1.5g); PROTEIN 30.4g; CARB 40.6g; FIBER 6.8g; CHOL 55mg; IRON 6.3mg; SODIUM 544mg; CALC 60mg

Wild Mushroom Stew with Gremolata

The Mushroom Stock (page 213) used here also makes a great base for mushroom-barley soup, a savory gravy for mashed potatoes, or a braised bean dish.

Yield: 4 servings (serving size: 2 cups stew)

4½ cups quartered shiitake mushrooms (about 8 ounces)

4½ cups quartered cremini mushrooms (about 8 ounces)

1 (8-ounce) package button mushrooms, quartered

1½ tablespoons olive oil, divided

2 cups thinly sliced leek (about 2 medium)

1 cup chopped fennel bulb (about 1 small bulb)

1 cup (1-inch-thick) slices carrot

¼ teaspoon salt, divided

2 cups Mushroom Stock

1½ tablespoons lower-sodium soy sauce

1 teaspoon minced fresh or ¼ teaspoon dried tarragon

1 teaspoon chopped fresh or ¼ teaspoon dried thyme

1 teaspoon chopped fresh or ¼ teaspoon dried sage

1 teaspoon honey

⅛ teaspoon black pepper

1 (14.5-ounce) can no-salt-added chopped tomatoes, undrained

1 tablespoon cornstarch

1 tablespoon water

2 tablespoons chopped fresh flat-leaf parsley

1 teaspoon grated lemon rind

1 garlic clove, minced

1. Preheat oven to 450°.

2. Combine mushrooms and 1 tablespoon oil in a single layer on a jelly-roll pan. Bake mushrooms at 450° for 30 minutes, stirring once.

3. Heat 1½ teaspoons oil in a Dutch oven over medium heat. Add leek, fennel, and carrot; cook 5 minutes. Sprinkle leek mixture with ⅛ teaspoon salt. Cover, reduce heat, and cook 10 minutes. Uncover; add mushroom mixture, stock, and next 7 ingredients. Bring to a boil. Reduce heat; simmer 5 minutes. Stir in remaining ⅛ teaspoon salt. Combine cornstarch and water. Stir cornstarch mixture into mushroom mixture, and cook 1 minute.

4. Combine parsley, lemon zest, and garlic. Serve gremolata with stew.

CALORIES 338; FAT 14g (sat 2g, mono 9.8g, poly 2g); PROTEIN 10.2g; CARB 44.6g; FIBER 7.6g; CHOL 0mg; IRON 4.1mg; SODIUM 656mg; CALC 137mg

Lentil-Edamame Stew

Fava beans are traditional in this stew, which we updated with edamame. You can also substitute green peas for the edamame. Halve the portion if you'd like to serve this as a hearty side dish.

Yield: 4 servings (serving size: about 1 cup stew)

1 cup dried lentils

¾ cup frozen shelled edamame (green soybeans)

2 tablespoons olive oil

1½ cups minced red onion

3 garlic cloves, minced

1 (14.5-ounce) can diced tomatoes, undrained

6 tablespoons fresh lemon juice

1 tablespoon chopped fresh parsley

1 tablespoon chopped fresh mint

½ teaspoon salt

½ teaspoon ground cumin

⅛ teaspoon ground red pepper

⅛ teaspoon ground cinnamon

Dash of ground cloves

Lemon slices (optional)

1. Place lentils in a large saucepan; cover with water to 2 inches above lentils. Bring to a boil; cover, reduce heat, and simmer 20 minutes or until tender. Drain well, and set aside.

2. Place edamame in a small saucepan; cover with water to 2 inches above edamame. Bring to a boil; cook 2 minutes or until edamame are tender. Remove from heat; drain well.

3. Heat oil in a Dutch oven over medium-high heat. Add onion, garlic, and tomatoes to pan; sauté 6 minutes or until onion is translucent, stirring often. Stir in lentils, edamame, juice, and remaining ingredients except lemon slices. Cook 2 minutes or until thoroughly heated, stirring often. Garnish with lemon slices, if desired.

CALORIES 320; FAT 8g (sat 1.1g, mono 5.2g, poly 1.4g); PROTEIN 18.6g; CARB 48.4g; FIBER 10.7g; CHOL 0mg; IRON 5.7mg; SODIUM 432mg; CALC 59mg

Thai-Coconut Bouillabaisse

Be sure to reserve the shells after peeling the shrimp; you'll need them to make the broth. *Bouillabaisse* is a classic Provençal seafood stew.

Yield: 6 servings (serving size: 2 clams, 2 mussels, ⅙ shrimp and fish, and ⅔ cup broth mixture)

Cooking spray

1 pound peeled and deveined jumbo shrimp (reserve shells)

1 cup chopped celery, divided

1 cup chopped carrot, divided

1 cup chopped onion, divided

2½ cups cold water

3 black peppercorns

1 bay leaf

1 teaspoon olive oil

1 cup chopped red bell pepper

½ cup chopped tomato

1 tablespoon minced fresh garlic

1 teaspoon red curry paste

4 (2 x ½-inch) lime rind strips

1 (13.5-ounce) can light coconut milk

12 littleneck clams, scrubbed

12 mussels, scrubbed and debearded

¼ cup chopped fresh basil

¼ cup chopped fresh cilantro

1 teaspoon salt

¼ teaspoon black pepper

1 (6-ounce) skinless halibut fillet or other lean white fish fillet, cut into 1-inch pieces

Lime wedges (optional)

1. Heat a medium saucepan over medium heat. Coat pan with cooking spray. Add shrimp shells to pan; cook 3 minutes, stirring frequently. Add ½ cup celery, ½ cup carrot, and ½ cup onion to pan; cook 1 minute, stirring occasionally. Stir in 2½ cups cold water, peppercorns, and bay leaf; bring to a boil. Reduce heat, and simmer 30 minutes, stirring occasionally. Strain mixture through a sieve over a bowl; discard solids.

2. Heat oil in a large saucepan over medium heat. Add remaining ½ cup celery, ½ cup carrot, and ½ cup onion to pan; cook 3 minutes, stirring occasionally. Add bell pepper; cook 1 minute, stirring occasionally. Stir in tomato, garlic, curry paste, and rind; cook 2 minutes, stirring frequently. Stir in broth mixture and coconut milk; bring to a boil. Add clams and mussels. Cover, reduce heat, and cook 2 minutes or until clams and mussels open. Remove from heat; discard any unopened shells. Stir in shrimp, basil, and remaining ingredients except lime wedges. Cover and let stand 5 minutes or until shrimp and halibut are done. Discard lime rind. Place 2 clams and 2 mussels in each of 6 bowls. Divide shrimp and fish evenly among bowls. Ladle ⅔ cup broth mixture over each serving. Serve with lime wedges, if desired.

CALORIES 226; FAT 6.9g (sat 3.5g, mono 1.2g, poly 1.2g); PROTEIN 30.4g; CARB 10.4g; FIBER 1.4g; CHOL 143mg; IRON 8mg; SODIUM 599mg; CALC 96mg

WINE TIP

In the south of France, bouillabaisse is traditionally served with a dry rosé, a great choice even with this not-so-traditional version. The kick of the red curry paste and cilantro, plus the exotic thick creaminess of the coconut milk, need a refreshing wine that has more weight and power than a white.

Lobster "Bouillabaisse"

Traditional bouillabaisse uses a variety of fish and shellfish. Enhanced with stock made from lobster shells, this version focuses on the king of crustaceans: lobster. If you'd rather not wrangle live lobsters, ask your fishmonger to steam the lobsters for you (and save the shells). This "bouillabaisse" is also nice (and less costly) with shrimp.

Yield: 8 servings (serving size: ½ lobster tail, ½ cup potato, ¼ cup chopped lobster, and ⅔ cup stock mixture)

5 cups water, divided

2 tablespoons plus ⅛ teaspoon salt, divided

4 (1½-pound) whole Maine lobsters

2 large peeled baking potatoes, cut into ¼-inch cubes (about 1⅓ pounds)

7 cups Shellfish Stock (page 169)

1 cup white wine

3 tablespoons tomato paste

⅛ teaspoon freshly ground black pepper

2 tablespoons minced fresh tarragon

Freshly ground black pepper

1. Bring 4 cups water and 2 tablespoons salt to a boil in a 5-gallon stockpot. Place a vegetable steamer or rack in the bottom of the pot. Add lobsters; steam, covered, 14 minutes or until done. Remove meat from cooked lobster claws. Cut each lobster tail in half, lengthwise; chill meat and tails.

2. Place potatoes in a saucepan; cover with water. Bring to a boil; cook 5 minutes or until tender. Drain; set aside.

3. Preheat oven to 300°.

4. Combine remaining 1 cup water, stock, wine, and tomato paste in a large saucepan; bring to a boil. Cook over medium-high heat 30 minutes or until reduced to 5 cups. Stir in remaining ⅛ teaspoon salt and pepper.

5. While stock reduces, place lobster and potato in a single layer on a baking sheet, keeping separate. Bake at 300° for 20 minutes or until thoroughly heated. Place half a lobster tail in each of 8 shallow soup bowls; place ½ cup potato and ¼ cup chopped lobster in each bowl. Ladle about ⅔ cup stock mixture over each serving; sprinkle each serving with ¾ teaspoon tarragon and black pepper.

CALORIES 270; FAT 2.6g (sat 0.4g, mono 0.5g, poly 1g); PROTEIN 36.5g; CARB 21g; FIBER 1.8g; CHOL 119mg; IRON 2.3mg; SODIUM 558mg; CALC 109mg

Mushroom Stock

This recipe is used in the Wild Mushroom Stew with Gremolata on page 207.

Yield: 2 cups (serving size: 1 cup stock)

5 cups water

1 cup dried porcini mushrooms
(about 1 ounce)

½ cup chopped celery

⅓ cup dry red wine

¼ cup dried lentils

2 thyme sprigs

1 sage sprig

1 whole garlic head, halved

1. Combine all ingredients in a large saucepan; bring to a boil. Reduce heat, and simmer until reduced to 2 cups (about 40 minutes). Strain stock through a sieve into a bowl; discard solids.

CALORIES 29; FAT 0.1g (sat 0.0g, mono 0.0g, poly 0.1g); PROTEIN 1.8g; CARB 5.1g; FIBER 1.3g; CHOL 0mg; IRON 0.7mg; SODIUM 5mg; CALC 18mg

NUTRITION TIP

Unlike most other vegetables, mushrooms contain two important B vitamins—niacin and riboflavin. The shiitake is a particularly healthful mushroom, since it contains lentinan, which may help fight cancer and bolster the immune system.

Chicken and Okra Stew

Look for okra pods between May and October, and choose pods that are firm, brightly colored, and short. Long okra pods tend to be tough. The "slime" that okra is known for will help thicken this stew.

Yield: 6 servings (serving size: 1⅓ cups stew)

4 teaspoons canola oil, divided

2 pounds skinless, boneless chicken thighs, quartered

1 habanero pepper

1½ cups chopped green bell pepper

1 cup finely chopped onion

⅔ cup finely chopped celery

2½ cups chopped plum tomato

2 tablespoons chopped fresh parsley

1 tablespoon chopped fresh oregano

¾ teaspoon salt

1 teaspoon freshly ground black pepper

⅛ teaspoon ground cloves

1 (14-ounce) can fat-free, lower-sodium chicken broth

1 pound fresh okra pods, cut into 1-inch pieces

1. Heat 2 teaspoons oil in a Dutch oven over medium-high heat. Add half of chicken to pan; cook 6 minutes, browning on all sides. Remove chicken from pan. Add remaining chicken to pan; cook 6 minutes, browning on all sides. Remove chicken from pan.

2. Cut habanero in half. Seed one half of pepper, and leave seeds in other half. Mince both pepper halves. Add remaining 2 teaspoons oil to pan; swirl to coat. Add minced habanero, bell pepper, onion, and celery; sauté 5 minutes or until tender, stirring occasionally. Add tomato; cook 3 minutes or until tomato softens. Add parsley and next 5 ingredients; bring to a boil. Return chicken to pan; cover, reduce heat, and simmer 10 minutes. Add okra; cover and simmer 15 minutes or until okra is just tender.

CALORIES 269; FAT 9.4g (sat 1.8g, mono 3.7g, poly 2.5g); PROTEIN 33g; CARB 13.4g; FIBER 4.8g; CHOL 126mg; IRON 2.8mg; SODIUM 594mg; CALC 106mg

Mexican Turkey Stew

While usually an ingredient in moles, roasted pumpkinseed kernels add another layer of nutty flavor to this posole-style broth. Look for them in specialty markets and health-food stores. Substitute ancho chile powder if guajillo is unavailable.

Yield: 8 servings (serving size: 1⅓ cups stew)

3 large Anaheim chiles, seeded and halved lengthwise

2 teaspoons canola oil

Cooking spray

1½ cups chopped onion

4 garlic cloves, minced

2 tablespoons ground guajillo chile powder

1½ teaspoons dried oregano

4 cups water

3 cups fat-free, lower-sodium chicken broth

1 (15-ounce) can golden or white hominy, drained

4 cups shredded cooked turkey breast

⅓ cup chopped fresh cilantro

¼ teaspoon salt

½ cup roasted unsalted pumpkinseed kernels

½ cup thinly sliced radishes

½ cup thinly sliced green onions

½ cup (2 ounces) crumbled queso fresco cheese

Lime wedges (optional)

Cilantro sprigs (optional)

1. Preheat broiler.

2. Place pepper halves, skin sides up, on a foil-lined baking sheet. Broil 6 minutes or until blackened. Place in a paper bag, and fold to close tightly. Let stand 15 minutes. Peel and chop; set aside.

3. Heat oil in a large Dutch oven coated with cooking spray over medium heat. Add onion to pan; cook 6 minutes, stirring occasionally. Add garlic; cook 1 minute, stirring occasionally. Add chile powder and oregano; cook 1 minute, stirring constantly. Stir in 4 cups water, broth, and hominy; bring to a boil. Reduce heat, and simmer, uncovered, 10 minutes. Stir in Anaheim chiles and turkey; cook 2 minutes. Stir in cilantro and salt; cook 3 minutes. Ladle about 1⅓ cups stew into each of 8 bowls. Top each serving with 1 tablespoon pumpkinseed kernels, 1 tablespoon radishes, 1 tablespoon green onions, and 1 tablespoon cheese. Serve with lime wedges and cilantro sprigs, if desired.

CALORIES 213; FAT 6.8g (sat 2.3g, mono 1.9g, poly 1.6g); PROTEIN 25.4g; CARB 13.5g; FIBER 3.2g; CHOL 56mg; IRON 1.7mg; SODIUM 483mg; CALC 88mg

BEER TIP

With Anaheim and guajillo chiles lending their subtle heat, reach for a flavorful chilled beer, like a Scottish-style ale. Look for a beer with a rich, malty sweetness, hinting of caramel, that works to balance the peppery posole. A beer with dark chocolate, toasted nut, and smoky notes complements the roasted pumpkinseeds in this richly layered stew.

Chicken Stew with Sweet Peppers

Try a mix of roasted red, yellow, and orange bell peppers to bring color to this stew.

Yield: 4 servings (serving size: 1½ cups stew)

2 teaspoons olive oil

1 cup finely chopped onion

¾ pound skinless, boneless chicken breast, cut into bite-sized pieces

3 cups chopped zucchini

1 cup finely chopped carrot

⅓ cup canned chopped green chiles, drained

¾ teaspoon dried oregano

½ teaspoon ground cumin

¼ teaspoon salt

¼ teaspoon black pepper

2 garlic cloves, minced

1 (15.5-ounce) can Great Northern beans, drained

1 (14½-ounce) can fat-free, lower-sodium chicken broth

1 cup chopped roasted bell peppers

4 teaspoons chopped fresh cilantro

1. Heat olive oil in a Dutch oven over medium-high heat. Add chopped onion and chicken; sauté 5 minutes or until lightly browned. Add zucchini and next 9 ingredients; bring to a boil. Cover, reduce heat, and simmer 30 minutes or until vegetables are tender.
2. Add bell peppers, and cook, uncovered, 10 minutes, stirring occasionally. Sprinkle with cilantro.

CALORIES 262; FAT 4.1g (sat 0.7g, mono 2g, poly 0.7g); PROTEIN 28.3g; CARB 28.8g; FIBER 7.8g; CHOL 49mg; IRON 3mg; SODIUM 455mg; CALC 96mg

MAKE-AHEAD TIP

This stew and the Peruvian Chicken Stew with Sweet Potatoes and Peanuts on the opposite page can be made ahead of time. A nice trick to freshen stew is to add the herbs right before serving, instead of before storing the stew.

Peruvian Chicken Stew with Sweet Potatoes and Peanuts

Cornmeal and potatoes are two of Peru's ancient staples; this recipe incorporates both. We also use a common Peruvian technique: thickening the broth with ground peanuts.

Yield: 6 servings (serving size: 1⅔ cups stew)

½ cup dry-roasted peanuts

1 tablespoon canola oil

1½ cups thinly sliced onion

6 cups water

½ cup yellow cornmeal

1 teaspoon salt

1 teaspoon ground cumin

⅛ teaspoon ground allspice

4 cups julienne-cut peeled sweet potato (about 1 pound)

1½ pounds skinless, boneless chicken breast, cut into bite-sized pieces

¼ cup chopped fresh cilantro

1. Place peanuts in a spice or coffee grinder; process until medium ground.

2. Heat oil in a large Dutch oven over medium-high heat. Add onion; sauté 10 minutes or until lightly browned. Stir in ground peanuts, water, and next 5 ingredients; bring to a boil. Reduce heat, and simmer 15 minutes. Stir in chicken; cook 10 minutes or until chicken is done. Stir in cilantro.

CALORIES 347; FAT 10g (sat 1.4g, mono 4.8g, poly 2.9g); PROTEIN 31.9g; CARB 31.8g; FIBER 4.4g; CHOL 66mg; IRON 2.1mg; SODIUM 504mg; CALC 65mg

Belgian Turkey Ragout

Our recipe is based on the Belgian beef dish *carbonnade à la flamande,* a thick stew with bacon, beer, onions, and sugar. With turkey instead of beef, it's also like the rich French stew called *ragout*. Purchase 3½ pounds of turkey thighs with skin and bone, or 2¼ pounds of skinless, boneless turkey thighs.

Yield: 8 servings (serving size: 1 cup stew)

3½ pounds turkey thighs

1 teaspoon salt, divided

½ teaspoon black pepper, divided

2 teaspoons olive oil

1 tablespoon butter

4 cups thinly sliced leek (about 5 large)

2 cups (½-inch) pieces carrot

3 tablespoons all-purpose flour

1 cup fat-free, lower-sodium chicken broth

1 tablespoon brown sugar

1 (12-ounce) bottle amber lager

1 tablespoon Dijon mustard

1 tablespoon white wine vinegar

2 tablespoons chopped fresh parsley

1. Preheat oven to 300°.

2. Remove skin from turkey; cut meat from bones. Discard skin and bones; cut meat into 1½-inch pieces. Sprinkle turkey with ½ teaspoon salt and ¼ teaspoon pepper.

3. Heat oil in a small ovenproof Dutch oven over medium-high heat. Add turkey; cook 6 minutes or until browned, stirring occasionally. Remove turkey and juices from pan. Reduce heat to medium; melt butter in pan. Add leek and carrot; cover and cook 12 minutes or until leek begins to brown, stirring occasionally.

4. Return turkey and juices to pan. Sprinkle flour over turkey mixture; stir well to coat. Add remaining ½ teaspoon salt, remaining ¼ teaspoon pepper, broth, sugar, and beer. Bring to a boil; cover. Place in oven. Bake at 300° for 50 minutes or until turkey is tender. Stir in mustard and vinegar; sprinkle with parsley.

CALORIES 378; FAT 4.4g (sat 1.6g, mono 1.5g, poly 0.7g); PROTEIN 61.5g; CARB 15.8g; FIBER 2.2g; CHOL 169mg; IRON 4.6mg; SODIUM 526mg; CALC 73mg

Ancho Pork and Hominy Stew

Ancho chile powder is different from chili powder, which is a mix of dried chiles, garlic, and other spices. It is made with only dried poblano chiles and lends a subtle sweetness to this stew.

Yield: 6 servings (serving size: 1⅓ cups stew)

2 tablespoons ancho chile powder

2 teaspoons dried oregano

1½ teaspoons smoked paprika

1 teaspoon ground cumin

½ teaspoon salt

1½ pounds pork tenderloin, trimmed and cut into ½-inch pieces

1 tablespoon olive oil, divided

2 cups chopped onion

1½ cups chopped green bell pepper

1 tablespoon minced garlic

2½ cups fat-free, lower-sodium chicken broth

1 (28-ounce) can hominy, drained

1 (14.5-ounce) can fire-roasted diced tomatoes, undrained

1. Combine first 5 ingredients in a large bowl; set 1½ teaspoons spice mixture aside. Add pork to remaining spice mixture in bowl, tossing well to coat.

2. Heat 2 teaspoons oil in a large Dutch oven over medium-high heat. Add pork mixture to pan; cook 5 minutes or until browned, stirring occasionally. Remove pork from pan; set aside. Add remaining 1 teaspoon oil to pan. Add onion, bell pepper, and garlic; sauté 5 minutes or until tender, stirring occasionally. Return pork to pan. Add reserved 1½ teaspoons spice mixture, broth, hominy, and tomatoes; bring to a boil. Partially cover, reduce heat, and simmer 25 minutes.

CALORIES 300; FAT 8.3g (sat 2.1g, mono 3.7g, poly 1.4g); PROTEIN 28.9g; CARB 26.9g; FIBER 6.1g; CHOL 76mg; IRON 3.2mg; SODIUM 523mg; CALC 51mg

Ropa Vieja

This Cuban stew is made by braising beef until it can be shredded—thus the name *Ropa Vieja* (translated as "old clothes"). Serve with tortillas, and include hot sauce on the side for those who like it fiery. Because the meat is shredded, it's also suitable for tacos and burritos.

Yield: 8 servings (serving size: about ¾ cup stew)

Cooking spray

2 (1-pound) flank steaks, trimmed

3 cups thinly vertically sliced red onion

2 cups red bell pepper strips (about 2 peppers)

2 cups green bell pepper strips (about 2 peppers)

4 garlic cloves, minced

6 tablespoons thinly sliced pitted green olives

1 teaspoon salt

1 teaspoon dried oregano

1 teaspoon ground cumin

½ teaspoon dried rosemary, crushed

½ teaspoon freshly ground black pepper

6 tablespoons sherry vinegar

3 cups fat-free, lower-sodium beef broth

1 tablespoon no-salt-added tomato paste

2 bay leaves

½ cup chopped fresh cilantro

1. Heat a large Dutch oven over medium-high heat. Coat Dutch oven with cooking spray. Add one steak to pan; cook 2½ minutes on each side or until browned. Remove steak from pan. Repeat procedure with cooking spray and remaining steak.

2. Reduce heat to medium. Add onion, bell peppers, and garlic to pan; cook 7 minutes or until tender, stirring frequently. Stir in olives and next 5 ingredients; cook 30 seconds or until fragrant. Stir in vinegar, scraping pan to loosen browned bits; cook 2 minutes or until liquid almost evaporates. Stir in broth, tomato paste, and bay leaves. Add steaks; bring to a simmer. Cover, reduce heat, and cook 1½ hours or until steaks are very tender. Discard bay leaves.

3. Remove steaks from pan; shred with two forks. Stir shredded beef and cilantro into pan.

CALORIES 229; FAT 9.1g (sat 3.4g, mono 3.9g, poly 0.6g); PROTEIN 26g; CARB 9.6g; FIBER 2g; CHOL 40mg; IRON 2.4mg; SODIUM 614mg; CALC 53mg

WINE TIP

A savory beef dish such as this needs a rich red wine, but preferably one that won't break the bank since this is a humble meal. Try a blend with zinfandel as the predominant grape.

Fall Stew

This stew is full of vegetables and flavor. You can substitute chuck roast for the lamb in the recipe, if you like. This is a good time to use your homemade White Chicken Stock (page 164).

Yield: 4 servings (serving size: 2 cups stew)

2 teaspoons olive oil

¾ pound lean boned leg of lamb or lean, boned chuck roast, cut into 1-inch cubes

1 cup chopped Vidalia or other sweet onion

1 cup chopped celery

¾ cup chopped carrot

3 garlic cloves, minced

½ cup dry red wine

1½ cups cubed baking potato

1 cup chopped peeled rutabaga

1 cup chopped peeled turnip

½ teaspoon salt

7 (10½-ounce) cans fat-free, lower-sodium chicken broth or 8 cups homemade chicken stock

2 bay leaves

½ cup chopped plum tomato

½ cup chopped zucchini

¼ cup chopped fresh cilantro

1 teaspoon dried oregano

1 teaspoon ground cumin

¼ teaspoon ground red pepper

¼ teaspoon black pepper

Cilantro sprigs (optional)

1. Heat oil in a large Dutch oven; add lamb, browning on all sides. Add onion, celery, carrot, and garlic; sauté 5 minutes. Add wine, and cook 3 minutes, stirring frequently.

2. Add potato and next 5 ingredients; bring to a boil. Reduce heat to medium; cook 1 hour and 20 minutes or until vegetables are tender. Add tomato and remaining ingredients except cilantro sprigs; cook an additional 10 minutes. Discard bay leaves. Garnish with cilantro sprigs, if desired.

CALORIES 312; FAT 10.2g (sat 2.6g, mono 5.4g, poly 1.4g); PROTEIN 26.3g; CARB 30.7g; FIBER 4.6g; CHOL 54mg; IRON 6.2mg; SODIUM 595mg; CALC 88mg

Hungarian Venison Stew

If you can't find venison, this recipe is good with beef stew meat. We found it tasted great with white or red wine. If you prefer less wine flavor, replace some or all of the wine with fat-free, lower-sodium beef broth.

Yield: 8 servings (serving size: about ¾ cup stew)

1.1 ounces all-purpose flour (about ¼ cup)

1½ teaspoons salt, divided

½ teaspoon freshly ground black pepper, divided

2 pounds venison, cut into 1-inch cubes

2 tablespoons butter

2 cups chopped onion

2 teaspoons minced garlic

2 cups dry white wine or fruity red wine

2 tablespoons sugar

1 tablespoon sweet Hungarian paprika

1 teaspoon ground red pepper

8 juniper berries

2 whole allspice berries

1 bay leaf

1. Preheat oven to 300°.
2. Lightly spoon flour into a dry measuring cup; level with a knife. Combine flour, ½ teaspoon salt, and ¼ teaspoon black pepper in a large zip-top plastic bag. Add venison; seal and shake to coat. Remove venison from bag; discard remaining flour mixture.
3. Melt butter in an ovenproof Dutch oven over medium-high heat. Add venison, onion, and garlic; sauté 5 minutes, browning venison on all sides. Add wine, scraping pan to loosen browned bits. Add remaining 1 teaspoon salt, remaining ¼ teaspoon black pepper, sugar, and remaining ingredients to pan; bring to a boil.
4. Cover and bake at 300° for 3 hours or until venison is tender. Remove berries and bay leaf before serving.

CALORIES 212; FAT 5.8g (sat 2.6g, mono 2g, poly 0.8g); PROTEIN 27.1g; CARB 11.9g; FIBER 1.1g; CHOL 104mg; IRON 4.6mg; SODIUM 527mg; CALC 24mg

INGREDIENT TIP

Pungent allspice and juniper berries lend the stew a spicy, complex flavor; be sure to remove the berries before pouring the stew into a bowl.

Hominy Chili with Beans

Hominy is made of dried corn kernels from which the hulls and germs have been removed. You can find it in the canned-vegetable section of the supermarket near the corn.

Yield: 4 servings (serving size: 1¼ cups soup)

2 teaspoons canola oil

2 teaspoons bottled minced garlic

4 teaspoons chili powder

1 teaspoon ground cumin

1 (15.5-ounce) can white hominy, drained

1 (15-ounce) can red beans, drained

1 (14.5-ounce) can no-salt-added diced tomatoes, undrained

1 (14.5-ounce) can no-salt-added stewed tomatoes, undrained and chopped

¼ cup reduced-fat sour cream

¼ cup (1 ounce) shredded reduced-fat sharp cheddar cheese

4 teaspoons minced fresh cilantro

1. Heat oil in a large saucepan over medium heat. Add garlic; sauté 1 minute. Stir in chili powder and next 5 ingredients; bring to a boil. Reduce heat; simmer, uncovered, 15 minutes. Spoon 1¼ cups chili into each of 4 bowls; top each serving with 1 tablespoon sour cream, 1 tablespoon cheese, and 1 teaspoon cilantro.

CALORIES 231; FAT 6.4g; (sat 1.9g, mono 2.1g, poly 1.3g); PROTEIN 8.6g; CARB 33.8g; FIBER 8.9g; CHOL 8mg; IRON 3.6mg; SODIUM 438mg; CALC 143mg

INGREDIENT TIP

If hominy is unavailable, you can substitute 1 (11-ounce) can vacuum-packed white corn or 1 (15.25-ounce) can whole-kernel corn, drained. Hominy imparts a distinctive flavor remarkably different from that of corn, so if you use corn, know that the dish will be more like a basic chili with beans.

Hearty Beef and Tomato Stew

You won't have a lot of hands-on time with this stew; the recipe involves mostly measuring and adding ingredients to the pot to simmer. To trim prep time, look for prechopped onions in the produce aisle. Serve with baguette slices.

Yield: 8 servings (serving size: 1½ cups stew)

2 teaspoons olive oil

2 pounds sirloin steak, trimmed and cut into ½-inch cubes

1 cup finely chopped onion (about 1 medium)

3 garlic cloves, minced

1 tablespoon tomato paste

1½ cups fat-free, lower-sodium beef broth

4 cups cubed red potato (1½ pounds)

2 cups sliced carrot

¾ cup pinot noir or other spicy dry red wine

2 teaspoons chopped fresh thyme

1 (16-ounce) package frozen pearl onions

1 (28-ounce) can crushed tomatoes, undrained

1 rosemary sprig

1 bay leaf

1 teaspoon salt

¾ teaspoon freshly ground black pepper

½ cup chopped fresh parsley

1. Heat oil in a large Dutch oven over medium-high heat. Add beef; cook 5 minutes or until browned, stirring frequently. Remove beef from pan, reserving 1 tablespoon drippings in pan. Add onion and garlic to pan; sauté 2 minutes or until onion begins to brown. Add tomato paste; cook 1 minute, stirring frequently. Add broth; bring to a boil. Return meat to pan. Add potato and next 7 ingredients; bring to a simmer. Cover and cook 1 hour and 15 minutes or until vegetables are tender, stirring occasionally. Discard rosemary and bay leaf. Stir in salt and pepper. Sprinkle with parsley.

CALORIES 329; FAT 7.5g (sat 2.6g, mono 3.3g, poly 0.4g); PROTEIN 31.1g; CARB 33.3g; FIBER 4.1g; CHOL 51mg; IRON 4.3mg; SODIUM 630mg; CALC 93mg

NUTRITION TIP

A double-dose of lycopene comes with tomato paste and canned tomatoes: You get 11 milligrams of lycopene per serving—more than twice the amount in a cup of raw tomatoes.

Two-Potato Lamb Stew with Roasted Garlic

Roast another head of garlic for making pasta sauces, topping pizzas, spreading onto bread, or stirring into mashed potatoes. Wrap separately in foil, and refrigerate for up to five days.

Yield: 8 servings (serving size: 1⅓ cups stew)

1 whole garlic head

Cooking spray

4 cups coarsely chopped onion

4 garlic cloves, minced

1.5 ounces all-purpose flour (about ⅓ cup)

2 pounds boneless leg of lamb, trimmed and cut into bite-sized pieces

2 teaspoons olive oil

1 teaspoon salt, divided

½ teaspoon freshly ground black pepper, divided

1 cup dry red wine

3 cups fat-free, lower-sodium beef broth

2½ cups (1-inch) cubed peeled sweet potato (about 10 ounces)

2½ cups (1-inch) cubed peeled Yukon gold potato (about 10 ounces)

2½ cups (½-inch) slices peeled parsnip (about 10 ounces)

1 tablespoon chopped fresh rosemary

1. Preheat oven to 350°.

2. Remove white papery skin from garlic head (do not peel or separate the cloves). Wrap garlic head in foil. Bake at 350° for 45 minutes or until tender; cool 10 minutes. Separate cloves; squeeze to extract garlic pulp. Discard skins. Heat a Dutch oven over medium-high heat. Coat pan with cooking spray. Add onion; sauté 10 minutes or until tender and golden brown. Add 4 minced garlic cloves; sauté 1 minute. Spoon onion mixture into a bowl.

3. Place flour in a shallow bowl or pie plate. Dredge lamb in flour, shaking off excess. Heat oil in pan over medium-high heat. Add half of lamb mixture; sprinkle with ¼ teaspoon salt and ⅛ teaspoon pepper. Cook 6 minutes, browning on all sides. Add browned lamb to onion mixture. Repeat procedure with remaining lamb mixture, ¼ teaspoon salt, and ⅛ teaspoon pepper.

4. Add wine to pan, scraping pan to loosen browned bits. Stir in lamb mixture and broth; bring to a boil. Cover, reduce heat, and simmer 1 hour or until lamb is just tender.

5. Stir in potatoes and parsnip. Cover and simmer 30 minutes. Stir in roasted garlic, remaining ½ teaspoon salt, remaining ¼ teaspoon pepper, and rosemary; simmer 10 minutes.

CALORIES 316; FAT 10.5g (sat 3.9g, mono 4.8g, poly 0.9g); PROTEIN 20.6g; CARB 35.4g; FIBER 4.9g; CHOL 58mg; IRON 2.5mg; SODIUM 526mg; CALC 60mg

Chunky Vegetarian Chili

This vegetarian chili recipe provides a great way for kids to eat fiber-rich foods. It can be taken on camping trips and in school lunches inside an insulated container.

Yield: 8 servings (serving size: 1 cup soup)

1 tablespoon vegetable oil

2 cups chopped onion

½ cup chopped yellow bell pepper

½ cup chopped green bell pepper

2 garlic cloves, minced

1 tablespoon brown sugar

1½ tablespoons chili powder

1 teaspoon ground cumin

1 teaspoon dried oregano

½ teaspoon salt

½ teaspoon black pepper

2 (16-ounce) cans stewed tomatoes, undrained

2 (15-ounce) cans no-salt-added black beans, rinsed and drained

1 (15-ounce) can no-salt-added kidney beans, rinsed and drained

1 (15-ounce) can no-salt-added pinto beans, rinsed and drained

1. Heat oil in a Dutch oven over medium-high heat. Add onion, bell peppers, and garlic; sauté 5 minutes or until tender. Add sugar and remaining ingredients, and bring to a boil. Reduce heat, and simmer 30 minutes.

CALORIES 142; FAT 2.2g (sat 0.3g, mono 0.8g, poly 0.9g); PROTEIN 6.9g; CARB 24.5g; FIBER 8.3g; CHOL 0mg; IRON 2.6mg; SODIUM 302mg; CALC 87mg

Pork and Hominy Chili

Mix canned hominy—a nutty, tender ingredient made from dried, hulled corn kernels—with chunks of pork and bold spices in this hearty, Mexican-inspired chili.

Yield: 4 servings (serving size: about 1½ cups soup)

2 teaspoons canola oil

8 ounces boneless center-cut pork chops, trimmed and cubed

1 cup chopped onion (about 1 medium)

¾ cup chopped green bell pepper

2 teaspoons bottled minced garlic

1 tablespoon chili powder

2 teaspoons ground cumin

¼ teaspoon salt

¼ teaspoon freshly ground black pepper

⅛ teaspoon ground red pepper

¼ cup no-salt-added tomato paste

1 (15.5-ounce) can golden hominy, rinsed and drained

1 (14.5-ounce) can no-salt-added diced tomatoes, undrained

1 (14-ounce) can fat-free, lower-sodium chicken broth

¼ cup reduced-fat sour cream

1. Heat oil in a large saucepan over medium-high heat. Add pork to pan; sauté 5 minutes or until lightly browned. Add onion, bell pepper, and garlic to pan; sauté 5 minutes or until tender. Stir in chili powder and next 4 ingredients. Cook 1 minute, stirring constantly. Stir in tomato paste, hominy, tomatoes, and broth; bring to a boil. Reduce heat, and simmer 10 minutes. Serve with sour cream.

CALORIES 238; FAT 7.8g (sat 2.5g, mono 3g, poly 1.3g); PROTEIN 17.6g; CARB 24.6g; FIBER 5.2g; CHOL 33mg; IRON 2.1mg; SODIUM 650mg; CALC 61mg

Turkey and Bean Chili

With ingredients like prechopped onion and less than 20 minutes cooking time, this flavorful chili comes together very quickly.

Yield: 6 servings (serving size: about 1 cup soup)

1 cup prechopped red onion

⅓ cup chopped seeded poblano pepper (about 1)

1 teaspoon bottled minced garlic

1¼ pounds ground turkey

1 tablespoon chili powder

2 tablespoons tomato paste

2 teaspoons dried oregano

1 teaspoon ground cumin

¼ teaspoon salt

¼ teaspoon black pepper

1 (19-ounce) can cannellini beans, rinsed and drained

1 (14.5-ounce) can diced tomatoes, undrained

1 (14-ounce) can fat-free, lower-sodium chicken broth

½ cup chopped fresh cilantro

6 lime wedges

1. Heat a large saucepan over medium heat. Add first 4 ingredients; cook 6 minutes or until turkey is done, stirring frequently to crumble. Stir in chili powder and next 8 ingredients; bring to a boil. Reduce heat, and simmer 10 minutes. Stir in cilantro. Serve with lime wedges.

CALORIES 211; FAT 6.5g (sat 1.7g, mono 1.9g, poly 1.6g); PROTEIN 22.5g; CARB 16.4g; FIBER 4.7g; CHOL 54mg; IRON 3.4mg; SODIUM 474mg; CALC 52mg

Beef and Beer Chili

Cook a pot of this flavorful chili in just 40 minutes for a quick weeknight meal that's sure to warm the soul. You can easily double the recipe and freeze extra for later.

Yield: 4 servings (serving size: 1½ cups soup)

1½ cups chopped red onion (about 1 medium)

1 cup chopped red bell pepper (about 1 small)

8 ounces ground beef, extra lean

2 garlic cloves, minced

1½ tablespoons chili powder

2 teaspoons ground cumin

1 teaspoon sugar

½ teaspoon salt

½ teaspoon dried oregano

1 (19-ounce) can no-salt-added red kidney beans, drained

1 (14.5-ounce) can no-salt-added diced tomatoes, undrained

1 (14-ounce) can fat-free, lower-sodium beef broth

1 (12-ounce) bottle beer

1 tablespoon yellow cornmeal

1 tablespoon fresh lime juice

1. Combine first 4 ingredients in a large Dutch oven over medium-high heat. Cook 5 minutes or until beef is browned, stirring to crumble. Stir in chili powder, cumin, sugar, and salt; cook 1 minute. Add oregano and next 4 ingredients to pan; bring to a boil. Reduce heat, and simmer 15 minutes. Stir in cornmeal; cook 5 minutes. Stir in juice.

CALORIES 232; FAT 3.3g (sat 0.8g, mono 1g, poly 0.3g); PROTEIN18.2g; CARB 27.2g; FIBER 6.6g; CHOL 30mg; IRON 3mg; SODIUM 592mg; CALC 69mg

Chili con Carne with Beans

Yield: 4 servings (serving size: 1½ cups soup)

1 cup chopped onion

4 teaspoons chili powder

1 tablespoon ground cumin

1 teaspoon bottled minced garlic

¼ teaspoon ground red pepper

1 pound ground sirloin

1½ cups canned crushed tomatoes

¼ teaspoon salt

1 (14.5-ounce) can diced tomatoes with green pepper, celery, and onion

1 (19-ounce) can no-salt-added kidney beans, rinsed and drained

1. Cook first 6 ingredients in a large nonstick skillet over medium-high heat until beef is browned, stirring to crumble. Add crushed tomatoes, salt, and diced tomatoes; bring to a boil. Reduce heat and simmer 4 minutes, stirring occasionally. Add beans; cook 2 minutes or until thoroughly heated.

CALORIES 304; FAT 6.2g (sat 2.1g, mono 2.1g, poly 0.8g); PROTEIN 31.1g; CARB 34.2g; FIBER 12.7g; CHOL 60mg; IRON 5.6mg; SODIUM 589mg; CALC 131mg

INGREDIENT TIP

Unlike pure "chile" powder made with ground dried chile peppers, "chili" powder typically contains a blend of seasonings such as cumin, paprika, garlic, and salt along with ground chiles. In 1892, German immigrant and Texas saloon owner William Gebhardt figured out a way to preserve his fall chile harvest by running them through a meat grinder, and then drying and pulverizing them. He was later inspired to add cumin, oregano, and black pepper to the mix.

Caribbean Black Bean Soup

A little of this spicy soup goes a long way, so it's best when served as an appetizer soup. If you want to decrease the heat, seed the jalapeños. (Pictured on cover.)

Yield: 8 servings (serving size: about 1 cup soup, 1 tablespoon cilantro, and 1 lime wedge)

1 tablespoon olive oil

2 cups chopped red onion (1 onion)

1 cup diced green bell pepper

1 cup diced red bell pepper

3 tablespoons finely chopped jalapeño pepper (2 peppers)

1 whole garlic head, peeled and minced

¼ cup no-salt-added tomato paste

4 cups organic vegetable broth, divided

1 teaspoon dried thyme

1 teaspoon ground cumin

½ teaspoon ground ginger

½ teaspoon ground allspice

¼ teaspoon ground red pepper

⅛ teaspoon salt

2 (15-ounce) cans no-salt-added black beans, rinsed and drained

½ cup coconut milk

½ cup chopped fresh cilantro

2 limes, quartered

1. Heat a large skillet over medium-high heat. Add oil to pan; swirl to coat. Add onion and next 3 ingredients; sauté 4 minutes. Add garlic; sauté 1 minute. Stir in tomato paste and 1 cup broth. Transfer vegetable mixture to a 5-quart electric slow cooker.

2. Stir in remaining 3 cups broth, thyme, and next 6 ingredients. Cover and cook on LOW for 8 hours.

3. Stir in coconut milk. Ladle soup into bowls; top with cilantro. Serve with lime wedges.

CALORIES 143; FAT 5g (sat 3g, mono 1.4g, poly 0.3g); PROTEIN 5.5g; CARB 20.5g; FIBER 5.6g; CHOL 0mg; IRON 2.3mg; SODIUM 333mg; CALC 59mg

Two-Bean Soup with Kale

This hearty bean soup warms up chilly nights. Use any type of canned beans you happen to have on hand, and add rotisserie chicken or Italian sausage for extra protein, if you wish.

Yield: 6 servings (serving size: about 1¼ cups soup)

3 tablespoons olive oil

1 cup chopped onion

½ cup chopped carrot

½ cup chopped celery

½ teaspoon salt, divided

2 garlic cloves, minced

4 cups organic vegetable broth, divided

7 cups stemmed, chopped kale (about 1 bunch)

2 (15-ounce) cans no-salt-added cannellini beans, rinsed, drained, and divided

1 (15-ounce) can no-salt-added black beans, rinsed and drained

½ teaspoon freshly ground black pepper

1 tablespoon red wine vinegar

1 teaspoon chopped fresh rosemary

1. Heat a large Dutch oven over medium-high heat. Add oil to pan; swirl to coat. Add onion, carrot, and celery; sauté 6 minutes or until tender. Stir in ¼ teaspoon salt and garlic; cook 1 minute. Stir in 3 cups vegetable broth and kale. Bring to a boil; cover, reduce heat, and simmer 3 minutes or until kale is crisp-tender.

2. Place half of cannellini beans and remaining 1 cup vegetable broth in a blender or food processor; process until smooth. Add pureed bean mixture, remaining cannellini beans, black beans, and pepper to soup. Bring to a boil; reduce heat, and simmer 5 minutes. Stir in remaining ¼ teaspoon salt, vinegar, and rosemary.

CALORIES 250; FAT 10.4g (sat 1.4g, mono 5.5g, poly 2.2g); PROTEIN 11.8g; CARB 30.5g; FIBER 9.2g; CHOL 0mg; IRON 3.8mg; SODIUM 593mg; CALC 189mg

All-American Chili

This traditional American chili is a comforting classic on a wintry night. Like most chilis, this version tastes even better the next day.

Yield: 8 servings (serving size: 1¼ cups soup)

6 ounces hot turkey Italian sausage

2 cups chopped onion

1 cup chopped green bell pepper

8 garlic cloves, minced

1 pound ground sirloin

1 jalapeño pepper, chopped

2 tablespoons chili powder

2 tablespoons brown sugar

1 tablespoon ground cumin

3 tablespoons tomato paste

1 teaspoon dried oregano

½ teaspoon freshly ground black pepper

¼ teaspoon salt

2 bay leaves

1¼ cups merlot or other fruity red wine

2 (28-ounce) cans no-salt-added whole tomatoes, undrained and coarsely chopped

2 (15-ounce) cans no-salt-added kidney beans, drained

½ cup (2 ounces) shredded reduced-fat sharp cheddar cheese

1. Heat a large Dutch oven over medium-high heat. Remove casings from sausage. Add sausage, onion, and next 4 ingredients to pan; cook 8 minutes or until sausage and beef are browned, stirring to crumble.

2. Add chili powder and next 7 ingredients and cook 1 minute, stirring constantly. Stir in wine, tomatoes, and kidney beans; bring to a boil. Cover, reduce heat, and simmer 1 hour, stirring occasionally. Uncover and cook 30 minutes, stirring occasionally. Discard bay leaves. Sprinkle each serving with cheddar cheese.

CALORIES 286; FAT 7.5g (sat 2.1g, mono 1.1g, poly 0.4g); PROTEIN 22.4g; CARB 28.5g; FIBER 6.5g; CHOL 48mg; IRON 5.1mg; SODIUM 460mg; CALC 169mg

slow cooker
tonight!

cooking class

A slow cooker is a busy cook's best friend. Follow our tips and techniques to ensure a wholesome, delicious meal every time you use this convenient appliance.

Benefits of Slow Cooking

In addition to allowing you to make meals ahead, your slow cooker offers these benefits:

• **Cleans up easily:** Usually you have only one container to wash (assuming you don't brown or sauté ingredients in a skillet before adding them to your cooker), or no container if you use heavy-duty plastic liners.

• **Environmentally friendly:** A slow cooker uses less electricity than the cooktop or oven. There's no extra heat escaping, so your kitchen stays cool.

• **Requires little attention:** You don't have to stand over a hot cooktop or watch the clock. The slow cooker works best when it's left alone to slowly simmer food.

• **Adaptable:** Most traditional recipes that call for long, slow, gentle cooking in a Dutch oven are adaptable to the slow cooker. Some of your family's favorite recipes can be ready when you walk through the door at the end of a hectic day.

• **Economical:** Tough, less-expensive cuts of meat transform into tender, moist, and richly flavored dishes when cooked in the slow cooker.

• **Healthier:** Seldom do you add fat when cooking meat or poultry in the slow cooker. During the long simmering time, any fat rises to the top of the cooking liquid; simply remove it before serving.

• **Portable and versatile:** You can position the slow cooker any place there's an electrical outlet. It's especially useful when you entertain or have limited counter space. Prepare hot drinks or appetizers in the slow cooker, and place the cooker where your guests will gather. Just make sure to use the LOW setting.

Best Cuts of Meat for Slow Cooking

Type of Meat (3 ounces cooked)	Calories	Fat (sat)
Chuck or rump roast	206	13.1g (4.9g)
Tip roast	199	11.3g (4.3g)
Lean beef stew meat	201	9.6g (3.6g)
Lean Boston butt roast	197	12.2g (4.4g)
Lamb stew meat	158	6.2g (2.2g)

Shopping for a Slow Cooker

With so many slow cookers on the market, it's hard to know which one to buy. Here are some tips to help you get started.

Size matters. The first thing to consider when selecting a slow cooker is which best suits your family. If you are cooking for yourself or a family of two, then a 3- to 4-quart size should work for you. Families of four or larger should look at a 5- or 6-quart slow cooker. Or, if you love to have leftovers, a 6-, 6½-, or 7-quart cooker is a good selection.

Keep a lid on it. A snug-fitting, see-through lid works best. Removing the cooker's lid during cooking releases a great deal of heat, so you want to be able to see the food through the lid.

Removable inserts. Slow cookers with removable inserts are easier to clean than one-piece units. Depending on the manufacturer, the insert may be dishwasher safe. Some inserts can go from the freezer to the cooker, and some can even be used to brown meat on the cooktop before slow cooking.

It's all in the timing. Many slow cookers come with programmable timers. This is an especially nice feature if you will be gone all day. If your slow cooker doesn't have one, purchase an external timer. Simply plug the external slow-cooker timer into the wall outlet, and then plug the cooker into the timer. It allows you to set the cooking time; when that time expires, the timer will automatically switch the cooker to warm.

Slow-Cooker Showdown

We tested our Provençal Beef Daube recipe (page 259) in six slow cookers—all with at least a 6-quart capacity—ranging in price from $35 to a hefty $280. The results varied more in appearance and flavor than anticipated. In our favorite cookers, the meat was more tender and succulent, and the cooking liquid was rich and well blended. In other cookers, flavors were less deliciously integrated. Our conclusion: The more successful pots seemed to cook at a slightly higher temp—even on the LOW settings, the stews bubbled a bit as they simmered.

Best Overall:
BREVILLE BSC560XL 7-QUART ($130)
Although this stainless cooker lacks a timer and operates with manual controls, it produced great results. We loved the lightweight cooking insert; it's safe for the cooktop. This model also includes a meat rack and a long, detachable cord. One drawback: A metal lid might tempt you to peek.

Best Value:
WEST BEND 84966 6-QUART ($80)
A close second, this model has a digital timer. The cooking insert is safe for cooktop use, and the warming element doubles as a griddle, so you can cook directly on it. There are three heat settings: HIGH, LOW, and WARM, a nice feature for entertaining or for families who eat in shifts.

Secrets of Slow Cooking

On a budget? Pressed for time? Transform tough, cheap cuts into delicious dinners that practically cook themselves. Try our top tips.

1. Brown Meat First for Better Flavor
Strictly speaking, meat doesn't need to be browned before it's added to the slow cooker, but it's a step we find worth the effort. The caramelized surface of the meat will lend rich flavor to the finished dish. And meat dredged in flour before browning will add body to the sauce (as in Provençal Beef Daube, page 259). Always brown and drain ground meat before putting it in the slow cooker. Otherwise, it may clump and add grease to the dish.

2. Spice Judiciously
Whole spices and dried herbs like cinnamon sticks, bay leaves, caraway seeds, and peppercorns will give intense flavor to a dish that cooks for several hours, so be careful not to overdo them. Chopped fresh herbs such as parsley remain vibrant if you stir them in near the end or when the dish is finished.

3. Use Less Liquid
Because the slow cooker generates steam that doesn't escape, there will be more liquid in the food when it's finished cooking than when it started. If you create or adapt a recipe for the slow cooker, decrease (by as much as half) the amount of liquid you normally use in the dish.

4. Know When to Go HIGH, and When to Go LOW
Generally, cooker temperatures range from 170° to 280°. Use the HIGH setting if you need to cook a more tender cut of meat relatively quickly. But for tougher cuts, it's best to use the LOW setting and cook longer to allow time for the meat to become tender.

5. Leave the Lid On!
Don't lift the lid until the dish is done. The steam generated during slow cooking is part of the cooking medium. Removing the lid will release this steam and increase cooking time. Moreover, when you lift the lid, temperatures can drop into the "danger zone" (between 40° and 140°) where bacteria multiply rapidly.

6. Account for Variables
Our Test Kitchen professionals find that some slow cookers—particularly some newer models—cook hotter than others. In one instance, liquid imperceptibly evaporated from the cooker, leaving far less sauce than when the same dish was prepared in a different model. Not all slow cookers are created equal, so don't rely on the stated cook time for a recipe until you know how your cooker behaves.

Our Test Kitchen's Top Slow-Cooker Tricks

1. Make-ahead magic. If your slow cooker has a removable insert, you can assemble the ingredients for some recipes in the insert the night before, and then refrigerate the whole thing. Starting with cold ingredients may increase the cook time.

2. Don't get burned. Although cooking time is more flexible in a slow cooker than in an oven, overcooking is possible, so test for doneness close to the time given in the recipe.

3. Remember time conversions. One hour on HIGH equals approximately 2 hours on LOW.

4. Cut uniform pieces. When cutting meat or vegetables, be sure the pieces are the same size so they cook evenly.

5. Trim the fat. Slow cooking requires little fat. Trim excess fat and skin from meats and poultry.

6. Add, don't stir. There's no need to stir ingredients unless a recipe specifically calls for it. Just layer the ingredients as the recipe directs.

7. You won't need much liquid. Use only the amount of liquid specified in a recipe.

8. Lay it on thick. You can thicken the juices and make gravy by removing the lid and cooking on HIGH for the last 20 to 30 minutes.

9. Finish fresh. To enhance the flavor, add seasonings and garnishes to the dish once it comes out of the slow cooker.

Slow-Cooker Safety

Slow cooking is a safe method for preparing food if you follow the standard procedures.

• Fill your slow cooker at least half full but no more than two-thirds full. This helps meat products reach a safe internal temperature quickly and cook evenly.

• Cool leftovers in shallow containers and store in the refrigerator within 2 hours after cooking is finished.

• Defrost any frozen foods before cooking a dish that includes meat, poultry, or seafood. This ensures that the contents of the insert reach a safe internal temperature quickly.

• Don't use your slow cooker to reheat leftovers, because the cooker will not heat the food fast enough, resulting in an increased risk of bacterial contamination. Instead, use a microwave or cooktop.

Quick Cleanup

Follow these tips to make cleaning your slow cooker a little easier.

• To minimize cleanup, buy clear, heavy-duty plastic liners made to fit 3- to 6½-quart oval and round slow cookers. Place the plastic liner inside the slow cooker before adding the recipe ingredients. Then, serve the meal directly from the slow cooker, with the liner in place. Once the cooker has cooled, just throw away the plastic liner along with the mess.

• If you don't have slow-cooker liners, be sure to coat the slow cooker with cooking spray before placing the food inside. This will make cleanup much easier.

• The best time to clean a slow-cooker insert is not long after you take the food out, once the insert has cooled slightly. Just make sure that the slow cooker isn't too hot. Cold water poured over a hot insert can cause it to crack.

• Never immerse a slow-cooker unit in water. Simply unplug it, and wipe it clean with a cloth.

Italian Beef Sandwiches

If you can't find Italian rolls, look for a sturdy bread that will soak up the juices in this moist, delightfully messy sandwich.

Yield: 8 servings (serving size: 1 sandwich and about ⅓ cup cooking liquid)

1 teaspoon dried Italian seasoning

1 teaspoon crushed red pepper

1 (2½-pound) rump roast, trimmed

1 (14-ounce) can fat-free, lower-sodium beef broth

1 garlic clove, minced

2 teaspoons olive oil

1 cup coarsely chopped green bell pepper (about 1 medium)

8 (2-ounce) Italian rolls

Giardiniera (pickled vegetables), chopped (optional)

1. Combine first 5 ingredients in a large zip-top plastic bag, and marinate in refrigerator overnight.

2. Place beef and marinade in an electric slow cooker; cover and cook on LOW for 8 hours or until beef is tender. Place beef on a cutting board (reserve cooking liquid); let stand 10 minutes. Thinly slice beef; place in a shallow dish. Pour cooking liquid over beef.

3. Heat a large nonstick skillet over medium-high heat. Add oil to pan; swirl to coat. Add bell pepper to pan; sauté 5 minutes or until tender. Slice rolls lengthwise, cutting to, but not through, other side. Hollow out top and bottom halves of rolls, leaving a ¾-inch-thick shell; reserve torn bread for another use. Arrange about 3 ounces beef and 2 tablespoons bell peppers on each roll. Drizzle 1 tablespoon cooking liquid over beef and peppers; top with giardiniera, if desired. Serve with remaining 2½ cups cooking liquid for dipping.

CALORIES 386; FAT 11.3g (sat 3.4g, mono 4.8g, poly 1.2g); PROTEIN 39.4g; CARB 29.2g; FIBER 1.8g; CHOL 102mg; IRON 5.4mg; SODIUM 479mg; CALC 52mg

Beef Brisket with Beer

Beef brisket is at its finest when you simmer it in a slow cooker and flavor it with beer and onions.

Yield: 12 servings (serving size: about 3 ounces brisket and ⅓ cup sauce)

1 (3-pound) beef brisket, trimmed

1 teaspoon salt

½ teaspoon freshly ground black pepper

¼ cup water

2 cups vertically sliced onion (about 1 large)

1½ cups chopped parsnip (about 2)

1 tablespoon balsamic vinegar

1 bay leaf

1 (12-ounce) bottle light beer

1. Rub brisket with salt and pepper. Heat a large heavy skillet over medium-high heat. Add brisket to pan; cook 10 minutes, browning on all sides. Remove brisket from pan. Add ¼ cup water to pan, stirring to loosen browned bits. Add onion and parsnip; sauté 5 minutes or until vegetables are tender.

2. Place onion mixture, vinegar, bay leaf, and beer in a large electric slow cooker. Place brisket on top of onion mixture. Cover and cook on LOW for 8 hours. Discard bay leaf. Cut brisket diagonally across grain into thin slices. Serve brisket with sauce.

CALORIES 160; FAT 5g (sat 1.9g, mono 2.1g, poly 0.2g); PROTEIN 20.5g; CARB 5.6g; FIBER 1.1g; CHOL 49mg; IRON 1.9mg; SODIUM 232mg; CALC 20mg

QUICK TIP

Round out your meal with a quick addition of creamy mashed potatoes. Prepackaged refrigerated potatoes are a good choice. Just be careful to watch the serving size, and pay close attention to the sodium.

Company Pot Roast

Dried shiitake mushrooms can replace the morels. Leftover meat and gravy make a delicious filling for hot roast beef sandwiches the next day.

Yield: 8 servings (serving size: 3 ounces roast, 1 onion wedge, about 3 carrot pieces, 4 potato halves, and about ¼ cup gravy)

1 (2-pound) boneless chuck roast, trimmed and cut in half

¼ cup lower-sodium soy sauce

2 garlic cloves, minced

1 cup beef broth

1 (0.35-ounce) package dried morels

1 tablespoon cracked black pepper

3 tablespoons sun-dried tomato paste

2 medium onions (about ¾ pound), quartered

1 (16-ounce) package carrots, cut into 2-inch pieces

16 small red potatoes (about 2 pounds), halved

1 tablespoon canola oil

1½ tablespoons all-purpose flour

3 tablespoons water

Rosemary sprigs (optional)

1. Combine roast, soy sauce, and garlic in a large zip-top plastic bag; seal bag, and marinate in refrigerator at least 8 hours, turning bag occasionally.

2. Bring broth to a boil in a small saucepan; add mushrooms. Remove from heat; cover and let stand 20 minutes. Drain mushrooms through a cheesecloth-lined colander over a bowl, reserving broth mixture.

3. Remove roast from bag, reserving marinade. Sprinkle roast with pepper, gently pressing pepper into roast. Combine reserved marinade, mushroom broth mixture, and tomato paste; stir well, and set aside.

4. Place mushrooms, onion, carrot, and potato in a 6-quart electric slow cooker; toss gently.

5. Heat a large skillet over medium-high heat. Add oil to pan; swirl to coat. Add roast, browning well on all sides. Place roast over vegetables in slow cooker. Pour tomato paste mixture into pan, scraping pan to loosen browned bits. Pour tomato paste mixture over roast and vegetables. Cover and cook on LOW for 10 hours or until roast is tender. Place roast and vegetables on a serving platter; keep warm. Reserve liquid in slow cooker; increase heat to HIGH.

6. Place flour in a small bowl. Gradually add 3 tablespoons water, stirring with a whisk until well blended. Add flour mixture to liquid in slow cooker. Cook, uncovered, 15 minutes or until slightly thick, stirring frequently. Serve gravy with roast and vegetables. Garnish with rosemary sprigs, if desired.

CALORIES 318; FAT 6.8g (sat 1.6g, mono 2.7g, poly 0.8g); PROTEIN 30.5g; CARB 33.1g; FIBER 5.2g; CHOL 40mg; IRON 3.9mg; SODIUM 552mg; CALC 70mg

Beef Pot Roast with Turnip Greens

Cipollini onions are small, flat Italian onions. If you can't find them, substitute pearl onions. Other large, full-flavored greens like mustard greens or kale will work as well.

Yield: 12 servings (serving size: 3 ounces roast, ¾ cup vegetable mixture, and ⅓ cup cooking liquid)

3.1 ounces all-purpose flour (about ¾ cup)

1 (3-pound) boneless chuck roast, trimmed

1 teaspoon kosher salt

½ teaspoon freshly ground black pepper

1 tablespoon olive oil

1 pound fresh turnip greens, trimmed and coarsely chopped

3 cups (2-inch) diagonally cut parsnips (about 1 pound)

3 cups cubed peeled Yukon gold potatoes (about 1 pound)

2 cups cipollini onions, peeled and quartered

2 tablespoons tomato paste

1 cup dry red wine

1 (14-ounce) can fat-free, lower-sodium beef broth

1 tablespoon black peppercorns

4 thyme sprigs

3 garlic cloves, crushed

2 bay leaves

1 bunch fresh flat-leaf parsley

Thyme sprigs (optional)

1. Place flour in a shallow dish. Sprinkle beef evenly with salt and pepper; dredge in flour. Heat a large skillet over medium-high heat. Add oil to pan; swirl to coat. Add beef; cook 10 minutes, browning on all sides. Place turnip greens in a 6-quart electric slow cooker; top with parsnip, potato, and onion. Transfer beef to slow cooker. Add tomato paste to skillet; cook 30 seconds, stirring constantly. Stir in wine and broth; bring to a boil, scraping pan to loosen browned bits. Cook 1 minute, stirring constantly. Pour broth mixture into slow cooker.

2. Place peppercorns and next 4 ingredients on a double layer of cheesecloth. Gather edges of cheesecloth together; tie securely. Add cheesecloth bundle to slow cooker. Cover and cook on LOW for 8 hours or until beef and vegetables are tender. Remove and discard cheesecloth bundle. Remove roast from slow cooker; slice. Serve with vegetable mixture and cooking liquid. Garnish with thyme sprigs, if desired.

CALORIES 424; FAT 21.3g (sat 8.1g, mono 9.4g, poly 0.9g); PROTEIN 33g; CARB 23.5g; FIBER 2.9g; CHOL 99mg; IRON 3.8mg; SODIUM 348mg; CALC 90mg

Brazilian Feijoada

Feijoada (pronounced fay-ZWAH-da), a Brazilian stew of pork and black beans, is traditionally served over rice with fresh orange slices for special occasions. Preparing it in a slow cooker makes it possible to serve on even the busiest weeknights.

Yield: 8 servings (serving size: about 1¼ cups bean mixture and 1 orange wedge)

2 cups dried black beans

4 applewood-smoked bacon slices

1 (1-pound) boneless pork shoulder (Boston butt), trimmed and cut into ½-inch cubes

¾ teaspoon salt, divided

½ teaspoon freshly ground black pepper, divided

3 bone-in beef short ribs, trimmed (about 2 pounds)

3 cups finely chopped onion (about 2 medium)

1¼ cups fat-free, lower-sodium chicken broth

4 garlic cloves, minced

1 (9-ounce) smoked ham hock

1 tablespoon white vinegar

8 orange wedges

1. Place beans in a small saucepan; cover with cold water. Bring to a boil; cook 2 minutes. Remove from heat; cover and let stand 1 hour. Drain.

2. Cook bacon in a large skillet over medium heat until crisp. Remove bacon from pan; crumble. Reserve drippings in pan. Sprinkle pork evenly with ⅛ teaspoon salt and ¼ teaspoon pepper. Increase heat to medium-high. Add pork to drippings in pan; cook 8 minutes, browning on all sides. Transfer pork to a 6-quart electric slow cooker. Sprinkle ribs evenly with ⅛ teaspoon salt and remaining ¼ teaspoon pepper. Add ribs to pan; cook 3 minutes on each side or until browned. Place ribs in slow cooker. Add drained beans, remaining ½ teaspoon salt, onion, and next 3 ingredients to slow cooker, stirring to combine. Cover and cook on LOW for 8 hours or until beans and meat are tender.

3. Remove ribs from slow cooker; let stand 15 minutes. Remove meat from bones; shred meat with 2 forks. Discard bones. Discard ham hock. Return beef to slow cooker. Stir in vinegar and crumbled bacon. Serve with orange wedges.

CALORIES 458; FAT 17.4g (sat 6.8g, mono 6.7g, poly 1.1g); PROTEIN 39.5g; CARB 35.8g; FIBER 11.6g; CHOL 96mg; IRON 6.4mg; SODIUM 533mg; CALC 102mg

Provençal Beef Daube

If you can't find niçoise olives, use another meaty variety, such as kalamata or gaeta.

Yield: 8 servings (serving size: about ¾ cup)

2 pounds boneless chuck roast, trimmed and cut into chunks

1 tablespoon extra-virgin olive oil

6 garlic cloves, minced

½ cup boiling water

½ ounce dried porcini mushrooms

¾ teaspoon salt, divided

Cooking spray

½ cup red wine

¼ cup fat-free, lower-sodium beef broth

⅓ cup pitted niçoise olives

½ teaspoon freshly ground black pepper

2 large carrots, peeled and thinly sliced

1 large onion, peeled and chopped

1 celery stalk, thinly sliced

1 (15-ounce) can whole tomatoes, drained and crushed

1 teaspoon whole black peppercorns

3 flat-leaf parsley sprigs

3 thyme sprigs

1 bay leaf

1 (1-inch) strip orange rind

1 tablespoon water

1 teaspoon cornstarch

1½ tablespoons fresh flat-leaf parsley leaves

1½ teaspoons chopped fresh thyme

1. Combine first 3 ingredients in a large zip-top plastic bag. Seal and marinate at room temperature 30 minutes, turning bag occasionally.
2. Combine ½ cup boiling water and mushrooms; cover and let stand 30 minutes. Drain through a sieve over a bowl, reserving mushrooms and ¼ cup soaking liquid. Chop mushrooms.
3. Heat a large skillet over medium-high heat. Sprinkle beef mixture with ¼ teaspoon salt. Coat pan with cooking spray. Add half of beef mixture to pan; sauté 5 minutes, turning to brown on all sides. Place browned beef mixture in a 6-quart electric slow cooker. Repeat procedure with cooking spray and remaining beef mixture. Add wine and broth to skillet; bring to a boil, scraping pan to loosen browned bits. Pour wine mixture into slow cooker. Add mushrooms, reserved ¼ cup soaking liquid, remaining ½ teaspoon salt, olives, and next 5 ingredients. Place peppercorns, parsley sprigs, thyme sprigs, bay leaf, and orange rind on a double layer of cheesecloth. Gather edges of cheesecloth together; tie securely. Add cheesecloth bundle to slow cooker. Cover and cook on LOW for 6 hours or until beef and vegetables are tender. Discard the cheesecloth bundle.
4. Combine 1 tablespoon water and cornstarch in a small bowl, stirring until smooth. Add cornstarch mixture to slow cooker; cook 20 minutes or until slightly thick, stirring occasionally. Sprinkle with parsley and chopped thyme.

CALORIES 360; FAT 22.5g (sat 8g, mono 10.6g, poly 1.1g); PROTEIN 30.2g; CARB 7.8g; FIBER 2.2g; CHOL 94mg; IRON 3.5mg; SODIUM 516mg; CALC 53mg

Thai Red Curry Beef

Jalapeño seeds add a slight kick to this Thai beef dish. If you want to decrease the heat, seed the jalapeño before mincing.

Yield: 8 servings (serving size: about ¾ cup beef mixture, ½ cup rice, and 1 tablespoon basil)

2 pounds lean beef stew meat

⅛ teaspoon salt

2 cups finely chopped onion (1 onion)

4 garlic cloves, minced

¾ cup lower-sodium beef broth

1 tablespoon dark brown sugar

3 tablespoons red curry paste

2 tablespoons fish sauce

2 tablespoons fresh lime juice

1 (13.5-ounce) can light coconut milk

1 jalapeño pepper, minced

2 cups bagged baby spinach leaves

4 cups hot cooked jasmine rice

½ cup fresh basil leaves

1. Heat a large nonstick skillet over medium-high heat. Add beef; cook 5 minutes or until browned, stirring occasionally. Drain. Place beef in a 4-quart electric slow cooker; sprinkle with salt.

2. Return pan to medium-high heat. Add onion and garlic; sauté 5 minutes or until tender. Spoon onion mixture over beef. Combine beef broth and next 6 ingredients; pour over beef. Cover and cook on LOW for 6 hours.

3. Stir in spinach. Cover and cook on LOW for 15 minutes or just until spinach wilts. Serve beef mixture over rice; sprinkle with basil leaves.

CALORIES 245; FAT 5.5g (sat 2.3g, mono 2g, poly 0.2g); PROTEIN 27.4g; CARB 20g; FIBER 1.3g; CHOL 50mg; IRON 2.8mg; SODIUM 624mg; CALC 42mg

Plum Pork Tenderloin

Serve with jasmine rice to help soak up some of the sauce. Snow peas make a great side dish for rounding out your meal.

Yield: 8 servings (serving size: 3 ounces pork and ½ cup sauce)

1 tablespoon ground cinnamon

1 tablespoon ground allspice

2 (1-pound) pork tenderloins, trimmed

Cooking spray

1 (9.3-ounce) jar plum sauce

½ cup water

2 plums, each cut into 6 wedges

1. Combine cinnamon and allspice; rub over pork. Place pork in a 5-quart electric slow cooker coated with cooking spray. Pour plum sauce over pork; add ½ cup water and plum wedges. Cover and cook on HIGH for 4 hours or until tender. Serve pork with sauce.

CALORIES 199; FAT 2.9g (sat 0.8g, mono 1g, poly 0.6g); PROTEIN 24.3g; CARB 17.6g; FIBER 1.3g; CHOL 74mg; IRON 1.7mg; SODIUM 238mg; CALC 23mg

INGREDIENT TIP

Ripe plums yield slightly to the touch, but don't squeeze them. Let the fruit sit in your palm. It should give a little. If you buy firm fruit, don't put it in the refrigerator or the kitchen window—put it in a paper bag in a dark place for a day or two to ripen.

Sauerbraten

The spicy-sweet gingersnaps soften the tang of white vinegar. Serve the tender marinated beef and sauce over spaetzle (tiny noodles or dumplings) for an authentic German feast.

Yield: 7 servings (serving size: 3 ounces roast and 6 tablespoons sauce)

1 cup water

2 tablespoons sugar

¾ cup white vinegar

1½ teaspoons salt

6 black peppercorns

5 whole cloves

3 bay leaves

1 lemon, sliced

1 (3-pound) rump roast, trimmed

1½ cups sliced onion (1 large)

15 gingersnaps, crumbled

Chopped fresh parsley (optional)

1. Place first 8 ingredients in a large heavy-duty zip-top plastic bag; seal bag. Turn bag to blend marinade. Place roast and onion in bag; seal bag, turning to coat. Marinate in refrigerator 24 hours, turning bag occasionally.

2. Remove roast from marinade, reserving marinade. Place roast in a 5-quart electric slow cooker. Strain reserved marinade through a sieve into a bowl, reserving 1½ cups; discard remaining liquid and solids. Pour 1½ cups strained marinade over roast. Cover and cook on LOW for 5 hours or until roast is tender.

3. Remove roast from slow cooker; cover and keep warm. Add gingersnap crumbs to liquid in slow cooker. Cover and cook on LOW for 8 minutes or until sauce thickens; stir with a whisk until smooth. Serve sauce with roast. Garnish with parsley, if desired.

CALORIES 202; FAT 5.6g (sat 1.7g, mono 2.2g, poly 0.3g); PROTEIN 20.7g; CARB 16.1g; FIBER 0.8g; CHOL 45mg; IRON 2.3mg; SODIUM 512mg; CALC 30mg

Pork with Apricots, Dried Plums, and Sauerkraut

Sauerkraut balances the sweetness of the apricot preserves and orange juice. Slow cooking tenderizes the pork and dried fruit.

Yield: 8 servings (serving size: 3 ounces pork and about ½ cup sauerkraut mixture)

1 (2-pound) pork tenderloin, trimmed

1 cup chopped onion (about 1 medium)

¾ cup apricot preserves

½ cup dried apricots

½ cup pitted dried plums

¼ cup fat-free, lower-sodium chicken broth

¼ cup orange juice

2 tablespoons cornstarch

1 teaspoon salt

½ teaspoon dried thyme

¼ teaspoon freshly ground black pepper

1 (10-ounce) package refrigerated sauerkraut

1. Place pork in an electric slow cooker. Combine onion and remaining ingredients in a large bowl; pour sauerkraut mixture over pork. Cover and cook on LOW for 7 hours. Remove pork from slow cooker. Let stand 10 minutes. Cut pork into ¼-inch-thick slices. Serve sliced pork with sauerkraut mixture.

CALORIES 261; FAT 2.5g (sat 0.8g, mono 0.9g, poly 0.4g); PROTEIN 24.6g; CARB 34.9g; FIBER 2.3g; CHOL 74mg; IRON 1.5mg; SODIUM 585mg; CALC 21mg

Curried Pork over Basmati Rice

Madras curry powder lends a little spice without being overpowering. Coconut milk stirred in at the end of the cooking time counters the burn with sweet creaminess. Reminiscent of many Indian-inspired dishes, this recipe relies on slow cooking to develop its richness.

Yield: 6 servings (serving size: about 1 cup pork mixture and ½ cup rice)

1 teaspoon canola oil

1½ pounds boneless pork loin, cut into 1-inch cubes

3½ cups cubed red potato

1 cup chopped onion

1 cup chopped red bell pepper

¼ cup fat-free, lower-sodium chicken broth

2 tablespoons all-purpose flour

1 tablespoon sugar

2 tablespoons tomato paste

1 tablespoon minced peeled fresh ginger

1½ teaspoons salt

1 teaspoon Madras curry powder

1 teaspoon ground cumin

2 garlic cloves, minced

½ cup coconut milk

3 cups hot cooked basmati rice

Cilantro sprigs (optional)

1. Heat a large skillet over medium-high heat. Add oil to pan; swirl to coat. Add pork; cook 4 minutes, browning on all sides.
2. Combine pork, potato, and next 11 ingredients in an electric slow cooker; stir well to dissolve flour. Cover and cook on LOW for 6 to 8 hours or until pork and potatoes are tender. Stir in coconut milk. Serve pork over rice. Garnish each serving with a cilantro sprig, if desired.

CALORIES 371; FAT 6.2g (sat 2.4g, mono 1.8g, poly 0.5g); PROTEIN 30.6g; CARB 47g; FIBER 3.4g; CHOL 71mg; IRON 2.9mg; SODIUM 682mg; CALC 29mg

Char Siu Pork Roast

Our recipe for *char siu,* the Chinese version of barbecue, transforms pork into a stress-free entrée. Serve with sticky or long-grain white rice and a steamed or stir-fried medley of bell peppers, carrots, snow peas, sliced baby corn, and water chestnuts.

Yield: 8 servings (serving size: 3 ounces pork and ¼ cup sauce)

¼ cup lower-sodium soy sauce

¼ cup hoisin sauce

3 tablespoons ketchup

3 tablespoons honey

2 teaspoons minced garlic

2 teaspoons grated peeled fresh ginger

1 teaspoon dark sesame oil

½ teaspoon five-spice powder

1 (2-pound) boneless pork shoulder (Boston butt), trimmed

½ cup fat-free, lower-sodium chicken broth

1. Combine first 8 ingredients in a small bowl, stirring well with a whisk. Place in a large zip-top plastic bag. Add pork to bag; seal. Marinate in refrigerator at least 2 hours, turning occasionally.
2. Place pork and marinade in an electric slow cooker. Cover and cook on LOW for 8 hours.
3. Remove pork from slow cooker with a slotted spoon; place on a cutting board or work surface. Cover with foil; keep warm.
4. Add broth to sauce in slow cooker. Cover and cook on LOW for 30 minutes or until sauce thickens. Shred pork with 2 forks; serve with sauce.

CALORIES 227; FAT 9.5g (sat 3.1g, mono 3.9g, poly 1.1g); PROTEIN 21.6g; CARB 12.7g; FIBER 0.4g; CHOL 73mg; IRON 1.7mg; SODIUM 561mg; CALC 30mg

Pork Vindaloo

Seasoned with ginger, garam masala, mustard seeds, and cumin, this fragrant Indian-spiced pork loin braises in a tomato-based sauce. The low-and-slow cooking method renders the pork melt-in-your-mouth tender.

Yield: 6 servings (serving size: 1 cup pork mixture, ½ cup rice, and 1 teaspoon cilantro)

1½ tablespoons minced peeled fresh ginger

2 teaspoons garam masala

2 teaspoons mustard seeds

½ teaspoon salt

1½ teaspoons ground cumin

½ teaspoon ground red pepper

1 (2-pound) boneless pork loin roast, trimmed and cut into 1-inch pieces

2 cups chopped onion

6 garlic cloves, minced

1.1 ounces all-purpose flour (about ¼ cup)

⅓ cup dry red wine

2½ cups coarsely chopped tomato (about 1 pound)

3 cups hot cooked basmati rice

2 tablespoons chopped fresh cilantro

1. Combine first 6 ingredients in a medium bowl. Add pork, tossing to coat.

2. Heat a large nonstick skillet over medium-high heat. Add pork to pan. Cook 5 minutes or until pork is lightly browned on all sides. Place pork in a 4-quart electric slow cooker.

3. Add onion and garlic to pan; reduce heat to medium, and sauté 5 minutes or until onion is crisp-tender. Stir in flour. Add wine, scraping pan to loosen browned bits. Add tomato to onion mixture. Spoon onion mixture over pork. Cover and cook on LOW for 7 hours or until pork is tender. Serve over rice; sprinkle with cilantro.

CALORIES 379; FAT 7.2g (sat 1.9g, mono 2.5g, poly 0.7g); PROTEIN 38.4g; CARB 36.2g; FIBER 2.7g; CHOL 95mg; IRON 3.1mg; SODIUM 279mg; CALC 43mg

Pork Carnitas

Serve with black beans and rice, if desired.

Yield: 10 servings (serving size: 3 ounces pork, 2 tortillas, 1 tablespoon onion, 1 tablespoon salsa, 1 tablespoon cilantro, and 1 lime wedge)

1 (3-pound) boneless pork shoulder (Boston butt), trimmed

10 garlic cloves, sliced

2 teaspoons ground cumin

1 teaspoon dried oregano

¾ teaspoon salt

½ teaspoon freshly ground black pepper

¾ cup orange juice

2 tablespoons fresh lime juice

2 chipotle chiles canned in adobo sauce, drained and chopped

20 (6-inch) flour or corn tortillas, warmed

⅔ cup chopped onion

⅔ cup bottled salsa

⅔ cup chopped fresh cilantro

10 lime wedges

1. Make ½-inch-deep slits on outside of roast; stuff with garlic. Combine cumin and next 3 ingredients in a small bowl. Place roast in a 3½-quart electric slow cooker. Sprinkle pork on all sides with spice mixture.

2. Combine juices and chipotle chiles. Pour juice mixture over pork. Cover and cook on LOW for 8 hours or until pork is tender.

3. Remove pork from slow cooker; shred with 2 forks. Skim fat from cooking liquid. Combine shredded pork and ½ cup cooking liquid; toss well.

4. Spoon 1½ ounces pork mixture onto each tortilla; top each with 1½ teaspoons onion, 1½ teaspoons salsa, and 1½ teaspoons cilantro. Serve with lime wedges.

CALORIES 334; FAT 12.6g (sat 3.9g, mono 5.1g, poly 1.7g); PROTEIN 29.4g; CARB 27.1g; FIBER 3g; CHOL 87mg; IRON 2.1mg; SODIUM 424mg; CALC 81mg

Sausage Jambalaya

Round out this meal with a small green salad and a slice of toasted French baguette.

Yield: 8 servings (serving size: about 1 cup jambalaya and ½ cup rice)

2 cups chopped onion

1 cup chopped celery

1 cup water

½ teaspoon Cajun seasoning

½ teaspoon dried thyme

1 pound skinless, boneless chicken thighs, cut into 1-inch cubes

8 ounces andouille sausage, sliced

1 (14.5-ounce) can diced tomatoes and green chiles, undrained

1 pound medium shrimp, peeled and deveined

4 cups hot cooked rice

Chopped green onions (optional)

1. Combine first 8 ingredients in a 4-quart electric slow cooker. Cover and cook on LOW for 6 hours. Stir in shrimp; cover and cook on LOW for 10 minutes or just until shrimp are done. Serve over rice. Sprinkle with green onions, if desired.

CALORIES 315; FAT 8.5g (sat 3g, mono 3.1g, poly 1.4g); PROTEIN 30g; CARB 27.9g; FIBER 1.3g; CHOL 149mg; IRON 3.6mg; SODIUM 404mg; CALC 61mg

QUICK TIP

To cut down on prep time, purchase prechopped onion and celery that you'll find in most grocers' produce departments. They are real time-savers.

Spiced Apple Pork Chops

Essential to the recipe, the thickness of the pork chops ensures that the chops stay tender and juicy throughout the long cook time. Mashed sweet potatoes and sautéed Brussels sprouts complete the comforting meal.

Yield: 4 servings (serving size: 1 pork chop and ¾ cup apple mixture)

4 (8-ounce) bone-in center-cut pork chops (about 1 inch thick)

¼ teaspoon salt

½ teaspoon freshly ground black pepper

1 teaspoon canola oil

Cooking spray

1 (8-ounce) container refrigerated prechopped onion (about 1¾ cups)

2 cups water

¼ cup firmly packed brown sugar

1 teaspoon ground cinnamon

½ teaspoon ground cloves

½ teaspoon ground ginger

1 (5-ounce) package dried apples

1. Sprinkle pork with salt and pepper. Heat a large nonstick skillet over medium-high heat. Add oil to pan; swirl to coat. Add pork to pan; cook 3 minutes on each side or until browned. Transfer pork to a 5-quart electric slow cooker coated with cooking spray, reserving drippings in pan. Reduce heat to medium. Add onion to drippings in pan; sauté 3 minutes or until tender. Stir in 2 cups water, scraping pan to loosen browned bits. Stir in brown sugar and next 3 ingredients. Remove pan from heat.

2. Add apples to slow cooker; pour onion mixture over apples. Cover and cook on LOW for 3 to 3½ hours or until tender. Serve pork chops with apple mixture.

CALORIES 391; FAT 9.7g (sat 2.6g, mono 3.7g, poly 1.3g); PROTEIN 31.7g; CARB 43.8g; FIBER 4.2g; CHOL 94mg; IRON 1.9mg; SODIUM 457mg; CALC 60mg

Thai-Style Pork

Peanut butter melds with classic Asian flavors to lend this one-dish meal a Thai flair. Lime makes a perfect accent.

Yield: 6 servings (serving size: ¾ cup rice, ⅔ cup pork mixture, and 1 teaspoon green onions)

1 (2-pound) boneless center-cut pork loin roast, trimmed

1 teaspoon olive oil

2 cups chopped red bell pepper

6 green onions, cut into 1-inch pieces

Cooking spray

2 tablespoons hoisin sauce

1 tablespoon lower-sodium soy sauce

1 tablespoon fresh lime juice

2 tablespoons creamy peanut butter

1 teaspoon cumin seeds, crushed

½ teaspoon salt

½ teaspoon crushed red pepper

2 garlic cloves, minced

4½ cups hot cooked basmati rice

2 tablespoons diagonally sliced green onions

1. Cut roast into 1-inch pieces. Heat a large nonstick skillet over medium heat. Add oil to pan; swirl to coat. Add pork; sauté 5 minutes or until browned.

2. Place pork, bell pepper, and green onion pieces in a 4-quart electric slow cooker coated with cooking spray; stir well.

3. Combine hoisin sauce and next 7 ingredients in a small bowl; stir until well blended. Pour mixture over pork and vegetables; stir well.

4. Cover and cook on LOW for 7 to 8 hours. Serve over rice; sprinkle with sliced green onions.

CALORIES 422; FAT 10.6g (sat 2.8g, mono 4.8g, poly 1.6g); PROTEIN 37.4g; CARB 42g; FIBER 2.4g; CHOL 95mg; IRON 3.6mg; SODIUM 547mg; CALC 38mg

FLAVOR TIP

With their crisp texture and sweet flavor, bell peppers are a nice complement to the pork in this dish. If you plan to use the peppers within a day or two, keep them at room temperature for better flavor.

Chinese Pork Tenderloin with Garlic-Sauced Noodles

Put the water for the pasta on to boil just before you remove the pork form the cooker to let it stand for 10 minutes.

Yield: 9 servings (serving size: 1⅓ cups noodle mixture, 1 teaspoon peanuts, 2 teaspoons cilantro, and 1 lime wedge)

2 (1-pound) pork tenderloins, trimmed

¼ cup lower-sodium soy sauce, divided

1 tablespoon hoisin sauce

1 tablespoon tomato sauce

1 teaspoon sugar

1 teaspoon grated peeled fresh ginger

2 garlic cloves, minced

3 tablespoons seasoned rice vinegar

1 teaspoon dark sesame oil

8 cups hot cooked Chinese-style noodles (about 16 ounces uncooked)

1 cup matchstick-cut carrots

¾ cup diagonally sliced green onions

¼ cup fresh cilantro leaves

⅓ cup chopped unsalted, dry-roasted peanuts

⅓ cup chopped fresh cilantro

9 lime wedges

1. Place tenderloins in a 5-quart electric slow cooker. Combine 1 tablespoon soy sauce and next 5 ingredients; drizzle over tenderloins. Cover and cook on LOW for 3½ hours. Remove pork from slow cooker, and place in a large bowl, reserving cooking liquid in slow cooker. Let pork stand 10 minutes.

2. Strain cooking liquid through a sieve into a bowl. Cover and keep warm. Shred pork with 2 forks.

3. Return cooking liquid to slow cooker; stir in remaining 3 tablespoons soy sauce, vinegar, and sesame oil. Cover and cook on HIGH 10 minutes. Turn slow cooker off. Add pork, noodles, and next 3 ingredients, tossing to coat. Spoon noodle mixture into bowls; sprinkle with peanuts and chopped cilantro. Serve with lime wedges.

CALORIES 303; FAT 5.7g (sat 1.2g, mono 2.3g, poly 1.4g); PROTEIN 28.3g; CARB 34.1g; FIBER 2.7g; CHOL 72mg; IRON 3.1mg; SODIUM 555mg; CALC 30mg

Rosemary Pork Sliders with Horseradish Aioli

Assemble the sliders before dinner. Or, consider showcasing a slider assembly station for your family or friends to make their own.

Yield: 12 servings (serving size: 2 sliders)

1 (1½-pound) boneless pork loin roast, trimmed

½ teaspoon freshly ground black pepper

Cooking spray

1 cup water

1 cup fat-free, lower-sodium chicken broth

½ cup vertically sliced shallots (2 large)

1 tablespoon chopped fresh rosemary

4 garlic cloves, minced

¾ cup canola mayonnaise

2 teaspoons prepared horseradish

24 (1.3-ounce) wheat slider buns, split and toasted

2 cups arugula

1. Sprinkle pork with pepper. Heat a large skillet over medium-high heat. Add pork; cook 3 minutes on each side or until browned. Transfer pork to a 3-quart slow cooker coated with cooking spray. Add 1 cup water and next 4 ingredients to slow cooker. Cover and cook on LOW for 8 hours or until tender.

2. Remove pork from slow cooker; place in a bowl. Shred pork with 2 forks. Pour cooking liquid through a sieve into a bowl, reserving shallots and garlic. Add ¾ cup strained cooking liquid, shallots, and garlic to pork; toss well. Discard remaining cooking liquid.

3. Combine mayonnaise and horseradish in a small bowl. Spoon about 2 tablespoons pork mixture on bottom half of each bun. Top evenly with arugula. Spread 1½ teaspoons mayonnaise mixture on cut side of each bun top. Cover sliders with bun tops.

CALORIES 421; FAT 20.2g (sat 2.9g, mono 8.3g, poly 3.4g); PROTEIN 26.1g; CARB 35.8g; FIBER 2.2g; CHOL 50mg; IRON 2.9mg; SODIUM 479mg; CALC 105mg

Braised Pork Loin with Port and Dried Plums

Yield: 10 servings (serving size: 3 ounces pork and ½ cup sauce)

1 (3¼-pound) boneless pork loin roast, trimmed

1½ teaspoons freshly ground black pepper

1 teaspoon salt

1 teaspoon dry mustard

1 teaspoon dried sage (not rubbed sage)

½ teaspoon dried thyme

1 tablespoon olive oil

2 cups sliced onion

1 cup finely chopped leek

1 cup finely chopped carrot

½ cup port or other sweet red wine

⅓ cup fat-free, lower-sodium chicken broth

⅓ cup water

1 cup pitted dried plums (about 20 dried plums)

2 bay leaves

2 tablespoons cornstarch

2 tablespoons water

1. Cut roast in half crosswise. Combine pepper and next 4 ingredients. Rub seasoning mixture over surface of roast halves.

2. Heat a large Dutch oven over medium-high heat. Add oil to pan; swirl to coat. Add pork, browning on all sides. Place pork in a 4½-quart electric slow cooker. Add onion, leek, and carrot to Dutch oven; sauté 5 minutes or until vegetables are golden. Stir in wine, broth, and ⅓ cup water, scraping pan to loosen browned bits. Pour wine mixture over pork in slow cooker; add plums and bay leaves. Cover and cook on LOW for 7 to 8 hours or until pork is tender.

3. Remove pork from slow cooker; reserve cooking liquid in slow cooker. Set pork aside; keep warm. Increase heat to HIGH. Combine cornstarch and 2 tablespoons water; stir well, and add to cooking liquid. Cook, uncovered, 15 minutes or until mixture is thick, stirring frequently. Discard bay leaves. Slice pork, and serve with sauce.

CALORIES 280; FAT 7.8g (sat 2.4g, mono 3.9g, poly 0.8g); PROTEIN 32.2g; CARB 17.7g; FIBER 2g; CHOL 93mg; IRON 2mg; SODIUM 340mg; CALC 40mg

Stuffed Squash

Serve this classic Middle Eastern meal in bowls so you can scoop up every drop of the tasty sauce with warm pita bread. Offer a salad of chopped lettuce, cucumber, and feta cheese.

Yield: 4 servings (serving size: 2 squash and 1 cup sauce)

8 medium yellow squash (about 3 pounds)

4 teaspoons minced garlic, divided

8 ounces lean ground lamb

¼ cup uncooked converted rice

¼ cup chopped fresh parsley

1 tablespoon chopped fresh mint

¼ teaspoon salt

¾ teaspoon ground allspice

¾ teaspoon ground cinnamon

½ teaspoon freshly ground black pepper

Cooking spray

½ cup finely chopped onion

2 teaspoons brown sugar

1 (15-ounce) can no-salt-added tomato sauce

1 (14.5-ounce) can petite diced tomatoes, undrained

8 teaspoons chopped fresh mint (optional)

1. Cut off narrow neck of each squash. Insert a small paring knife into cut ends of squash. Carefully twist knife to remove pulp. (Do not pierce sides of squash.)

2. Combine 2 teaspoons garlic, lamb, and next 7 ingredients in a bowl. Stuff lamb mixture evenly into squash to within ¼ inch of opening. Place squash horizontally, slightly overlapping, in a 5-quart electric slow cooker coated with cooking spray.

3. Combine remaining 2 teaspoons garlic, onion, and next 3 ingredients; pour over squash. Cover and cook on LOW for 6 hours or until squash is tender and filling is done. Serve squash with sauce; sprinkle with additional mint, if desired.

CALORIES 347; FAT 14.7g (sat 5.9g, mono 5.5g, poly 1.4g); PROTEIN 15.8g; CARB 38.4g; FIBER 5.7g; CHOL 41mg; IRON 3.5mg; SODIUM 507mg; CALC 137mg

Pork and Slaw Sandwiches

Yield: 15 servings (serving size: 1 sandwich)

1 (3-pound) boneless pork loin roast, trimmed

1 cup water

1¾ cups barbecue sauce

2 tablespoons brown sugar

1½ tablespoons hot sauce

½ teaspoon freshly ground black pepper

2½ cups packaged cabbage-and-carrot coleslaw

¼ cup canola mayonnaise

1 tablespoon white vinegar

¼ teaspoon sugar

⅛ teaspoon salt

15 (2-ounce) hamburger buns

1. Place pork and 1 cup water in a 3- to 4-quart electric slow cooker. Cover and cook on LOW for 7 hours or until meat is tender.

2. Drain pork, discarding cooking liquid. Return pork to slow cooker; shred with 2 forks. Stir in barbecue sauce and next 3 ingredients (through pepper). Cover and cook on LOW for 1 hour.

3. Combine coleslaw and next 4 ingredients in a bowl; toss well. Place about ⅓ cup pork mixture and about 2 tablespoons slaw on bottom half of each bun; cover with bun tops.

CALORIES 330; FAT 8.7g (sat 2.1g, mono 3.8g, poly 2.1g); PROTEIN 23.4g; CARB 38.1g; FIBER 1.3g; CHOL 59mg; IRON 2.3mg; SODIUM 565mg; CALC 78mg

QUICK TIP

Using packaged cabbage-and-carrot coleslaw shaves time off the prep. Long gone are the days when you'd have to shred your own.

Indian Lamb Curry

A combo of tomato juice and flour creates a thick sauce. Serve with a piece of naan to sop up any extra.

Yield: 8 servings (serving size: ½ cup rice, ⅔ cup lamb curry, 1 tablespoon yogurt, and 1 tablespoon cilantro)

2 pounds boneless leg of lamb, trimmed and cut into 1-inch cubes

1 (14.5-ounce) can diced tomatoes, undrained

2 tablespoons all-purpose flour

2 cups finely chopped white onion

2 tablespoons grated peeled fresh ginger

2 teaspoons mustard seeds

2 teaspoons garam masala

2 teaspoons ground cumin

½ teaspoon salt

¼ teaspoon ground red pepper

4 garlic cloves, minced

4 cups hot cooked basmati rice

½ cup plain fat-free yogurt

½ cup chopped fresh cilantro

1. Heat a large nonstick skillet over medium-high heat. Add lamb; sauté 5 minutes or until browned. Remove lamb from pan; place in a 4-quart electric slow cooker.

2. Drain tomatoes, reserving juice. Place flour in a small bowl; gradually add tomato juice, stirring with a whisk until smooth. Stir tomatoes, tomato juice mixture, onion, and next 7 ingredients into lamb. Cover and cook on LOW for 8 hours or until lamb is tender. Serve lamb curry over rice; top with yogurt, and sprinkle with cilantro.

CALORIES 302; FAT 6.4g (sat 2.1g, mono 2.3g, poly 0.6g); PROTEIN 27.5g; CARB 32g; FIBER 1.4g; CHOL 75mg; IRON 3.8mg; SODIUM 372mg; CALC 72mg

Tarragon Lamb Shanks with Cannellini Beans

Yield: 12 servings (serving size: about 3 ounces lamb and ⅔ cup bean mixture)

4 (1½-pound) lamb shanks

1 (19-ounce) can cannellini beans or other white beans, rinsed and drained

1½ cups diced peeled carrot

1 cup chopped onion

¾ cup chopped celery

2 garlic cloves, thinly sliced

2 teaspoons dried tarragon

½ teaspoon salt

¼ teaspoon freshly ground black pepper

1 (28-ounce) can diced tomatoes, undrained

1. Trim fat from lamb shanks. Place beans and next 4 ingredients in a 7-quart electric slow cooker; stir well. Place lamb shanks on bean mixture; sprinkle with tarragon, salt, and pepper. Pour tomatoes over lamb. Cover and cook on LOW for 11 hours or until lamb is very tender.

2. Remove lamb shanks from slow cooker. Pour bean mixture through a colander or sieve over a bowl, reserving liquid. Let liquid stand 5 minutes; skim fat from surface of liquid. Return bean mixture to liquid. Remove lamb from bones; discard bones. Serve lamb with bean mixture.

CALORIES 353; FAT 10.3g (sat 3.7g, mono 4.1g, poly 1g); PROTEIN 50.3g; CARB 12.9g; FIBER 2.9g; CHOL 145mg; IRON 4.9mg; SODIUM 554mg; CALC 80mg

Veal Paprikash

Yield: 7 servings (serving size: ¾ cup veal mixture, ¾ cup noodles, ½ teaspoon parsley, and 1 teaspoon chives)

1 (2¼-pound) lean boneless veal tip round roast, trimmed and cut into 1-inch cubes

1 (8-ounce) package presliced fresh mushrooms

1½ cups sliced carrot

1 cup slivered onion

2 tablespoons chopped fresh parsley

4 garlic cloves, minced

2 bay leaves

2.25 ounces all-purpose flour (about ½ cup)

1 tablespoon Hungarian sweet paprika

¾ teaspoon salt

½ teaspoon dried thyme

½ teaspoon freshly ground black pepper

¼ cup dry white wine

½ cup reduced-fat sour cream

5¼ cups hot cooked medium egg noodles (about 10 ounces uncooked pasta)

3½ teaspoons chopped fresh parsley

7 teaspoons chopped fresh chives

1. Place first 7 ingredients in a 3½-quart electric slow cooker; toss well. Combine flour and next 4 ingredients (through pepper) in a small bowl; gradually add wine, stirring until well blended. Add flour mixture to slow cooker; stir well. Cover and cook on LOW for 6 hours or until veal and vegetables are tender. Discard bay leaves.
2. Turn slow cooker off, and let mixture stand 5 minutes. Stir in sour cream. Serve veal mixture over egg noodles; sprinkle with parsley and chives.

CALORIES 410; FAT 7.2g (sat 2.9g, mono 1.9g, poly 1g); PROTEIN 40.3g; CARB 43.7g; FIBER 3.3g; CHOL 170mg; IRON 3.4mg; SODIUM 390mg; CALC 75mg

INGREDIENT TIP

When storing a bunch of fresh herbs, such as chives or parsley, wrap the stems in a damp paper towel, and store them in a  *zip-top plastic bag in the refrigerator. Wash herbs just before using; pat them dry with a paper towel.*

Sweet and Sour Chicken

Substitute pork tenderloin in place of chicken thighs, if desired.

Yield: 6 servings (serving size: ⅔ cup chicken mixture and ½ cup rice)

1 cup chopped onion (about 1 medium)

⅓ cup sugar

⅓ cup ketchup

¼ cup orange juice

3 tablespoons cornstarch

3 tablespoons cider vinegar

2 tablespoons lower-sodium soy sauce

1 tablespoon grated peeled fresh ginger

1 pound skinless, boneless chicken thighs, cut into 1-inch pieces

2 (8-ounce) cans pineapple chunks in juice, drained

1 large green bell pepper, cut into ¾-inch pieces

1 large red bell pepper, cut into ¾-inch pieces

3 cups hot cooked white rice

1. Combine first 12 ingredients in an electric slow cooker. Cover and cook on LOW for 6 hours or HIGH for 4 hours. Serve over rice.

CALORIES 332; FAT 3.4g (sat 0.9g, mono 1g, poly 0.9g); PROTEIN 18.4g; CARB 57g; FIBER 1.8g; CHOL 63mg; IRON 2.3mg; SODIUM 348mg; CALC 38mg

Turkey Thighs with Olives and Dried Cherries

Turkey thighs are easy to find, but you also can use a cut-up chicken, if you prefer. This dish is great served with couscous.

Yield: 8 servings (serving size: 3 ounces turkey and about ⅓ cup cooking liquid)

1 cup thinly sliced leek (about 1 large)

1 cup ruby port or other sweet red wine

¾ cup dried cherries

¾ cup pitted kalamata olives

⅓ cup fresh orange juice (about 1 orange)

1 teaspoon paprika

1 teaspoon crushed red pepper

4 thyme sprigs

1 (3-inch) cinnamon stick

3½ pounds turkey thighs, skinned

¼ teaspoon salt

1 tablespoon ground cumin

1. Combine first 9 ingredients in an electric slow cooker, stirring well.

2. Rinse turkey with cold water; pat dry. Sprinkle with salt and cumin. Place in slow cooker. Cover and cook on LOW for 6 hours. Discard thyme sprigs and cinnamon stick. Serve turkey with cooking liquid.

CALORIES 335; FAT 10.5g (sat 2.4g, mono 4.9g, poly 2.2g); PROTEIN 29g; CARB 17.8g; FIBER 2.8g; CHOL 121mg; IRON 5mg; SODIUM 388mg; CALC 56mg

NUTRITION TIP

Turkey skin contains plenty of fat; removing it reduces the fat by about one-third. The skin is easy to remove from thighs.

Mediterranean Roast Turkey

Serve this slow-cooker roast with mashed potatoes and garnish with fresh thyme sprigs, if desired.

Yield: 8 servings (serving size: about 4 ounces turkey and about ⅓ cup onion mixture)

2 cups chopped onion (about 1 large)

½ cup pitted kalamata olives

½ cup julienne-cut drained oil-packed sun-dried tomato halves

2 tablespoons fresh lemon juice

1½ teaspoons minced garlic

1 teaspoon Greek seasoning mix

½ teaspoon salt

¼ teaspoon freshly ground black pepper

1 (4-pound) boneless turkey breast, trimmed

½ cup fat-free, lower-sodium chicken broth, divided

3 tablespoons all-purpose flour

1. Combine first 9 ingredients in an electric slow cooker. Add ¼ cup chicken broth. Cover and cook on LOW for 7 hours.

2. Combine remaining ¼ cup broth and flour in a small bowl; stir with a whisk until smooth. Add broth mixture to slow cooker. Cover and cook on LOW for 30 minutes. Cut turkey into slices. Serve with onion mixture.

CALORIES 314; FAT 4.9g (sat 0.9g, mono 2.6g, poly 0.8g); PROTEIN 57g; CARB 7g; FIBER 0.9g; CHOL 141mg; IRON 3.1mg; SODIUM 468mg; CALC 34mg

Orange-Rosemary Chicken

While this recipe cooks, the aroma of oranges will make your mouth water. The chicken comes out supermoist and juicy.

Yield: 4 servings (serving size: 1 chicken breast half, or 1 chicken thigh and 1 chicken drumstick)

1 large orange

2 tablespoons butter, softened

2 teaspoons chopped fresh rosemary

½ teaspoon kosher salt

½ teaspoon freshly ground black pepper

2 garlic cloves, minced

1 (3½-pound) roasting chicken

Cooking spray

1. Grate rind from half of orange to measure 2 teaspoons. Cut orange half into quarters. Combine orange rind, butter, and next 4 ingredients in a small bowl. (Reserve remaining orange half for another use.)

2. Remove and discard giblets and neck from chicken. Trim excess fat. Starting at neck cavity, loosen skin from breast and drumsticks by inserting fingers, gently pushing between skin and meat. Rub half of butter mixture under loosened skin. Rub remaining butter mixture over surface of chicken. Lift wing tips up and over back; tuck under chicken. Place orange pieces in cavity.

3. Place chicken, breast side up, on a small rack coated with cooking spray. Place rack inside a 5-quart electric slow cooker.

4. Cover and cook on LOW for 4 hours or until a thermometer inserted into meaty part of thigh registers 165°.

5. Remove chicken from slow cooker. Let stand 15 minutes. Discard skin.

CALORIES 296; FAT 11.3g (sat 5g, mono 3.2g, poly 1.6g); PROTEIN 41.7g; CARB 5.1g; FIBER 0.9g; CHOL 147mg; IRON 2.2mg; SODIUM 433mg; CALC 42mg

Chicken Korma

If you prefer milder foods, reduce or omit the crushed red pepper. Add warm naan on the side of this classic Indian dish.

Yield: 8 servings (serving size: about 1 cup chicken mixture, ½ cup rice, and 1½ teaspoons cilantro)

2 pounds skinless, boneless chicken thighs, cut into bite-sized pieces

2 cups coarsely chopped onion (1 onion)

2 tablespoons minced peeled fresh ginger

2 teaspoons curry powder

1 teaspoon ground coriander

½ teaspoon ground cumin

½ teaspoon crushed red pepper

4 garlic cloves, minced

2 cups (½-inch) cubed peeled baking potato

1 teaspoon salt

1 (14.5-ounce) can petite diced tomatoes, undrained

2 bay leaves

1 (3-inch) cinnamon stick

½ cup plain fat-free yogurt

4 cups hot cooked long-grain brown rice

¼ cup chopped fresh cilantro

1. Heat a large nonstick skillet over medium-high heat. Add chicken; sauté 8 minutes or until lightly browned. Remove chicken from pan; place in a 5-quart electric slow cooker. Add onion to pan; sauté 3 minutes. Add ginger and next 5 ingredients; sauté 2 minutes. Pour mixture over chicken in slow cooker. Stir in potato and next 4 ingredients.

2. Cover and cook on LOW for 6 hours. Discard bay leaves and cinnamon stick. Turn slow cooker off; let stand 15 minutes. Stir in yogurt. Serve chicken mixture over rice. Sprinkle with cilantro.

CALORIES 297; FAT 5.6g (sat 1.4g, mono 1.7g, poly 1.5g); PROTEIN 26.7g; CARB 34.1g; FIBER 3.7g; CHOL 94mg; IRON 4.1mg; SODIUM 507mg; CALC 63mg

Garlic Chicken

The garlic becomes creamy and mellows as it cooks. Spread it on chunks of crusty French baguette and soak up the fabulous sauce as you enjoy every morsel of this supertender chicken. If you're tight on time, substitute 3 pounds of chicken pieces rather than cut up the whole chicken. Also, look for garlic cloves that are already peeled.

Yield: 5 servings (serving size: 4 ounces chicken, about 3 tablespoons sauce, and about 8 garlic cloves)

½ cup fat-free, lower-sodium chicken broth

3 tablespoons dry white wine

2 tablespoons cognac

1 (3⅓-pound) whole chicken, skinned and cut into 8 pieces

1½ teaspoons extra-virgin olive oil

1½ teaspoons butter

¼ teaspoon salt

⅛ teaspoon freshly ground black pepper

40 garlic cloves, peeled (about 4 whole heads)

2 teaspoons fresh thyme leaves

4 teaspoons chopped fresh parsley (optional)

1. Combine first 3 ingredients in a small bowl.

2. Discard giblets and neck from chicken. Rinse chicken and pat dry. Heat oil and butter in a 12-inch nonstick skillet over medium-high heat until butter melts. Sprinkle chicken pieces evenly with salt and pepper. Add chicken pieces to pan; cook 2½ minutes on each side or until golden. Remove chicken from pan; place in a 4-quart electric slow cooker.

3. Reduce heat to medium. Add garlic to drippings in pan; sauté 1 minute or until garlic begins to brown. Stir in broth mixture, scraping pan to loosen browned bits. Boil 2 minutes or until sauce is reduced to about 1 cup. Pour sauce over chicken; sprinkle with thyme. Cover and cook on LOW for 4 hours or until chicken is done. Serve sauce with chicken. Garnish with chopped parsley, if desired.

CALORIES 254; FAT 7.1g (sat 2.1g, mono 2.7g, poly 1.3g); PROTEIN 32.9g; CARB 8.3g; FIBER 0.6g; CHOL 105mg; IRON 1.7mg; SODIUM 297mg; CALC 63mg

Mediterranean Chicken

Capturing the simplicity found in sun-drenched Mediterranean cuisine, these braised chicken thighs melt under the influence of bright, vibrant lemon, briny olives and capers, and juicy plum tomatoes. Serve with rosemary mashed potatoes or over hot basmati rice.

Yield: 6 servings (serving size: 2 chicken thighs and ½ cup sauce)

1 small lemon

1¾ cups coarsely chopped onion

¼ cup pitted kalamata olives, halved (12 olives)

2 tablespoons drained capers

1 (14.5-ounce) can whole plum tomatoes, drained and coarsely chopped

12 bone-in chicken thighs (about 3 pounds), skinned

¼ teaspoon freshly ground black pepper

1 tablespoon olive oil

Chopped fresh rosemary (optional)

Chopped fresh parsley (optional)

1. Grate rind and squeeze juice from lemon to measure 1 teaspoon and 1 tablespoon, respectively. Place lemon rind in a small bowl. Cover and refrigerate. Combine lemon juice, onion, and next 3 ingredients in a 5-quart electric slow cooker.
2. Sprinkle chicken with pepper. Heat a large nonstick skillet over medium-high heat. Add oil to pan; swirl to coat. Place half of chicken in pan; cook 3 minutes on each side or until browned. Place chicken in slow cooker. Repeat procedure with remaining chicken. Cover and cook on LOW for 4 hours or until chicken is done.
3. Place chicken thighs on plates. Stir reserved lemon rind into sauce. Serve sauce over chicken. Garnish with rosemary and parsley, if desired.

CALORIES 220; FAT 8.9g (sat 1.8g, mono 4.4g, poly 1.7g); PROTEIN 26.5g; CARB 7.2g; FIBER 1.4g; CHOL 107mg; IRON 1.8mg; SODIUM 387mg; CALC 35mg

FLAVOR TIP

Piquant, sharp, and tangy are just a few words to describe capers. Use capers sparingly to infuse sauces, salads, pizzas, dressings, and pasta or vegetable dishes with flavor.

Sweet and Spicy Satsuma Turkey

Fresh mandarin oranges, riesling, and orange marmalade provide the highlights for the sweet profile, while crushed red pepper adds the spicy kick to this Asian-inspired turkey dish. Serve with hot steamed rice as an accompaniment to soak up the delicious sauce.

Yield: 8 servings (serving size: 5 ounces turkey and ½ cup sauce)

3 cups thinly sliced red onion (1 large onion)

¾ cup riesling or other slightly sweet white wine

⅔ cup fresh orange juice (2 large oranges)

⅓ cup orange marmalade

2 teaspoons tamarind paste

½ teaspoon crushed red pepper

3¾ pounds bone-in turkey thighs, skinned

2 teaspoons five-spice powder

1 teaspoon salt

1 tablespoon canola oil

2 cups fresh Satsuma mandarin orange sections (about 7 oranges)

1½ tablespoons cornstarch

Sliced green onions (optional)

1. Combine first 6 ingredients in a 5-quart oval electric slow cooker.
2. Rinse turkey with cold water; pat dry. Sprinkle turkey with five-spice powder and salt. Heat a large nonstick skillet over medium-high heat. Add oil to pan; swirl to coat. Add turkey; cook 3 to 4 minutes on each side or until browned. Place turkey in a single layer over onion mixture in slow cooker, overlapping slightly. Add orange sections. Cover and cook on LOW for 4 hours.
3. Remove turkey from slow cooker. Remove bones from turkey; discard bones. Shred turkey and place on a platter. Pour cooking liquid and orange sections into a medium saucepan, reserving ¼ cup cooking liquid. Combine reserved cooking liquid and cornstarch in a small bowl, stirring with a whisk until smooth. Stir cornstarch mixture into orange mixture in saucepan. Bring to a boil; cook, stirring constantly, 1 minute or until sauce thickens.
4. Serve sauce over turkey. Sprinkle with green onions, if desired.

CALORIES 277; FAT 5.7g (sat 1.4g, mono 2g, poly 1.6g); PROTEIN 28.6g; CARB 24.7g; FIBER 1.8g; CHOL 109mg; IRON 2.8mg; SODIUM 398mg; CALC 59mg

Braised Turkey and Asian Vegetables

Five-spice powder–dusted turkey thighs become tender and moist from slow cooking atop a medley of Asian vegetables. Wheat-flour udon noodles would be a perfect complement to the flavorful broth.

Yield: 8 servings (serving size: 5 ounces turkey, ¾ cup vegetable-broth mixture, and 1 tablespoon green onions)

2 (3½-ounce) packages shiitake mushrooms

1 cup thinly sliced red bell pepper

5 baby bok choy, quartered lengthwise

1 (15-ounce) can precut baby corn, drained

1 (8-ounce) can sliced bamboo shoots, drained

2 tablespoons hoisin sauce

2 tablespoons oyster sauce

1 tablespoon lower-sodium soy sauce

2 teaspoons grated peeled fresh ginger

2 teaspoons dark sesame oil

3 garlic cloves, minced

1 tablespoon canola oil

4 bone-in turkey thighs (about 4 pounds), skinned

1 teaspoon five-spice powder

½ teaspoon freshly ground black pepper

2 cups thinly sliced napa (Chinese) cabbage

½ cup chopped green onions

1. Remove stems from mushrooms; slice mushrooms. Place mushrooms, bell pepper, and next 3 ingredients in a 7-quart electric slow cooker. Combine hoisin sauce and next 5 ingredients in a small bowl. Stir into vegetable mixture in slow cooker.

2. Heat a large nonstick skillet over medium-high heat. Add canola oil to pan; swirl to coat. Sprinkle turkey thighs evenly with five-spice powder and black pepper. Add half of turkey to pan. Cook 3 minutes on each side or until browned. Add turkey to slow cooker. Repeat procedure with remaining turkey. Cover and cook on LOW for 5 hours or until turkey is tender.

3. Remove turkey from bones; cut meat into bite-sized pieces. Discard bones. Stir cabbage into vegetable mixture. Serve vegetables and broth in individual bowls. Top with turkey; sprinkle evenly with green onions.

CALORIES 249; FAT 7.4g (sat 1.7g, mono 2.5g, poly 2.3g); PROTEIN 32.6g; CARB 11.3g; FIBER 2.6g; CHOL 116mg; IRON 3.7mg; SODIUM 466mg; CALC 143mg

Chicken Verde

Make your friends "green" with envy at your slow-cooker savvy by serving up this savory Southwestern-style entrée, loaded with tomatillos, onion, and roasted poblano and jalapeño peppers. Corn tortillas and a simple green salad round out the menu.

Yield: 6 servings (serving size: 1 chicken breast half, ¾ cup sauce, and about 1 tablespoon cilantro)

5 poblano chiles (about ¾ pound)

4 jalapeño peppers (about 4½ ounces)

5½ cups chopped tomatillos (about 1¾ pounds; about 16 small)

2 cups chopped onion (1 large)

1 tablespoon sugar

5 garlic cloves, minced

1 (4.5-ounce) can chopped green chiles, undrained

6 (8-ounce) bone-in chicken breast halves, skinned

1½ teaspoons ground cumin

½ teaspoon freshly ground black pepper

1 tablespoon canola oil

¼ cup chopped fresh cilantro

⅓ cup reduced-fat sour cream (optional)

1. Preheat broiler.

2. Place poblano chiles and jalapeño peppers on a foil-lined baking sheet. Broil 10 minutes or until blackened and charred, turning occasionally. Place peppers in a paper bag; fold to close tightly. Let stand 15 minutes. Peel chiles and peppers; cut in half lengthwise. Discard seeds and membranes. Chop poblano chiles. Finely chop jalapeño peppers.

3. Combine poblano chiles, jalapeño peppers, tomatillos, and next 4 ingredients in a large bowl.

4. Sprinkle chicken with cumin and pepper. Heat a large nonstick skillet over medium-high heat. Add oil to pan; swirl to coat. Add half of chicken to pan. Cook 2½ minutes on each side or until browned. Place chicken in a 6-quart electric slow cooker. Repeat procedure with remaining chicken. Pour tomatillo mixture over chicken. Cover and cook on LOW for 3½ hours or until chicken is tender.

5. Remove chicken from slow cooker; keep warm. Pour sauce into a medium saucepan. Bring to a boil; reduce heat, and simmer, uncovered, 25 minutes or until reduced to 4½ cups.

6. Serve chicken with sauce. Sprinkle with chopped cilantro. Garnish with sour cream, if desired.

CALORIES 282; FAT 6g (sat 0.9g, mono 2.1g, poly 1.7g); PROTEIN 37.1g; CARB 20.6g; FIBER 5g; CHOL 86mg; IRON 2.4mg; SODIUM 168mg; CALC 55mg

Chicken Cacciatore

The Italian word cacciatore translates to "hunter" in English, referring to a dish prepared with tomatoes, mushrooms, and onions—"hunter-style."

Yield: 8 servings (serving size: 1 thigh and 1 drumstick, about 1 cup vegetable mixture, and ½ cup pasta)

8 bone-in chicken thighs
(2¼ pounds), skinned

8 bone-in chicken drumsticks
(1¾ pounds), skinned

½ teaspoon salt, divided

½ teaspoon freshly ground black pepper

1 tablespoon olive oil

Cooking spray

1 (8-ounce) package mushrooms, quartered

2 tablespoons minced garlic

1 large onion, sliced

1 green bell pepper, vertically sliced

1 red bell pepper, vertically sliced

½ cup dry white wine

1.5 ounces all-purpose flour (about ⅓ cup)

2 tablespoons chopped fresh oregano

2 tablespoons chopped fresh thyme

1 (28-ounce) can whole plum tomatoes, undrained and chopped

4 cups hot cooked fettuccine

Chopped fresh thyme (optional)

1. Sprinkle chicken with ¼ teaspoon salt and pepper. Heat a large nonstick skillet over medium-high heat. Add oil to pan; swirl to coat. Add half of chicken to pan; cook 5 minutes on each side or until lightly browned. Place chicken in a 5-quart electric slow cooker coated with cooking spray. Repeat procedure with remaining chicken. Place mushrooms on top of chicken.

2. Add garlic, onion, and bell peppers to pan; sprinkle vegetables with remaining ¼ teaspoon salt. Reduce heat to medium, and cook 5 minutes or until vegetables are crisp-tender, stirring often. Add wine, scraping pan to loosen brown bits. Cook 1 minute. Stir in flour. Stir in oregano, thyme, and tomatoes.

3. Pour tomato mixture over mushrooms in slow cooker. Cover and cook on LOW for 3 hours or until chicken is very tender. Serve over fettuccine. Sprinkle with additional thyme, if desired.

CALORIES 361; FAT 7.6g (sat 1.7g, mono 2.9g, poly 1.7g); PROTEIN 32.5g; CARB 35.6g; FIBER 3.4g; CHOL 106mg; IRON 3.5mg; SODIUM 476mg; CALC 59mg

Pulled Chicken Sandwiches

Yield: 8 servings (serving size: 1 sandwich)

3 cups thinly sliced onion

1 teaspoon canola oil

1¾ pounds skinless, boneless chicken breast halves

1 cup ketchup

2 tablespoons cider vinegar

2 tablespoons molasses

1 tablespoon Dijon mustard

1 teaspoon onion powder

1 teaspoon ground cumin

½ teaspoon garlic powder

½ teaspoon hot sauce

8 (1.2-ounce) whole-wheat hamburger buns, toasted

1. Place onion in a 4-quart oval electric slow cooker. Heat a large nonstick skillet over medium-high heat. Add oil to pan; swirl to coat. Add half of chicken, and cook 3 to 4 minutes on each side or until golden brown. Place chicken in a single layer on top of onion. Repeat procedure with remaining chicken.

2. Combine ketchup and next 7 ingredients; pour over chicken. Cover and cook on LOW for 4 hours until chicken is tender and sauce is thick.

3. Remove chicken from slow cooker. Shred chicken with 2 forks, and stir into sauce. Spoon ¾ cup chicken mixture onto bottom of each bun; cover with bun tops.

CALORIES 271; FAT 3.6g (sat 0.7g, mono 1.1g, poly 1.2g); PROTEIN 27g; CARB 33.6g; FIBER 3.6g; CHOL 58mg; IRON 2.1mg; SODIUM 613mg; CALC 76mg

Provençale Chicken Supper

Use bone-in chicken breasts for this French-country dish.

Yield: 4 servings (serving size: 1 chicken breast half and 1 cup bean mixture)

4 (6-ounce) chicken breast halves, skinned

2 teaspoons dried basil

⅛ teaspoon salt

⅛ teaspoon freshly ground black pepper

1 cup diced yellow bell pepper

1 (15.5-ounce) can cannellini beans or other white beans, rinsed and drained

1 (14.5-ounce) can diced tomatoes with basil, garlic, and oregano, undrained

Basil sprigs (optional)

1. Place chicken in an electric slow cooker; sprinkle with basil, salt, and black pepper. Add bell pepper, beans, and tomatoes. Cover and cook on LOW for 8 hours. Garnish with basil sprigs, if desired.

CALORIES 281; FAT 2.2g (sat 0.6g, mono 0.5g, poly 0.5g); PROTEIN 44.9g; CARB 18.1g; FIBER 4.7g; CHOL 99mg; IRON 3.2mg; SODIUM 495mg; CALC 86mg

SUBSTITUTION TIP

The flavor of fresh herbs is generally better than dried, but we've used dried basil here for convenience. If you prefer fresh, use 2 tablespoons instead and stir it in at the end.

Lemon-Rosemary Chicken

Five ingredients and 10 minutes is all it takes to prep this citrusy chicken for dinner.

Yield: 4 servings (serving size: ¼ of chicken)

2 tablespoons butter, softened

2 tablespoons chopped fresh rosemary

2 garlic cloves, minced

¼ teaspoon salt

¼ teaspoon freshly ground black pepper

1 (4-pound) whole chicken

1 lemon, cut in half crosswise

1. Combine first 5 ingredients in a small bowl.

2. Remove and discard giblets and neck from chicken. Trim excess fat. Starting at neck cavity, loosen skin from breast and drumsticks by inserting fingers, gently pushing between skin and meat. Rub butter mixture under loosened skin and rub over breast and drumsticks. Lift wing tips up and over back; tuck under chicken. Place lemon halves inside cavity.

3. Place chicken, breast side up, on a small rack. Place rack inside slow cooker. Cover and cook on HIGH for 3 hours or until a thermometer inserted into thigh registers 165°.

CALORIES 315; FAT 12.1g (sat 5.2g, mono 3.4g, poly 1.8g); PROTEIN 47.2g; CARB 2.1g; FIBER 0.7g; CHOL 166mg; IRON 2.5mg; SODIUM 362mg; CALC 36mg

FLAVOR TIP

Rosemary is one of the most aromatic and pungent of all herbs. Its needlelike leaves have a pronounced lemon-pine flavor.

Sweet Glazed Chicken Thighs

Yield: 6 servings (serving size: ½ cup rice, 1 chicken thigh, about ⅓ cup sauce, and 1½ teaspoons green onions)

2 pounds skinless, boneless chicken thighs

½ teaspoon freshly ground black pepper

¼ teaspoon salt

1 teaspoon olive oil

Cooking spray

1 cup pineapple juice

2 tablespoons light brown sugar

2 tablespoons lower-sodium soy sauce

3 tablespoons water

2 tablespoons cornstarch

3 cups hot cooked rice

3 tablespoons sliced green onions

1. Sprinkle chicken with pepper and salt. Heat a large nonstick skillet over medium-high heat. Add oil to pan; swirl to coat. Add chicken to pan. Cook 2 to 3 minutes on each side or until browned. Transfer chicken to a 4-quart electric slow cooker coated with cooking spray. Stir pineapple juice into drippings, scraping pan to loosen browned bits. Remove from heat; stir in brown sugar and soy sauce. Pour juice mixture over chicken. Cover and cook on LOW for 2½ hours.

2. Transfer chicken to a serving platter with a slotted spoon. Increase heat to HIGH. Combine 3 tablespoons water and cornstarch in a small bowl; add to sauce in slow cooker, stirring with a whisk. Cook 2 minutes or until sauce thickens, stirring constantly with whisk.

3. Place rice on each of 6 plates. Top with chicken thighs and sauce. Sprinkle each serving with green onions.

CALORIES 339; FAT 7.1g (sat 1.7g, mono 2.5g, poly 1.6g); PROTEIN 32.4g; CARB 33.7g; FIBER 0.6g; CHOL 125mg; IRON 2.8mg; SODIUM 363mg; CALC 35mg

Cuban Beans and Rice

Dried beans are inexpensive and a convenient choice for economical meals. They also lend themselves well to slow cooking because, unlike on the cooktop, there is no risk of burning during the long simmering period. This meatless entrée reheats well the next day for lunch. Store leftover bean mixture and rice in separate containers in the refrigerator.

Yield: 10 servings (serving size: 1 cup bean mixture and ½ cup rice)

1 pound dried black beans

2 cups water

2 cups organic vegetable broth

2 cups chopped onion

1½ cups chopped red bell pepper

1 cup chopped green bell pepper

2 tablespoons olive oil

1½ teaspoons salt

2 teaspoons fennel seeds, crushed

2 teaspoons ground coriander

2 teaspoons ground cumin

2 teaspoons dried oregano

2 tablespoons sherry or red wine vinegar

2 (10-ounce) cans diced tomatoes and green chiles, drained

5 cups hot cooked rice

Hot sauce (optional)

1. Sort and wash beans; place in a large bowl. Cover with water to 2 inches above beans; cover and let stand 8 hours. Drain beans.

2. Place beans, 2 cups water, and next 10 ingredients in an electric slow cooker; stir well. Cover and cook on HIGH for 5 hours or until beans are tender. Stir in vinegar and tomatoes. Serve over rice. Sprinkle with hot sauce, if desired.

CALORIES 314; FAT 3.3g (sat 0.5g, mono 2.1g, poly 0.4g); PROTEIN 12g; CARB 57.2g; FIBER 6.2g; CHOL 0mg; IRON 3.8mg; SODIUM 584mg; CALC 33mg

Old-Fashioned Chicken Fricassee

A classic stew with chicken breasts and vegetables simmering in white wine is sure to bring comfort to your table.

Yield: 4 servings (serving size: 1 chicken breast half, ⅔ cup sauce, and 1 tablespoon parsley)

3 tablespoons all-purpose flour

1 teaspoon paprika

1 teaspoon poultry seasoning

½ teaspoon salt

½ teaspoon freshly ground black pepper

4 (6-ounce) chicken breast halves, skinned

2 teaspoons butter

2 cups sliced carrot

1½ cups chopped onion

½ cup chopped celery

3 garlic cloves, minced

1 cup fat-free, lower-sodium chicken broth

¼ cup dry white wine

¼ cup chopped fresh parsley

1. Combine first 5 ingredients in a large heavy-duty zip-top plastic bag. Add chicken; seal bag, and toss to coat. Remove chicken from bag, shaking off excess flour. Reserve flour mixture.

2. Melt butter in a large nonstick skillet over medium-high heat until it melts. Add chicken, skinned side down; cook 5 minutes or until chicken is browned, turning after 3 minutes. Remove chicken from pan. Place chicken in a 4-quart oval electric slow cooker.

3. Add carrot, onion, celery, and garlic to slow cooker. Combine reserved flour mixture, broth, and wine in a medium bowl, stirring with a whisk until blended. Add to slow cooker. Cover and cook on LOW for 3 hours or until chicken is tender. Serve chicken with sauce, and sprinkle with parsley.

CALORIES 262; FAT 4g (sat 1.7g, mono 0.9g, poly 0.6g); PROTEIN 34.5g; CARB 18.5g; FIBER 3.5g; CHOL 84mg; IRON 2.2mg; SODIUM 595mg; CALC 70mg

Saucy Chicken over Rice

Yield: 6 servings (serving size: ½ cup rice, 1 drumstick, 1 thigh, and about ½ cup sauce)

6 skinned chicken thighs (about 2 pounds)

6 skinned chicken drumsticks (about 1¾ pounds)

1 teaspoon canola oil

⅓ cup finely chopped onion

2 garlic cloves, minced

⅓ cup dry white wine

1 (14½-ounce) can stewed tomatoes, undrained and chopped

½ teaspoon dried Italian seasoning

½ teaspoon salt-free lemon-herb seasoning

¼ teaspoon salt

¼ teaspoon dried tarragon

¼ teaspoon crushed red pepper

3 cups hot cooked rice

1. Trim fat from chicken. Heat a large nonstick skillet over medium-high heat. Add oil to pan; swirl to coat. Add half of chicken; cook 5 to 7 minutes or until browned, turning occasionally. Place chicken in a 5-quart electric slow cooker. Repeat procedure with remaining chicken.

2. Add onion and garlic to pan; sauté 2 minutes. Add wine, scraping pan to loosen browned bits. Add tomatoes; remove from heat. Stir in Italian seasoning and next 4 ingredients. Pour tomato mixture over chicken in slow cooker. Cover and cook on LOW for 5 hours. Serve chicken and tomato sauce over rice.

CALORIES 405; FAT 8.9g (sat 2.2g, mono 3g, poly 2.3g); PROTEIN 47.1g; CARB 28.3g; FIBER 1.7g; CHOL 173mg; IRON 4.1mg; SODIUM 487mg; CALC 49mg

Chickpeas in Curried Coconut Broth

Yield: 6 servings (serving size: 1⅓ cups chickpea mixture and 1 cup rice)

2 teaspoons canola oil

1½ cups chopped onion

2 garlic cloves, minced

2 (19-ounce) cans chickpeas (garbanzo beans), rinsed and drained

2 (14.5-ounce) cans no-salt-added diced tomatoes, undrained

1 (13.5-ounce) can light coconut milk

1 tablespoon curry powder

2 tablespoons chopped pickled jalapeño pepper

1 teaspoon salt

½ cup chopped fresh cilantro

6 cups hot cooked basmati rice

1. Heat a large nonstick skillet over medium heat. Add oil to pan; swirl to coat. Add onion and garlic; sauté 5 minutes or until onion is tender. Place onion mixture, chickpeas, and next 5 ingredients in a 3½-quart electric slow cooker; stir well. Cover and cook on LOW for 6 to 8 hours. Stir in cilantro. Serve over rice.

CALORIES 369; FAT 4.3g (sat 0.9g, mono 1.4g, poly 1.1g); PROTEIN 10.5g; CARB 71.1g; FIBER 6.4g; CHOL 0mg; IRON 4mg; SODIUM 620mg; CALC 55mg

Hoppin' John

Hoppin' John is said to bring good luck all year when eaten on New Year's Day.

Yield: 6 servings (serving size: 1⅔ cups)

2 (16-ounce) packages frozen black-eyed peas

1¼ cups sliced green onions, divided

2 cups hot water

¾ cup chopped red bell pepper

2 tablespoons minced seeded jalapeño pepper

2 teaspoons hot sauce

¼ teaspoon salt

¼ teaspoon freshly ground black pepper

1 vegetable-flavored or chicken-flavored bouillon cube

1 (14.5-ounce) can diced tomatoes with pepper, celery, and onion, undrained

1 tablespoon tomato paste

⅔ cup uncooked converted rice

1. Place peas, ¾ cup green onions, 2 cups hot water, and next 6 ingredients in a 4-quart electric slow cooker; stir well. Cover and cook on HIGH for 4 hours. Stir in tomatoes, tomato paste, and rice; cover and cook on HIGH for 1 hour or until peas and rice are tender and most of liquid is absorbed. Stir in remaining ½ cup green onions.

CALORIES 349; FAT 1.5g (sat 0.5g, mono 0.3g, poly 0.7g); PROTEIN 17.6g; CARB 67g; FIBER 11.8g; CHOL 0mg; IRON 4.9mg; SODIUM 632mg; CALC 87mg

Spanish Tortilla (*Tortilla de Patatas*)

We recommend using a slow-cooker liner for this recipe and hitting it with some cooking spray before adding the potato mixture. It makes serving and cleanup a cinch.

Yield: 4 servings (serving size: 1 wedge)

2 teaspoons olive oil

2 cups thinly sliced peeled baking potato

1⅓ cups chopped onion

1 cup chopped red bell pepper

Cooking spray

3 large eggs

6 large egg whites

¼ teaspoon salt

½ teaspoon freshly ground black pepper

2 tablespoons grated fresh Parmesan cheese

2 tablespoons chopped fresh parsley

2 tablespoons drained capers

1. Heat a large nonstick skillet over medium-high heat. Add oil to pan; swirl to coat. Add potato, onion, and bell pepper. Cook 8 minutes or until onion is tender and potato just begins to brown, stirring occasionally.

2. Coat a 3-quart electric slow cooker with cooking spray. Place potato mixture in slow cooker. Combine egg, egg whites, salt, and pepper, stirring with a whisk. Pour egg mixture over vegetables in slow cooker. Cover and cook on LOW for 2½ hours or just until egg is set in center.

3. Turn off slow cooker. Let stand, covered, 10 minutes. Sprinkle with cheese, parsley, and capers. Cut into wedges.

CALORIES 200; FAT 7.6g (sat 2.1g, mono 3.5g, poly 0.9g); PROTEIN 15.2g; CARB 28.9g; FIBER 2.7g; CHOL 161mg; IRON 2.3mg; SODIUM 483mg; CALC 109mg

Mediterranean Succotash

Traditional Southern succotash is a combination of lima beans, corn, and tomatoes. In our version, Mediterranean vegetables are the stars.

Yield: 8 servings (serving size: ¾ cup succotash, about ⅔ cup couscous, and 1 tablespoon cheese)

1 cup organic vegetable broth

1 cup chopped zucchini

1 cup chopped red bell pepper

½ cup pitted kalamata olives, halved

2 garlic cloves, minced

2 (15-ounce) cans cannellini beans, rinsed and drained

1 (14.5-ounce) can diced tomatoes, undrained

¼ cup chopped fresh parsley

2 tablespoons balsamic vinegar

2 tablespoons fresh lemon juice

¼ teaspoon freshly ground black pepper

1 (10-ounce) package couscous

2 ounces crumbled feta cheese (about ½ cup)

1. Place first 7 ingredients in a 4-quart electric slow cooker; stir well. Cover and cook on LOW for 4 hours. Stir in parsley and next 3 ingredients.

2. Cook couscous according to package directions, omitting salt and fat. Serve succotash over couscous; sprinkle with cheese.

CALORIES 263; FAT 4.2g (sat 1.4g, mono 2.2g, poly 0.4g); PROTEIN 11g; CARB 45.1g; FIBER 5.8g; CHOL 6mg; IRON 1.9mg; SODIUM 553mg; CALC 117mg

the extras

Hot Mulled Ginger-Spiced Cider

By preparing this cider in an electric slow cooker, you free up the cooktop. However, you can also heat it in a pot on the stove, if you prefer.

Yield: 12 servings (serving size: 1 cup)

3 whole cloves

2 (4 x 1–inch) strips orange rind

2 whole allspice

1 (3-inch) cinnamon stick

1 (½-inch) piece peeled fresh ginger

12 cups apple cider

½ cup apple jelly

¼ teaspoon ground nutmeg

1. Place first 5 ingredients on a 5-inch-square double layer of cheesecloth. Gather edges of cheesecloth together; tie securely.

2. Place cheesecloth bag, cider, jelly, and nutmeg in an electric slow cooker. Cover and cook on HIGH for 4 hours. Remove and discard cheesecloth bag.

3. Ladle cider into mugs.

CALORIES 174; FAT 0g; PROTEIN 1g; CARB 43.8g; FIBER 0g; CHOL 0mg; IRON 0mg; SODIUM 0mg; CALC 0mg

Ginger-Lemon Hot Toddies

Ginger infuses this lemony hot toddy with spiciness—the perfect antidote to chilly winter weather. After you add the alcohol, turn the slow cooker to LOW and allow guests to help themselves.

Yield: 14 servings (serving size: about 1 cup)

8 cups water

2 cups fresh lemon juice (about 14 small lemons)

2 cups honey

5 tablespoons finely chopped crystallized ginger

1 (3-inch) piece peeled fresh ginger, cut into ¼-inch-thick slices

¾ cup golden rum

¾ cup brandy

Lemon rind strips (optional)

1. Place first 5 ingredients in a 4½-quart electric slow cooker. Cover and cook on HIGH for 4 hours. Remove and discard ginger slices.
2. Stir in rum and brandy. Ladle mixture into mugs, and garnish with lemon rind strips, if desired.

CALORIES 226; FAT 0g; PROTEIN 0.5g; CARB 45.6g; FIBER 0.1g; CHOL 0mg; IRON 0.3mg; SODIUM 7mg; CALC 10mg

Mocha Hot Chocolate

Serve this coffee-flavored hot chocolate with a batch of your favorite biscotti.

Yield: 9 servings (serving size: ⅔ cup)

1 (1½-quart) container chocolate light ice cream

3 cups 2% reduced-fat milk

2 tablespoons instant espresso granules

1. Spoon ice cream into a 3-quart electric slow cooker. Add milk and espresso. Cover and cook on LOW for 3 hours or until thoroughly heated.

2. Ladle hot chocolate into mugs.

CALORIES 187; FAT 6.3g (sat 3.7g, mono 1.5g, poly 0.2g); PROTEIN 6.7g; CARB 25.1g; FIBER 1.3g; CHOL 33mg; IRON 0mg; SODIUM 93mg; CALC 175mg

Spiced Caramel Cider

If you'd prefer a beverage with less spice, try substituting apple juice for the apple cider. It's fantastic either way.

Yield: 12 servings (serving size: about 1 cup)

½ cup sugar

3 tablespoons water

1 tablespoon butter

⅓ cup whipping cream

5 whole allspice

5 whole cloves

2 (3-inch) cinnamon sticks

10 cups apple cider

¼ cup fresh orange juice

1 tablespoon fresh lemon juice

Cinnamon sticks (optional)

1. Place sugar and 3 tablespoons water in a small, heavy saucepan over medium-low heat. Cook 3 minutes or until sugar melts, stirring gently. Continue cooking 5 minutes or until golden (do not stir). Remove from heat; let stand 1 minute. Add butter, stirring until melted. Gradually add whipping cream, stirring constantly. Cook over medium heat 1 minute or until caramel sauce is smooth, stirring constantly. Remove from heat.

2. Place allspice, cloves, and cinnamon sticks on a double layer of cheesecloth. Gather edges of cheesecloth together; tie securely. Place in a 4-quart electric slow cooker. Add cider, orange juice, and caramel sauce, stirring until caramel sauce dissolves. Cover and cook on LOW for 3 hours. Remove and discard cheesecloth bag. Stir in lemon juice.

3. Ladle cider into mugs. Garnish with cinnamon sticks, if desired.

CALORIES 180; FAT 3g (sat 1.9g, mono 0.9g, poly 0.1g); PROTEIN 1g; CARB 38.4g; FIBER 0g; CHOL 10mg; IRON 0mg; SODIUM 9mg; CALC 6mg

Berry-Lemonade Tea

Here's a refreshingly fruity mix of tea and lemonade that is delicious hot or cold—depending on the season. You can even spike it!

Yield: 12 servings (serving size: 1 cup tea and 1 lemon slice)

12 regular sized tea bags

8 cups water

5 cups refrigerated natural lemonade

⅓ cup honey

1 (12-ounce) package frozen mixed berries

2 lemons, each cut into 6 slices

1. Remove paper tags from tea bags. Place tea bags, 8 cups water, and next 3 ingredients in a 5-quart electric slow cooker. Cover and cook on LOW for 3 hours.

2. Pour tea through a sieve into a bowl; discard solids. Serve warm or over ice. Garnish with lemon slices.

CALORIES 87; FAT 0.1g; PROTEIN 0.3g; CARB 23.4g; FIBER 0.8g; CHOL 0mg; IRON 0.1mg; SODIUM 6mg; CALC 5mg

Cheesy Spinach-Crab Dip

This cheesy crab dip makes a savory party appetizer with minimal preparation time. Serve warm with pita chips or whole-grain crackers.

Yield: 20 servings (serving size: ¼ cup)

1½ cups lump crabmeat, drained and shell pieces removed

4 ounces shredded 50% reduced-fat jalapeño cheddar cheese, (about 1 cup)

3 ounces grated fresh Parmesan cheese (about ¾ cup)

½ cup fat-free milk

½ cup grated onion (about ½ large onion)

½ cup canola mayonnaise

1 tablespoon sherry vinegar

½ teaspoon ground red pepper

2 garlic cloves, minced

1 (10-ounce) package frozen chopped spinach, thawed, drained, and squeezed dry

1 (8-ounce) tub fat-free cream cheese

1 (8-ounce) carton fat-free sour cream

1 teaspoon grated lemon rind

1. Place first 12 ingredients in a 3-quart electric slow cooker; stir well. Cover and cook on LOW for 2 hours. Stir in lemon rind.

CALORIES 118; FAT 6.9g (sat 1.7g, mono 3.3g, poly 1.4g); PROTEIN 9.6g; CARB 4.1g; FIBER 0.9g; CHOL 26mg; IRON 0.4mg; SODIUM 300mg; CALC 165mg

FLAVOR TIP

For those who like their dips hot and spicy, increase the ground red pepper or add crushed red pepper for an additional kick.

Roasted Garlic–White Bean Dip

This white bean dip gets its flavor from a combination of garlic, rosemary, and kalamata olives and its smooth texture from ricotta cheese. If time allows, pick up a baguette and make your own crostini at home, or just serve with crackers.

Yield: 15 servings (serving size: ¼ cup)

¼ cup olive oil

6 garlic cloves, thinly sliced

2 (15.5-ounce) cans cannellini beans, rinsed and drained

⅓ cup water

1 cup fat-free ricotta cheese

3 ounces grated fresh Parmesan cheese (about ¾ cup)

1 teaspoon chopped fresh rosemary

¼ teaspoon freshly ground black pepper

¼ cup pitted kalamata olives, coarsely chopped

½ teaspoon grated lemon rind

Chopped fresh rosemary (optional)

Freshly ground black pepper (optional)

1. Heat a small saucepan over low heat. Add oil to pan; swirl to coat. Add garlic; cook 5 minutes. Place beans and ⅓ cup water in a food processor. Add garlic mixture, ricotta cheese, and next 3 ingredients; process until smooth.

2. Place bean mixture in a 3-quart electric slow cooker. Cover and cook on LOW for 2 hours.

3. Stir in olives and lemon rind. Garnish with rosemary and pepper, if desired.

CALORIES 129; FAT 6g (sat 1.4g, mono 3.8g, poly 0.5g); PROTEIN 7.5g; CARB 11g; FIBER 2.7g; CHOL 7mg; IRON 0.9mg; SODIUM 249mg; CALC 138mg

Blue Cheese–Artichoke Dip

Blue cheese amps up the flavor for a little twist on the traditional artichoke appetizer. The dip holds up well for about two hours after the cook time. Serve with pita chips or toasted baguette slices.

Yield: 20 servings (serving size: ¼ cup)

1 cup chopped onion

¾ cup chopped red bell pepper

1 garlic clove, minced

4 ounces blue cheese, crumbled (about 1 cup)

¼ teaspoon freshly ground black pepper

2 (14-ounce) cans artichoke hearts, drained and coarsely chopped

1 (8-ounce) block fat-free cream cheese, softened

1 (8-ounce) carton reduced-fat sour cream

1. Heat a medium nonstick skillet over medium-high heat. Add onion and bell pepper; sauté 5 minutes. Add garlic; sauté 1 minute. Remove from heat.

2. Place onion mixture in a 2½-quart electric slow cooker. Add blue cheese and remaining ingredients; stir until blended. Cover and cook on LOW for 2 hours or until cheese melts and mixture is thoroughly heated, stirring occasionally.

CALORIES 76; FAT 3.3g (sat 1.9g, mono 0.7g, poly 0.1g); PROTEIN 4.8g; CARB 7.7g; FIBER 3.7g; CHOL 12mg; IRON 0.3mg; SODIUM 188mg; CALC 99mg

INGREDIENT TIP

If you really love blue cheese, then pull out all the stops and choose Gorgonzola for this dip. Among blues, Gorgonzola is moist, creamy, savory, earthy, and slightly spicier than other blues. However, any blue will do.

Buffalo-Style Drummettes with Blue Cheese Dip

Heating the chicken drummettes in the oven helps to brown them. You can also brown them, in batches, in a skillet on the cooktop.

Yield: 15 servings (serving size: 2 drummettes, about 1 tablespoon dip, 2 carrot sticks, and 2 celery sticks)

Cooking spray

3 pounds chicken wing drummettes, skinned (30 drummettes)

¼ teaspoon freshly ground black pepper

¾ cup thick hot sauce

2 tablespoons cider vinegar

1 teaspoon reduced-sodium Worcestershire sauce

2 garlic cloves, minced

Blue Cheese Dip

30 carrot sticks

30 celery sticks

1. Preheat oven to 450°.

2. Line a jelly-roll pan with foil; coat foil with cooking spray. Place chicken on prepared pan; sprinkle with pepper. Lightly coat chicken with cooking spray. Bake, uncovered, at 450° for 7 minutes or until lightly browned.

3. Combine hot sauce and next 3 ingredients in an oval 4-quart electric slow cooker coated with cooking spray.

4. Remove chicken from pan; drain on paper towels. Place chicken in slow cooker, tossing gently to coat with sauce. Cover and cook on HIGH for 3 hours or until chicken is very tender. Serve with Blue Cheese Dip, carrot sticks, and celery sticks.

CALORIES 95; FAT 4.8g (sat 1.7g, mono 1.6g, poly 0.7g); PROTEIN 7.9g; CARB 4.4g; FIBER 0.5g; CHOL 25mg; IRON 0.4mg; SODIUM 248mg; CALC 42mg

Blue Cheese Dip

Yield: 18 servings (serving size: about 1 tablespoon)

4 ounces ⅓-less-fat cream cheese (about ½ cup)

½ cup fat-free sour cream

2 tablespoons canola mayonnaise

2 garlic cloves, minced

3 tablespoons blue cheese, crumbled and divided

1. Place cream cheese in a medium bowl; beat with a mixer until smooth. Add sour cream, mayonnaise, garlic, and half of blue cheese, beating until smooth.

2. Stir in remaining blue cheese.

CALORIES 38; FAT 3.1g (sat 1.2g, mono 1.1g, poly 0.4g); PROTEIN 1.1g; CARB 1.5g; FIBER 0g; CHOL 6.9mg; IRON 0mg; SODIUM 62mg; CALC 24mg

Lamb Meatballs

Lemon zest adds a nice bright lift to the spicy sauce and complements the Greek-inspired flavors of these meatballs.

Yield: 14 servings (serving size: 2 meatballs and about 2 tablespoons sauce)

¼ cup grated onion, drained

¼ cup dried currants

½ teaspoon ground cumin

¼ teaspoon ground allspice

¼ teaspoon ground cinnamon

¼ teaspoon crushed red pepper

2 garlic cloves, minced

1 large egg

2 tablespoons chopped fresh mint

½ pound ground lamb

½ pound ground turkey

¾ cup fresh breadcrumbs

1 tablespoon olive oil

Cooking spray

1 (24-ounce) jar spicy red pepper pasta sauce

1 teaspoon grated lemon rind

1. Combine first 9 ingredients in a large bowl. Add lamb, turkey, and breadcrumbs; stir well. Shape into 28 (1-inch) meatballs.

2. Heat a large skillet over medium-high heat. Add oil to pan; swirl to coat. Add meatballs to pan. Cook 2 minutes on each side or until browned. Transfer meatballs to a 4-quart electric slow cooker coated with cooking spray.

3. While meatballs cook, combine pasta sauce and lemon rind in a medium bowl. Pour sauce over meatballs. Cover and cook on HIGH for 2 hours or until meatballs are done.

CALORIES 134; FAT 6.3g (sat 2.1g, mono 2.3g, poly 0.4g); PROTEIN 9.6g; CARB 10g; FIBER 1.3g; CHOL 37mg; IRON 0.7mg; SODIUM 190mg; CALC 31mg

Gruyère-Bacon Dip

Serve this with assorted vegetable dippers. It's also tasty as a condiment spread on turkey burgers.

Yield: 16 servings (serving size: 2 tablespoons)

½ cup chopped onion

Cooking spray

4 ounces shredded Gruyère cheese (about 1 cup)

½ cup canola mayonnaise

1 teaspoon Worcestershire sauce

½ teaspoon dry mustard

⅛ teaspoon freshly ground black pepper

1 (8-ounce) block fat-free cream cheese, softened

2 tablespoons chopped green onions

4 center-cut bacon slices, cooked and crumbled

1. Heat a large nonstick skillet over medium-high heat. Add onion to pan; sauté 5 minutes or until tender. Remove from heat.

2. Place onion in a 2½-quart electric slow cooker coated with cooking spray. Add cheese and next 5 ingredients. Stir until blended. Cover and cook on LOW for 1½ hours or until cheese melts, stirring after 45 minutes. Top with green onions and bacon.

CALORIES 102; FAT 8.3g (sat 2.1g, mono 3.9g, poly 1.7g); PROTEIN 4.9g; CARB 1.7g; FIBER 0.1g; CHOL 13mg; IRON 0.1mg; SODIUM 198mg; CALC 124mg

Fresh Whole-Wheat Pitas

These are sublime straight out of the oven and stuffed with your favorite salad or sandwich fixings. Leftovers make tasty chips. White whole-wheat flour is available through King Arthur (www.kingarthurflour.com) or Bob's Red Mill (www.bobsredmill.com).

Yield: 8 servings (serving size: 1 pita)

1 tablespoon sugar

1 package dry yeast (about 2¼ teaspoons)

1 cup plus 2 tablespoons warm water (100° to 110°)

10 ounces bread flour (about 2¼ cups)

4.75 ounces white whole-wheat flour (about 1 cup), divided

2 tablespoons 2% Greek yogurt

1 tablespoon extra-virgin olive oil

¾ teaspoon salt

Olive oil–flavored cooking spray

1. Dissolve sugar and yeast in 1 cup plus 2 tablespoons warm water in a large bowl; let stand 5 minutes. Lightly spoon flours into dry measuring cups; level with a knife. Add bread flour, 3 ounces (about ¾ cup) whole-wheat flour, yogurt, oil, and salt to the yeast mixture; beat with a mixer at medium speed until smooth. Turn dough out onto a floured surface. Knead dough until smooth and elastic (about 10 minutes); add enough of remaining whole-wheat flour, 1 tablespoon at a time, to prevent dough from sticking to hands (dough will feel sticky). Place dough in a large bowl coated with cooking spray, turning to coat top. Cover and let rise in a warm place (85°), free from drafts, 45 minutes or until doubled in size.

2. Position oven rack on lowest shelf.

3. Preheat oven to 500°.

4. Divide dough into 8 portions. Working with one portion at a time, gently roll each portion into a 5½-inch circle. Place 4 dough circles on each of 2 baking sheets heavily coated with cooking spray. Bake, one sheet at a time, at 500° for 8 minutes or until puffed and browned. Cool on a wire rack.

CALORIES 211; FAT 2.9g (sat 0.4g, mono 1.5g, poly 0.4g); PROTEIN 7g; CARB 39.9g; FIBER 3.1g; CHOL 0mg; IRON 2.5mg; SODIUM 225mg; CALC 11mg

NUTRITION TIP

White whole-wheat flour is simply made from white wheat instead of the more traditional red wheat. White wheat doesn't have the genes for bran color, and it also has a milder flavor than red wheat. Nutritionally, though, it's considered equal to red wheat.

Ciabatta

This bread gets its name from its shape; ciabatta is Italian for "slipper." Letting the sponge rest for 12 hours develops complex yeast flavor, a soft interior, and a crisp, thin crust.

Yield: 2 loaves, 16 servings (serving size: 1 slice)

Sponge:

4.75 ounces bread flour (about 1 cup)

½ cup warm fat-free milk (100° to 110°)

¼ cup warm water (100° to 110°)

1 tablespoon honey

1 package dry yeast (about 2¼ teaspoons)

Dough:

16.63 ounces bread flour, divided (about 3½ cups)

½ cup semolina or pasta flour

¾ cup warm water (100° to 110°)

½ cup warm fat-free milk (100° to 110°)

1½ teaspoons salt

1 package dry yeast (about 2¼ teaspoons)

3 tablespoons semolina or pasta flour, divided

1. To prepare sponge, weigh or lightly spoon 1 cup flour into a dry measuring cup; level with a knife. Combine 1 cup flour and next 4 ingredients in a large bowl, stirring well with a whisk. Cover; chill 12 hours.

2. To prepare dough, let sponge stand at room temperature 30 minutes. Weigh or lightly spoon 3½ cups bread flour and ½ cup semolina flour into dry measuring cups, and level with a knife. Add 3 cups bread flour, ½ cup semolina flour, ¾ cup warm water, ½ cup warm milk, salt, and 1 package yeast to sponge, and stir well to form a soft dough. Turn dough out onto a floured surface. Knead until smooth and elastic (about 8 minutes), and add enough of remaining bread flour, 1 tablespoon at a time, to prevent dough from sticking to hands. Divide dough in half.

3. Working with one portion at a time (cover remaining dough to prevent drying), roll each into a 13 x 5–inch oval. Place, 3 inches apart, on a large baking sheet sprinkled with 2 tablespoons semolina flour. Taper ends of dough to form a "slipper." Sprinkle 1 tablespoon semolina flour over dough. Cover and let rise in a warm place (85°), free from drafts, 45 minutes or until doubled in size. (Gently press two fingers into dough. If indentation remains, dough has risen enough.)

4. Preheat oven to 425°.

5. Uncover dough. Bake at 425° for 18 minutes or until the loaves are lightly browned and sound hollow when tapped. Remove from pan, and cool on a wire rack.

CALORIES 150; FAT 0.1g (sat 0g, mono 0.1g, poly 0g); PROTEIN 6.3g; CARB 32.1g; FIBER 1.3g; CHOL 0mg; IRON 2.1mg; SODIUM 227mg; CALC 21mg

Garlic-Thyme Focaccia

Two kinds of salt add flavor and crunch. For a spicy variation, infuse the oil with
$1/2$ teaspoon crushed red pepper along with the garlic; strain through a sieve before
brushing the flavored oil onto the dough.

Yield: 10 servings (serving size: 1 piece)

1 teaspoon sugar

1 package dry yeast (about
$2^{1}/4$ teaspoons)

1 cup warm water (100° to 110°)

$1/2$ teaspoon fine sea salt

11.25 ounces all-purpose flour,
divided (about $2^{1}/3$ cups plus
2 tablespoons)

Cooking spray

1 tablespoon olive oil

2 garlic cloves, thinly sliced

1 tablespoon chopped fresh thyme

$3/4$ teaspoon coarse sea salt

Thyme sprigs (optional)

1. Dissolve sugar and yeast in 1 cup warm water in a large bowl; let
stand 5 minutes. Stir in fine sea salt. Weigh or lightly spoon flour into
dry measuring cups and spoons; level with a knife. Add 2 cups plus
2 tablespoons flour, stirring to form a soft dough. Turn dough out
onto a floured surface. Knead dough until smooth and elastic (about
8 minutes); add enough of remaining $1/3$ cup flour, 1 tablespoon at a
time, to prevent dough from sticking to hands.
2. Place dough in a large bowl coated with cooking spray, turning to
coat top. Cover and let rise in a warm place (85°), free from drafts,
45 minutes or until doubled in size. (Gently press two fingers into
dough. If indentation remains, dough has risen enough.)
3. Heat oil in a small skillet over medium-low heat. Add garlic; cook 5
minutes or until fragrant. Remove garlic from oil with a slotted spoon;
discard garlic, and remove pan from heat.
4. Place dough on a baking sheet coated with cooking spray; pat
into a 12 x 8–inch rectangle. Brush garlic oil over dough; sprinkle with
thyme. Cover and let rise 25 minutes or until doubled in size.
5. Preheat oven to 425°.
6. Make indentations in top of dough using the handle of a wooden
spoon or your fingertips; sprinkle dough evenly with coarse sea salt.
Bake at 425° for 14 minutes or until lightly browned. Remove from
pan; cool on a wire rack. Garnish with thyme sprigs.

CALORIES 128; FAT 1.7g (sat 0.2g, mono 1g, poly 0.3g); PROTEIN 3.5g; CARB 24.2g; FIBER 1.1g;
CHOL 0mg; IRON 1.6mg; SODIUM 289mg; CALC 7mg

INGREDIENT TIP

*Thyme comes in dozens of varieties, but
most cooks use French thyme. Because
the leaves are so small, they often don't
require chopping, but you'll want to chop
them for this recipe.*

Baguette

Try your hand at making this classic French bread—you'll love the result.

Yield: 2 loaves, 12 servings per loaf (serving size: 1 slice)

1 package dry yeast (about 2¼ teaspoons)

1¼ cups warm water (100° to 110°)

14.25 ounces bread flour, divided (about 3 cups)

1 teaspoon salt

Cooking spray

1 teaspoon cornmeal

1. Dissolve yeast in warm water in a large bowl; let stand 5 minutes. Lightly spoon flour into dry measuring cups; level with a knife. Add 2¾ cups flour to yeast mixture; stir until a soft dough forms. Cover and let stand 15 minutes. Turn dough out onto a lightly floured surface; sprinkle evenly with salt. Knead until salt is incorporated and dough is smooth and elastic (about 6 minutes); add enough of remaining flour, 1 tablespoon at a time, to prevent dough from sticking to hands (dough will feel slightly sticky).

2. Place dough in large bowl coated with cooking spray, turning to coat top. Cover and let rise in a warm place (85°), free from drafts, 40 minutes or until doubled in size. (Gently press two fingers into dough. If an indentation remains, dough has risen enough.) Punch dough down; cover and let rest 5 minutes. Divide in half. Working with one portion at a time (cover remaining dough to prevent drying), roll each portion on a floured surface into a 12-inch rope, slightly tapered at ends. Place ropes on a large baking sheet sprinkled with cornmeal. Lightly coat dough with cooking spray, and cover; let rise 20 minutes or until doubled in size.

3. Preheat oven to 450°.

4. Uncover dough. Cut 3 (¼-inch-deep) diagonal slits across top of each loaf. Bake at 450° for 20 minutes or until browned on bottom and sounds hollow when tapped.

CALORIES 53; FAT 0.2g (sat 0g, mono 0.1g, poly 0.1g); PROTEIN 2.1g; CARB 11.2g; FIBER 0.5g; CHOL 0mg; IRON 0.8mg; SODIUM 97mg; CALC 1mg

Buttered Sweet Potato Knot Rolls

Serve these beautifully colored rolls for a holiday dinner. If you have leftover baked, mashed sweet potatoes, you can substitute them for the canned sweet potatoes called for in this recipe.

Yield: 24 servings (serving size: 1 roll)

1 package dry yeast (about 2¼ teaspoons)

1 cup warm 2% reduced-fat milk (100° to 110°)

¾ cup canned mashed sweet potatoes

3 tablespoons butter, melted and divided

1¼ teaspoons salt

2 large egg yolks, lightly beaten

23.75 ounces bread flour, divided (about 5 cups)

Cooking spray

1. Dissolve yeast in warm milk in a large bowl; let stand 5 minutes.
2. Add sweet potatoes, 1 tablespoon butter, salt, and egg yolks, stirring mixture with a whisk.
3. Lightly spoon flour into dry measuring cups; level with a knife. Add 4½ cups flour; stir until a soft dough forms.
4. Turn dough out onto a floured surface. Knead until smooth and elastic (about 8 minutes); add enough of remaining flour, 1 tablespoon at a time, to prevent dough from sticking to hands (dough will feel very soft and tacky).
5. Place dough in a large bowl coated with cooking spray, turning to coat top. Cover and let rise in a warm place (85°), free from drafts, 45 minutes or until doubled in size. (Gently press two fingers into dough. If indentation remains, dough has risen enough.) Punch dough down. Cover and let rest 5 minutes.
6. Line 2 baking sheets with parchment paper. Divide dough into 24 equal portions. Working with one portion at a time (cover remaining dough to prevent drying), shape each portion into a 9-inch rope. Carefully shape rope into a knot; tuck top end of knot under roll. Place roll on a prepared pan.
7. Repeat procedure with remaining dough, placing 12 rolls on each pan. Lightly coat rolls with cooking spray; cover and let rise 30 minutes or until doubled in size.
8. Preheat oven to 400°.
9. Uncover rolls. Bake at 400° for 8 minutes with 1 pan on bottom rack and 1 pan on second rack from top. Rotate pans; bake an additional 7 minutes or until rolls are golden brown on top and sound hollow when tapped.
10. Remove rolls from pans; place on wire racks. Brush rolls with remaining 2 tablespoons butter. Serve warm or at room temperature.

CALORIES 134; FAT 2.6g (sat 1.2g, mono 0.7g, poly 0.3g); PROTEIN 4.3g; CARB 23g; FIBER 0.9g; CHOL 22mg; IRON 1.4mg; SODIUM 147mg; CALC 21mg

Parmesan–Corn Bread Muffins

The flavorful cheese in this recipe is a nice balance with the sweetness of cornmeal.

Yield: 10 servings (serving size: 1 muffin)

4.5 ounces all-purpose flour (about 1 cup)

⅔ cup yellow cornmeal

2 tablespoons sugar

2 teaspoons baking powder

¼ teaspoon salt

⅔ cup nonfat buttermilk

3 tablespoons canola oil

2 large egg whites, lightly beaten

Cooking spray

¼ cup (1 ounce) grated fresh Parmesan cheese

1. Preheat oven to 425°.

2. Lightly spoon flour and cornmeal into dry measuring cups; level with a knife. Combine flour, cornmeal, sugar, baking powder, and salt in a medium bowl, stirring with a whisk. Make a well in center of mixture. Combine buttermilk, oil, and egg whites; add to flour mixture, stirring just until moist.

3. Spoon batter into 10 muffin cups coated with cooking spray. Sprinkle evenly with cheese. Bake at 425° for 10 minutes or until muffins spring back when touched lightly in center. Remove muffins from pan immediately; place on a wire rack. Serve warm.

CALORIES 151; FAT 4.9g (sat 1.1g mono 1.2g poly 2.4g); PROTEIN 4.3g; CARB 21.9g; FIBER 0.6g; CHOL 2mg; IRON 1mg; SODIUM 229mg; CALC 110mg

Whole-Grain Cornsticks

You can prepare these in muffin tins, but a cast-iron cornstick pan yields a crisper crust.

Yield: 1 dozen (serving size: 1 cornstick)

3.6 ounces whole-wheat flour (about ¾ cup)

¾ cup yellow cornmeal

3 tablespoons grated fresh Parmesan cheese

2 teaspoons baking powder

1½ teaspoons chili powder

1 teaspoon salt

¾ cup plus 2 tablespoons fat-free milk

2 tablespoons olive oil

2 tablespoons honey

1 large egg, lightly beaten

¾ cup frozen whole-kernel corn, thawed

⅓ cup minced red onion

2 tablespoons minced jalapeño pepper

Cooking spray

1. Preheat oven to 425°.
2. Lightly spoon flour into a dry measuring cup; level with a knife. Combine flour and next 5 ingredients in a large bowl. Make a well in center of mixture. Combine milk, oil, honey, and egg. Add to flour mixture, stirring just until moist. Fold in corn, onion, and jalapeño.
3. Place a cast-iron cornstick pan in 425° oven for 5 minutes. Remove from oven; immediately coat with cooking spray. Spoon batter into pan. Bake at 425° for 18 minutes or until lightly browned. Remove from pan immediately; serve warm.

CALORIES 120; FAT 3.6g (sat 0.8g, mono 2.1g, poly 0.4g); PROTEIN 4g; CARB 19g; FIBER 2g; CHOL 19mg; IRON 0.7mg; SODIUM 325mg; CALC 96mg

Parmesan and Cracked Pepper Grissini

Yield: 12 servings (serving size: 2 breadsticks)

1 package dry yeast (about 2¼ teaspoons)

1 cup warm water (100° to 110°)

14.25 ounces bread flour, divided (about 3 cups)

1¼ teaspoons salt

Cooking spray

1 teaspoon water

1 large egg white, lightly beaten

½ cup (2 ounces) grated fresh Parmesan cheese

1 tablespoon cracked black pepper

2 teaspoons cornmeal, divided

1. Dissolve yeast in 1 cup warm water in a large bowl; let stand 5 minutes.

2. Weigh or lightly spoon flour into dry measuring cups; level with a knife. Add 2¾ cups flour and salt to yeast mixture; stir until a soft dough forms. Turn dough out onto a floured surface. Knead until smooth and elastic (about 8 minutes); add enough of remaining flour, 1 tablespoon at a time, to prevent dough from sticking to hands (dough will feel tacky).

3. Place dough in a large bowl coated with cooking spray, turning to coat top. Cover and let rise in a warm place (85°), free from drafts, 45 minutes or until doubled in size. (Gently press two fingers into dough. If indentation remains, dough has risen enough.)

4. Punch dough down. Cover and let rest 5 minutes. Turn dough out onto a lightly floured surface; roll into a 12 x 8–inch rectangle.

5. Combine 1 teaspoon water and egg white, stirring with a whisk; brush evenly over dough. Sprinkle dough with cheese and pepper. Lightly coat dough with cooking spray; cover with plastic wrap. Gently press toppings into dough; remove plastic wrap.

6. Sprinkle each of 2 baking sheets with 1 teaspoon cornmeal. Cut dough in half lengthwise to form 2 (12 x 4–inch) rectangles. Cut each rectangle crosswise into 12 (1-inch) strips.

7. Working with 1 strip at a time (cover remaining strips to prevent drying), gently roll each strip into a log. Holding ends of log between forefinger and thumb of each hand, gently pull log into a 14-inch rope, slightly shaking it up and down while pulling. (You can also roll each strip into a 14-inch rope on a lightly floured surface.) Place rope on a prepared pan, curving into a series of shapes so that rope fits on pan.

8. Repeat procedure with remaining strips, placing 12 on each pan. Lightly coat ropes with cooking spray. Cover and let rise 20 minutes or until doubled in size.

9. Preheat oven to 450°.

10. Uncover dough; bake at 450° for 6 minutes with 1 pan on bottom rack and 1 pan on second rack from top. Rotate pans; bake an additional 6 minutes or until golden brown.

11. Remove breadsticks from pans; cool completely on wire racks.

CALORIES 148; FAT 1.9g (sat 0.9g, mono 0.4g, poly 0.3g); PROTEIN 6.4g; CARB 25.9g; FIBER 1.1g; CHOL 3mg; IRON 1.8mg; SODIUM 326mg; CALC 64mg

Chunky Applesauce

We left the skins on the McIntosh apples to provide texture and color to this favorite fruit dish.

Yield: 14 servings (serving size: ½ cup)

Cooking spray

4 pounds Golden Delicious apples, peeled and cut into ½-inch slices

2 pounds McIntosh apples, cut into ½-inch slices

½ cup water

¼ cup sugar

6 (3-inch) cinnamon sticks

2 tablespoons fresh lemon juice

¼ cup unsalted butter (optional)

1. Coat a 5-quart electric slow cooker with cooking spray. Combine apples, next 4 ingredients, and butter, if desired, in slow cooker. Cover and cook on LOW for 6 hours. Stir until desired consistency. Serve warm or chilled.

CALORIES 117; FAT 0.1g; PROTEIN 0.3g; CARB 29.9g; FIBER 4.3g; CHOL 0mg; IRON 6.4mg; SODIUM 0mg; CALC 7mg

INGREDIENT TIP

For chunkier applesauce, do not mash the mixture after cooking.

Grilled Asparagus with Balsamic Vinegar

If you're looking for a change of pace from plain old steamed asparagus, here's a refreshing option. It's easy, quick, and flavorful.

Yield: 4 servings

1 pound thin asparagus spears

1 teaspoon olive oil

¼ teaspoon kosher salt

⅛ teaspoon freshly ground black pepper

Cooking spray

1 tablespoon balsamic vinegar

1. Prepare grill.

2. Snap off and discard tough ends of asparagus. Place asparagus in a bowl or shallow dish; drizzle with oil. Sprinkle with salt and pepper, tossing well to coat. Place asparagus on a grill rack coated with cooking spray; grill 2 minutes on each side or until crisp-tender. Place asparagus in a bowl; drizzle with vinegar. Serve immediately.

CALORIES 25; FAT 1.2g (sat 0.2g, mono 0.8g, poly 0.2g); PROTEIN 1.3g; CARB 3g; FIBER 0g; CHOL 0mg; IRON 1.3mg; SODIUM 120mg; CALC 16mg

FLAVOR TIP

Some traditionally produced balsamic vinegars are aged for decades. They're quite expensive but definitely worth the splurge.

Santa Fe Black Beans

Yield: 14 servings (serving size: ½ cup beans, about 1 tablespoon cheese, about 1½ teaspoons cilantro, and about 1½ teaspoons pumpkinseed kernels)

1 (1-pound) package dried black beans

3 cups fat-free, lower-sodium chicken broth

2 cups finely chopped onion (about 1 large)

1 tablespoon chopped chipotle chile, canned in adobo sauce

1 teaspoon salt

4 garlic cloves, minced

1 tablespoon fresh lime juice

4 ounces crumbled queso fresco (about 1 cup)

½ cup chopped fresh cilantro

½ cup unsalted pumpkinseed kernels

1. Sort and wash beans; place in a large Dutch oven. Cover with water to 2 inches above beans; bring to a boil. Cook 2 minutes; remove from heat. Cover and let stand 1 hour. Drain beans.

2. Place beans in a 3-quart electric slow cooker. Stir in chicken broth and next 4 ingredients. Cover and cook on LOW for 10 hours or until beans are tender.

3. Stir in lime juice. Mash bean mixture with a potato masher until slightly thick. Sprinkle with queso fresco, cilantro, and pumpkinseed kernels.

CALORIES 165; FAT 4.4g (sat 1.8g, mono 1.2g, poly 0.9g); PROTEIN 9.8g; CARB 23.1g; FIBER 3.5g; CHOL 6mg; IRON 2mg; SODIUM 347mg; CALC 9mg

Simple Garlicky Lima Beans

This is a delicious, basic way to cook any kind of fresh shell bean or pea. You can add these cooked beans to salads. For another variation, drizzle with olive oil and lemon juice, and sprinkle with crushed red pepper or a few shavings of Parmesan cheese.

Yield: 8 servings (serving size: ½ cup)

4 cups fresh lima beans

2½ cups water

1 tablespoon olive oil

2 garlic cloves, crushed

3 fresh thyme sprigs

1 bay leaf

½ teaspoon sea salt

¼ teaspoon freshly ground black pepper

1. Sort and wash beans; drain. Combine beans and next 5 ingredients in a medium saucepan. Bring to a boil. Cover, reduce heat, and simmer 20 minutes or until tender. Discard thyme sprigs and bay leaf. Stir in salt and pepper.

CALORIES 105; FAT 2.4g (sat 0.4g, mono 1.3g, poly 0.5g); PROTEIN 5.4g; CARB 16.2g; FIBER 3.9g; CHOL 0mg; IRON 2.5mg; SODIUM 152mg; CALC 30mg

Southern-Style Green Beans

Infused with deep bacon and onion flavor, these tender beans are just like your grandmother used to make. Serve with pepper sauce for an extra kick, if desired.

Yield: 8 servings (serving size: ½ cup beans and 1½ teaspoons bacon)

3 center-cut bacon slices

1 cup chopped onion

1 cup fat-free, lower-sodium chicken broth

¼ teaspoon salt

1½ pounds green beans, trimmed

Hot pepper sauce (optional)

1. Cook bacon in a large nonstick skillet over medium heat 6 minutes or until crisp. Remove bacon from pan, reserving 1 teaspoon drippings in pan; crumble bacon. Add onion to drippings in pan; sauté 5 minutes or until tender.

2. Combine onion, broth, salt, and green beans in a 4-quart electric slow cooker. Cover and cook on LOW for 8 hours or until beans are very tender. Transfer beans from slow cooker to a serving bowl, using a slotted spoon. Sprinkle with crumbled bacon. Serve with hot pepper sauce, if desired.

CALORIES 38; FAT 0.8g (sat 0.4g, mono 0.6g, poly 0.1g); PROTEIN 2.1g; CARB 7g; FIBER 3.4g; CHOL 3mg; IRON 0.4mg; SODIUM 181mg; CALC 46mg

Lemon-Rosemary Beets

A little lemon juice brings out the vivid color in these beets and keeps the flavors bright, too.

Yield: 7 servings (serving size: ½ cup)

2 pounds beets (about 6), peeled and cut into wedges

2 tablespoons fresh lemon juice

2 tablespoons extra-virgin olive oil

2 tablespoons honey

1 tablespoon cider vinegar

¾ teaspoon kosher salt

½ teaspoon freshly ground black pepper

2 rosemary sprigs

½ teaspoon grated lemon rind

1. Place first 8 ingredients in a 4-quart electric slow cooker. Cover and cook on LOW for 8 hours or until beets are tender. Remove and discard rosemary sprigs; stir in lemon rind.

CALORIES 112; FAT 4.2g (sat 0.6g, mono 3.1g, poly 0.4g); PROTEIN 2.2g; CARB 17.8g; FIBER 3.7g; CHOL 0mg; IRON 1.2mg; SODIUM 239mg; CALC 22mg

Broccoli with Red Pepper Flakes and Toasted Garlic

The bold, straightforward flavors of garlic and crushed red pepper make this classic Mediterranean broccoli dish especially appealing.

Yield: 4 servings (serving size: 1 cup)

2 teaspoons olive oil

6 cups broccoli florets (about 1 head)

¼ teaspoon kosher salt

¼ teaspoon crushed red pepper

3 garlic cloves, thinly sliced

¼ cup water

1 Heat olive oil in a large nonstick skillet over medium-high heat. Add broccoli, kosher salt, crushed red pepper, and sliced garlic. Sauté 2 minutes. Add ¼ cup water. Cover, reduce heat to low, and cook 2 minutes or until broccoli is crisp-tender.

CALORIES 53; FAT 2.7g (sat 0.4g, mono 1.7g, poly 0.4g); PROTEIN 3.3g; CARB 6.4g; FIBER 3.2g; CHOL 0mg; IRON 1mg; SODIUM 147mg; CALC 55mg

INGREDIENT TIP

For chefs and many home cooks, kosher salt, a cousin of table salt, has become the standard. Kosher salt, named as such because it's used by Jewish butchers, is chemically identical to table salt. But it has fewer additives and comes in coarser particles, which makes it easy to pinch and sprinkle.

Steamed Brussels Sprouts and Cauliflower with Walnuts

This quick and versatile side dish is good with beef and pork roasts or chicken. A serving boasts nearly one-fourth of daily fiber needs while the walnuts add a dose of heart-healthy unsaturated fat.

Yield: 6 servings (serving size: about ¾ cup)

6 tablespoons coarsely chopped walnuts

2¼ cups trimmed Brussels sprouts (about 1 pound), halved

3 cups cauliflower florets

½ teaspoon kosher salt

¼ teaspoon freshly ground black pepper

½ teaspoon fresh lemon juice

1. Place walnuts in a small skillet over medium heat; cook 3 minutes or until walnuts are lightly browned, shaking pan frequently. Remove from heat.

2. Steam Brussels sprouts, covered, 10 minutes or until tender. Add cauliflower to pan; steam, covered, 2 minutes or just until tender. Drain. Combine Brussels sprouts, cauliflower, salt, pepper, and juice in a medium bowl; toss to combine. Sprinkle evenly with walnuts.

CALORIES 104; FAT 3.5g (sat 0.4g, mono 0.5g, poly 2.5g); PROTEIN 6.4g; CARB 15.2g; FIBER 6.3g; CHOL 0mg; IRON 1.8mg; SODIUM 222mg; CALC 68mg

FLAVOR TIP

Toasting the walnuts heightens their flavor, much like meat is flavored by browning. It intensifies their nuttiness so you can use just a few nuts and still get big flavor.

Honey-Orange Carrots

Brighten up any weeknight meal with this healthy side dish loaded with vitamins.

Yield: 13 servings (serving size: ½ cup)

3 pounds carrots, diagonally cut into 3-inch pieces

2 tablespoons water

½ cup honey

½ teaspoon salt

2 tablespoons butter, cut into pieces

½ teaspoon grated orange rind

1. Place carrots, 2 tablespoons water, and honey in a 4-quart electric slow cooker.

2. Sprinkle salt over carrots. Sprinkle butter pieces over mixture. Cover and cook on LOW for 8 hours or until carrots are very tender. Transfer carrots to a bowl; stir in orange rind.

CALORIES 98; FAT 2g (sat 1.2g, mono 0.5g, poly 0.2g); PROTEIN 1.1g; CARB 20.5g; FIBER 2.9g; CHOL 5mg; IRON 0.4mg; SODIUM 176mg; CALC 36mg

QUICK TIP

Use a Microplane® grater to quickly grate the orange rind.

Balsamic Collard Greens

Serve these greens with pork tenderloin and garlic mashed potatoes.

Yield: 5 servings (serving size: ½ cup collard greens and 2½ teaspoons bacon)

3 bacon slices

1 cup chopped onion

1 (16-ounce) package chopped fresh collard greens

¼ teaspoon salt

2 garlic cloves, minced

1 bay leaf

1 (14.5-ounce) can fat-free, lower-sodium chicken broth

3 tablespoons balsamic vinegar

1 tablespoon honey

1. Cook bacon in a large Dutch oven over medium heat until crisp. Remove bacon from pan; crumble. Add onion to drippings in pan; sauté 5 minutes or until tender. Add collard greens, and cook 2 to 3 minutes or until greens begin to wilt, stirring occasionally.

2. Place collard green mixture, salt, and next 3 ingredients in a 3-quart electric slow cooker. Cover and cook on LOW for 3½ to 4 hours.

3. Combine balsamic vinegar and honey in a small bowl. Stir vinegar mixture into collard greens just before serving. Remove and discard bay leaf. Sprinkle with bacon.

CALORIES 82; FAT 1.8g (sat 0.8g, mono 0.8g, poly 0.4g); PROTEIN 5g; CARB 13.6g; FIBER 3.8g; CHOL 6mg; IRON 0.3mg; SODIUM 260mg; CALC 144mg

Poblano Corn Pudding

Guaranteed to heat up any meal, this corn pudding is a tasty menu item for a Mexican-themed buffet.

Yield: 8 servings (serving size: ½ cup)

4 large poblano chiles (10 ounces)

Cooking spray

½ cup 1% low-fat milk

¼ cup yellow cornmeal

1.1 ounces all-purpose flour (about ¼ cup)

2 tablespoons sugar

2 tablespoons butter, melted

1 teaspoon baking powder

¼ teaspoon salt

2 large eggs, lightly beaten

1 (8¼-ounce) can cream-style corn

2 cups frozen whole-kernel corn

4 ounces reduced-fat cheddar cheese with jalapeño peppers, shredded (about 1 cup)

1. Preheat broiler.

2. Place poblano chiles on a foil-lined baking sheet. Broil 8 minutes or until blackened and charred, turning after 6 minutes. Place in a paper bag; fold to close tightly. Let stand 15 minutes. Peel and discard skins. Discard seeds and stems. Chop chiles.

3. Coat an oval 3-quart electric slow cooker with cooking spray. Place milk and next 7 ingredients in slow cooker; stir with a whisk until blended. Stir in chiles, corn, and cheese. Cover and cook on LOW for 2½ hours or until set. Remove lid. Cook on LOW for 15 minutes.

CALORIES 183; FAT 5.8g (sat 2.9g, mono 1.6g, poly 0.5g); PROTEIN 9.1g; CARB 26.5g; FIBER 1.7g; CHOL 65mg; IRON 1.1mg; SODIUM 353mg; CALC 185mg

Spicy Black-Eyed Peas

Yield: 7 servings (serving size: ½ cup)

3 cups shelled black-eyed peas

2 cups fat-free, lower-sodium chicken broth

2 cups chopped sweet onion

2 tablespoons finely chopped jalapeño pepper

½ teaspoon dried thyme

¼ teaspoon salt

¼ teaspoon freshly ground black pepper

4 garlic cloves, minced

1 (12-ounce) smoked turkey leg

1 bay leaf

Hot sauce (optional)

1. Place all ingredients except hot sauce in a 3-quart electric slow cooker; stir well. Cover and cook on LOW for 8 hours or until peas are tender. Discard bay leaf and turkey leg. Serve peas with a slotted spoon, and sprinkle with hot sauce, if desired.

CALORIES 135; FAT 2.8g (sat 1g, mono 0.7g, poly 0.8g); PROTEIN 10.4g; CARB 17g; FIBER 4g; CHOL 22mg; IRON 1.5mg; SODIUM 287mg; CALC 101mg

FREEZER TIP

Freeze your summer bounty of black-eyed peas for fresh flavor in the fall. Fill a heavy-duty zip-top plastic bag with unrinsed peas, and place in the freezer. Use within three months for best taste.

Loaded Twice-Baked Potatoes

For a main dish, split the potatoes from the top, and open slightly; pile on more toppings, and enjoy the entire potato.

Yield: 8 servings (serving size: 1 potato half)

4 small baking potatoes (about 6 ounces each)

Cooking spray

⅛ teaspoon kosher salt

¼ cup fat-free milk

¼ cup plain fat-free Greek yogurt

2 ounces shredded reduced-fat sharp cheddar cheese (about ½ cup), divided

¼ teaspoon kosher salt

¼ teaspoon freshly ground black pepper

1 tablespoon chopped fresh chives

2 bacon slices, cooked and crumbled

1. Scrub potatoes; rinse and pat dry with paper towels. Coat potatoes with cooking spray; pierce potatoes with a fork. Rub ⅛ teaspoon kosher salt evenly over potatoes; place in an oval 6-quart electric slow cooker. Cover and cook on LOW for 8 hours or until potatoes are tender. Cool slightly.

2. Cut each potato in half lengthwise; scoop out pulp into a medium microwave-safe bowl, leaving a ⅛-inch-thick shell. Mash pulp with a potato masher. Stir in milk, yogurt, ¼ cup cheese, ¼ teaspoon kosher salt, and pepper. Microwave at HIGH 1 minute or until thoroughly heated.

3. Spoon potato mixture evenly into shells; sprinkle evenly with remaining ¼ cup cheese. Arrange potato halves in bottom of slow cooker. Cover and cook on HIGH for 25 minutes or until thoroughly heated and cheese melts. Sprinkle each potato half with about ½ teaspoon chives and about 1 teaspoon bacon.

CALORIES 194; FAT 12.7g (sat 1.2g, mono 0.6g, poly 0.1g); PROTEIN 4.9g; CARB 15.8g; FIBER 1.9g; CHOL 7mg; IRON 1mg; SODIUM 193mg; CALC 126mg

Sweet Potato Gratin

A sprinkle of Parmesan and thyme adds a unique twist to this savory-sweet potato gratin.

Yield: 12 servings (serving size: ½ cup)

1 tablespoon butter, softened

1 cup thinly sliced sweet onion

2 pounds sweet potatoes (about 3 large), peeled and thinly sliced

1 tablespoon all-purpose flour

1 teaspoon chopped fresh thyme

½ teaspoon kosher salt

½ teaspoon freshly ground black pepper

2 ounces grated fresh Parmesan cheese (about ½ cup), divided

Cooking spray

½ cup organic vegetable broth

1. Melt butter in a medium nonstick skillet over medium heat. Add onion; sauté 5 minutes or until lightly browned. Combine onion, sweet potato, next 4 ingredients, and ¼ cup cheese in a large bowl, tossing to coat with flour. Coat a 4-quart electric slow cooker with cooking spray. Transfer vegetable mixture to slow cooker.
2. Pour broth over potato mixture. Sprinkle with remaining ¼ cup cheese. Cover and cook on LOW for 4 hours or until potato is tender.

CALORIES 90; FAT 2.5g (sat 1.3g, mono 0.6g, poly 0.1g); PROTEIN 3.4g; CARB 13.8g; FIBER 2.2g; CHOL 6mg; IRON 1mg; SODIUM 216mg; CALC 93mg

Charred Summer Vegetables

Serve with grilled pork, chicken, or fish. Add the vegetables to a hot cast-iron skillet, cover, and cook 5 minutes without stirring so the natural sugars caramelize and add flavor.

Yield: 6 servings (serving size: ⅔ cup)

Cooking spray

2½ cups fresh corn kernels (about 5 ears)

2 cups chopped green beans (about 8 ounces)

1 cup chopped zucchini (about 4 ounces)

1 cup chopped red bell pepper

2 tablespoons finely chopped shallots

1 tablespoon chopped fresh flat-leaf parsley

2 tablespoons fresh lemon juice

4 teaspoons extra-virgin olive oil

½ teaspoon salt

½ teaspoon chopped fresh thyme

¼ teaspoon freshly ground black pepper

1. Heat a 12-inch cast-iron skillet over high heat. Coat pan with cooking spray. Add corn kernels, chopped green beans, chopped zucchini, and chopped bell pepper to pan; stir to combine. Cover and cook 5 minutes. Combine shallots and remaining ingredients in a bowl, stirring well. Add shallot mixture to corn mixture; toss to coat.

CALORIES 102; FAT 3.2g (sat 0.3g, mono 1.7g, poly 0.3g); PROTEIN 3.3g; CARB 18.5g; FIBER 2.7g; CHOL 0mg; IRON 0.8mg; SODIUM 210mg; CALC 31mg

Poppy Seed Fruited Slaw

If you prefer slaws without mayo, you'll like this fruited variation. You can combine and refrigerate the dressing up to a day ahead. Serve with baked chicken, or take it to a picnic or backyard barbecue.

Yield: 6 servings (serving size: 1 cup)

Coleslaw:

½ cup orange sections

1 cup halved seedless red grapes

1 (16-ounce) package cabbage-and-carrot coleslaw

Dressing:

¼ cup sugar

1 tablespoon minced fresh onion

3 tablespoons cider vinegar

1 teaspoon poppy seeds

4 teaspoons canola oil

½ teaspoon dry mustard

¼ teaspoon salt

1. To prepare coleslaw, chop orange sections. Combine chopped oranges, grapes, and coleslaw in a large bowl.

2. To prepare dressing, combine ¼ cup sugar and remaining ingredients, stirring with a whisk until sugar dissolves. Add dressing mixture to cabbage mixture, and toss well. Cover and chill 30 minutes before serving.

CALORIES 114; FAT 3.6g (sat 0.3g, mono 1.9g, poly 1.1g); PROTEIN 1.6g; CARB 21.3g; FIBER 1g; CHOL 0mg; IRON 0.7mg; SODIUM 114mg; CALC 56mg

QUICK TIP

Once the rind and white pith have been removed from your orange, hold the fruit in your palm. Gently follow the natural sections of the orange with a knife to cut out wedges or sections.

Figs and Prosciutto with Mint and Shaved Parmigiano-Reggiano

Ripe figs are the secret to this simple yet refined salad. It's best made just before serving.

Yield: 8 servings (serving size: 4 fig quarters, about ½ ounce prosciutto, and ⅛ ounce cheese)

8 fresh figs, quartered

2 teaspoons extra-virgin olive oil

¼ teaspoon cracked black pepper

1 ounce Parmigiano-Reggiano cheese, thinly shaved

12 mint leaves, thinly sliced

4 ounces thinly sliced prosciutto

1. Place figs in a bowl; drizzle with oil. Sprinkle figs with pepper; toss gently.

2. Place fig mixture in center of a platter; top with cheese and mint. Top with prosciutto.

CALORIES 90; FAT 3.4g (sat 1.2g, mono 1.8g, poly 0.3g); PROTEIN 4.8g; CARB 9.5g; FIBER 1.4g; CHOL 11mg; IRON 0.3mg; SODIUM 270mg; CALC 64mg

NUTRITION TIP

The dense texture and subtle, sweet flavor of fresh figs are hard to beat.

Figs are a good source of fiber, manganese, potassium, and vitamin B$_6$.

Spinach Strawberry Salad

This simple starter salad is an ideal accompaniment to grilled or roasted chicken or pork.

Yield: 4 servings (serving size: 2 cups salad)

1½ cups quartered strawberries

¼ cup **Easy Herb Vinaigrette**

1 tablespoon finely chopped fresh mint

1 (6-ounce) package fresh baby spinach

2 tablespoons sliced almonds, toasted

¼ teaspoon freshly ground black pepper

1. Combine first 4 ingredients in a large bowl; toss gently to coat. Sprinkle with almonds and pepper; serve immediately.

CALORIES 136; FAT 10.3g (sat 0.7g, mono 6g, poly 3g); PROTEIN 2.1g; CARB 11g; FIBER 3.6g; CHOL 0mg; IRON 1.7mg; SODIUM 113mg; CALC 50mg

Easy Herb Vinaigrette

Since this recipe makes plenty of dressing to keep on hand, having a salad with dinner is effortless any night of the week.

Yield: about 1⅔ cups (serving size: 2 tablespoons vinaigrette)

9 tablespoons white wine vinegar

1½ tablespoons wildflower honey

½ teaspoon fine salt

1 cup canola oil

3 tablespoons chopped fresh basil

3 tablespoons minced fresh chives

1. Combine first 3 ingredients in a medium bowl; slowly whisk in oil until combined. Stir in basil and chives. Store, covered, in refrigerator for up to 5 days.

CALORIES 160; FAT 17.2g (sat 1.2g, mono 10.2g, poly 5.1g); PROTEIN 0.1g; CARB 2.1g; FIBER 0.1g; CHOL 0mg; IRON 0mg; SODIUM 89mg; CALC 2mg

Pike Place Market Salad

This salad calls for herb salad mix, which can be found prebagged in the supermarket, or you can use any combination of lettuces and herbs. Any fresh cherry or berry (such as blackberries or blueberries) will do nicely. The dressing and caramelized walnuts can be made a day ahead—store the nuts in an airtight container and the dressing in the refrigerator.

Yield: 4 servings (serving size: 2 cups salad)

Walnuts:

1 tablespoon sugar

3 tablespoons coarsely chopped walnuts

Cooking spray

Dressing:

½ cup apple cider

3 tablespoons water

¼ teaspoon cornstarch

1 tablespoon finely chopped shallots

1 tablespoon champagne vinegar

⅛ teaspoon salt

⅛ teaspoon freshly ground black pepper

Remaining ingredients:

8 cups herb salad mix

2 cups berries and/or pitted sweet cherries

¼ cup (1 ounce) blue cheese, crumbled

1. Place sugar in a small skillet over medium heat; cook 90 seconds or until sugar dissolves, stirring as needed so sugar dissolves evenly and doesn't burn. Reduce heat; stir in walnuts. Cook over low heat 30 seconds or until golden. Spread mixture onto foil coated with cooking spray. Cool completely; break into small pieces.

2. Place cider in a small saucepan over medium-high heat; bring to a boil. Cook until reduced to 2 tablespoons (about 5 minutes). Combine water and cornstarch in a small bowl; add to pan. Bring cider mixture to a boil, stirring constantly; cook 30 seconds. Remove from heat. Stir in shallots, vinegar, salt, and pepper; let cool.

3. Place salad mix in a large bowl. Drizzle with dressing; toss gently to coat. Divide evenly among 4 plates; top with berries, cheese, and walnuts. Serve immediately.

CALORIES 165; FAT 6.7g (sat 1.8g, mono 0.7g, poly 3g); PROTEIN 5.2g; CARB 24.6g; FIBER 4.5g; CHOL 6mg; IRON 1.9mg; SODIUM 199mg; CALC 116mg

WINE NOTE

This market salad is a kaleidoscope of bold flavors and compelling textures, from the berries to the caramelized walnuts to the crumbled blue cheese. It needs a powerhouse of a wine to match it all; try a Gewürztraminer with bright tropical fruit flavors. It is a great counterpoint to the saltiness of the cheese.

Mixed Lettuce, Pear, and Goat Cheese Salad with Citrus Dressing

If you can't find Meyer lemons, use regular lemon juice and add a pinch of sugar to approximate the flavor.

Yield: 8 servings (serving size: about 1 cup lettuce mixture, about ¼ cup pear, and 1½ tablespoons cheese)

Dressing:

1 tablespoon finely chopped shallots

1 teaspoon Dijon mustard

¼ cup fresh orange juice

4 teaspoons fresh Meyer lemon juice

¼ teaspoon kosher salt

⅛ teaspoon freshly ground black pepper

4 teaspoons extra-virgin olive oil

Salad:

2 tablespoons fresh orange juice

2 firm ripe Bosc pears, cored and thinly sliced

6 cups mixed baby lettuces

1 head Boston or butter lettuce, torn (about 2 cups)

¾ cup (3 ounces) crumbled goat cheese

1. Combine shallots and mustard in a medium bowl, stirring with a whisk. Stir in ¼ cup orange juice and next 3 ingredients. Gradually add oil, stirring constantly with a whisk.

2. Combine 2 tablespoons orange juice and pears, tossing to coat. Combine lettuces in a large bowl. Drizzle with dressing; toss gently to coat. Arrange about 1 cup lettuce mixture on each of 8 salad plates. Top each serving with about ¼ cup pear and 1½ tablespoons cheese.

CALORIES 100; FAT 5.6g (sat 2.5g, mono 2.4g, poly 0.4g); PROTEIN 3.5g; CARB 10.2g; FIBER 2.5g; CHOL 8mg; IRON 1.1mg; SODIUM 141mg; CALC 67mg

Mixed Citrus Green Salad

The dressing on this salad also works well on fruit salads without greens.

Yield: 7 servings (serving size: 2 cups salad, 1 tablespoon dressing, and 3 walnut halves)

1 cup red seedless grapes, halved

2 (5 ounce) bags mixed salad greens

1 (11-ounce) can mandarin oranges, drained

1 (8-ounce) container pineapple chunks, drained

1 (8-ounce) container red grapefruit, drained

7 tablespoons Orange-Poppy Seed Dressing

21 walnut halves, toasted

1. Combine first 5 ingredients in a large bowl. Arrange 2 cups salad on each of 7 plates; drizzle each with 1 tablespoon Orange-Poppy Seed Dressing (reserve remaining dressing for another use). Top each serving with 3 walnut halves.

CALORIES 173; FAT 8.6g (sat 1.4g, mono 2.3g, poly 3.8g); PROTEIN 3.3g; CARB 23.5g; FIBER 2.3g; CHOL 4mg; IRON 0.8mg; SODIUM 53mg; CALC 60mg

Orange-Poppy Seed Dressing

Yield: 1 cup plus 2 tablespoons (serving size: 1 tablespoon dressing)

½ cup fresh orange juice

¼ cup honey

¼ cup canola oil

2 tablespoons champagne vinegar

⅛ teaspoon salt

1 teaspoon poppy seeds

1. Place first 5 ingredients in a blender; process until blended. Add poppy seeds; pulse once. Cover and refrigerate.

CALORIES 17; FAT 1.2g (sat 0.1g, mono 0.7g, poly 0.4g); PROTEIN 0g; CARB 1.7g; FIBER 0g; CHOL 0mg; IRON 0mg; SODIUM 7mg; CALC 1mg

Orange, Arugula, and Kalamata Olive Salad

Blood oranges add vibrant red color, so use them if you can find them. Pit the olives by crushing them with the blade of a chef's knife.

Yield: 8 servings (serving size: about 1¼ cups)

2 tablespoons fresh lemon juice

1½ teaspoons extra-virgin olive oil

½ teaspoon salt

⅛ teaspoon freshly ground black pepper

8 cups trimmed arugula (about 8 ounces)

2 cups thinly sliced fennel bulb

¾ cup vertically sliced red onion

12 sliced pitted kalamata olives

2 cups coarsely chopped orange sections (about 2 pounds)

1. Combine first 4 ingredients. Combine arugula, fennel, onion, and olives in a large bowl. Drizzle lemon mixture over arugula mixture; toss gently to coat. Top with orange sections.

CALORIES 62; FAT 2.6g (sat 0.3g, mono 1.8g, poly 0.3g); PROTEIN 1.4g; CARB 9.4g; FIBER 2.3g; CHOL 0mg; IRON 0.6mg; SODIUM 254mg; CALC 65mg

Orange-Fig Jam

Serve this honey-colored jam alongside goat cheese or ⅓-less-fat cream cheese with assorted crackers. The recipe makes a lot, so store in decorative jars in your refrigerator to serve to unexpected guests and at impromptu parties. Tie on a pretty ribbon to present as a hostess gift.

Yield: 64 servings (serving size: 1 tablespoon)

1¾ cups water

1½ cups sugar

¼ cup Grand Marnier (orange-flavored liqueur)

¼ cup fresh orange juice

2 (7-ounce) packages dried Calimyrna figs, coarsely chopped

1 teaspoon grated orange rind

1. Place all ingredients except orange rind in a 2½-quart electric slow cooker; stir until sugar dissolves. Cover and cook on LOW for 6 hours. Stir in orange rind.

2. Place half of fig mixture in a food processor; process until smooth. Pour into a bowl. Repeat procedure with remaining fig mixture. Ladle jam into hot sterilized jars. Cover jars with metal lids; screw on bands. Cool to room temperature. Chill thoroughly; store in refrigerator.

CALORIES 37; FAT 0.1g; PROTEIN 0.2g; CARB 9g; FIBER 0.6g; CHOL 0mg; IRON 0.1mg; SODIUM 1mg; CALC 10mg

Chunky Peach-Ginger Chutney

If you use frozen peaches, there's no need to thaw them first. This chutney thickens as it stands, as well as when it chills. Serve the chutney warm or chilled with grilled or roasted pork, chicken, or lamb.

Yield: 4¼ cups (serving size: ¼ cup)

2 cups chopped onion

4 cups fresh or frozen sliced peeled peaches

1 cup golden raisins

1 cup firmly packed light brown sugar

¼ cup crystallized ginger

1 teaspoon mustard seeds

½ teaspoon ground ginger

¼ teaspoon ground cinnamon

¼ teaspoon ground cloves

1.1 ounces all-purpose flour (about ¼ cup)

¼ cup cider vinegar

1. Place a large nonstick skillet over medium-high heat. Add chopped onion, and sauté 5 minutes or until tender.
2. Place onion, peaches, and next 7 ingredients in a 3-quart electric slow cooker; stir well. Weigh or lightly spoon flour into a dry measuring cup; level with a knife. Combine flour and vinegar in a small bowl; stir with a whisk until well blended. Add flour mixture to peach mixture; stir well. Cover and cook on LOW for 5 hours.

CALORIES 120; FAT 0.2g (sat 0g, mono 0.1g, poly 0.1g); PROTEIN 1g; CARB 29.3g; FIBER 1.4g; CHOL 0mg; IRON 1mg; SODIUM 8mg; CALC 28mg

Overnight Apple Butter

Make a sweet, rich apple butter spread that is perfect slathered on a toasted English muffin or served over pork chops. One taste and you'll never believe it's fat free.

Yield: 4 cups (serving size: ¼ cup)

1 cup packed brown sugar

½ cup honey

¼ cup apple cider

1 tablespoon ground cinnamon

¼ teaspoon ground cloves

⅛ teaspoon ground mace

10 medium apples, peeled and cut into large chunks (about 2½ pounds)

1. Place all ingredients in a 5-quart electric slow cooker; stir well. Cover and cook on LOW for 10 hours or until apples are very tender.
2. Place a large sieve over a bowl; spoon one-third of apple mixture into sieve. Press mixture through sieve using the back of a spoon or ladle. Discard pulp. Repeat procedure with remaining apple mixture. Return apple mixture to slow cooker. Increase heat to HIGH. Cook, uncovered, on HIGH for 1½ hours or until mixture is thick, stirring occasionally. Spoon into a bowl; cover and chill for up to a week.

CALORIES 132; FAT 0g; PROTEIN 0.1g; CARB 35.3g; FIBER 3.1g; CHOL 0mg; IRON 0.7mg; SODIUM 6mg; CALC 18mg

Salsa Arrabbiata

A tomato-based pasta sauce, salsa arrabbiata—literally "angry sauce"—is made in countless versions in Italy, sometimes with meat, sometimes without, but always with some kind of hot pepper.

Yield: 6 servings (serving size: 1⅓ cups)

6 quarts water

2 teaspoons salt

1 pound uncooked campanelle pasta

1½ tablespoons olive oil

1½ cups (¼-inch-thick) onion wedges

3 bay leaves

1 (3-ounce) prosciutto end piece, cut into ½-inch pieces

½ cup pepperoncini peppers, drained, seeded, and thinly sliced

1 (28-ounce) can plum tomatoes, undrained and chopped

1 cup (4 ounces) grated fresh Parmigiano-Reggiano cheese

1. Bring 6 quarts water and 2 teaspoons salt to a boil in a large stockpot. Stir in campanelle pasta; partially cover, and return to a boil, stirring frequently. Cook 6 minutes or until pasta is almost al dente, stirring occasionally. Drain pasta in a colander over a bowl, reserving 1 cup cooking liquid.

2. While pasta cooks, heat oil in a Dutch oven over medium-high heat. Add onion, bay leaves, and prosciutto; sauté 5 minutes or until onion softens. Add peppers, and sauté 1 minute. Stir in reserved 1 cup cooking liquid and tomatoes; bring to a boil. Reduce heat, and simmer 10 minutes or until sauce thickens. Discard bay leaves.

3. Add pasta to Dutch oven; cook 1 minute, stirring well to coat, or until pasta is al dente. Remove from heat; stir in cheese.

CALORIES 331; FAT 7.7g (sat 2.7g, mono 2.8g, poly 0.8g); PROTEIN 15.1g; CARB 50.6g; FIBER 2g; CHOL 18mg; IRON 2.6mg; SODIUM 965mg; CALC 182mg

FLAVOR TIP

The spicy heat comes from small, whole, pickled peppers that are labeled pepperoncini or pepperoncino. Although these are milder than pickled cherry peppers, they provide plenty of spice.

Clam Sauce

While some clam sauces call for anchovies or a hot red chile, ours relies on tomatoes and basil for flavor.

Yield: 4 servings (serving size: 1 cup)

3 (6½-ounce) cans minced clams, undrained

1 tablespoon olive oil

2 garlic cloves, minced

1⅓ cups chopped tomato

2 tablespoons minced fresh parsley

1 teaspoon crushed red pepper

½ cup dry white wine

4 cups hot cooked fettuccine (about 8 ounces uncooked pasta)

2 tablespoons chopped fresh basil

1. Drain clams in a colander over a bowl, reserving liquid.

2. Heat oil in a large nonstick skillet over medium heat. Add garlic; cook 30 seconds, stirring constantly. Add tomato, parsley, and pepper; cook 1 minute. Add wine; cook 30 seconds. Add reserved clam liquid and pasta, tossing to coat; cook 3 minutes or until liquid almost evaporates, stirring frequently. Stir in clams and basil. Serve immediately.

CALORIES 289; FAT 6.3g (sat 1.1g, mono 3.3g, poly 1.1g); PROTEIN 9.8g; CARB 48.5g; FIBER 2.8g; CHOL 64mg; IRON 3.7mg; SODIUM 316mg; CALC 49mg

Mushroom Sauce

Because fresh porcini mushrooms are hard to come by in this country, we've combined dried porcini with fresh cremini (baby portobellos) to create this flavorful sauce.

Yield: 4 servings (serving size: about 1½ cups)

1½ cups dried porcini mushrooms (about 1½ ounces)

2 teaspoons olive oil

½ cup finely chopped prosciutto (about 2 ounces)

½ cup finely chopped onion

4 cups sliced cremini or button mushrooms (about 8 ounces)

½ teaspoon grated lemon rind

½ teaspoon salt

¼ teaspoon black pepper

2 garlic cloves, minced

1 cup fat-free, lower-sodium chicken broth

¾ cup dry red wine

1 tablespoon cornstarch

1 tablespoon water

4 cups hot cooked cavatappi (about 2 cups uncooked pasta)

1. Combine boiling water and porcini mushrooms in a bowl; cover and let stand 30 minutes. Drain. Rinse and coarsely chop porcini mushrooms.

2. Heat oil in a medium skillet over medium-high heat. Add prosciutto, and sauté 1 minute. Add onion; sauté 3 minutes or until tender. Stir in porcini mushrooms, cremini mushrooms, and next 4 ingredients; cook 4 minutes or until browned, stirring frequently. Stir in broth and wine, scraping pan to loosen browned bits. Bring to a boil; cook 3 minutes. Combine cornstarch and 1 tablespoon water in a small bowl. Add cornstarch mixture to pan; bring to a boil. Cook 1 minute, stirring constantly. Add pasta, tossing to coat.

CALORIES 304; FAT 5.1g (sat 1g, mono 2.6g, poly 1g); PROTEIN 15.4g; CARB 48.9g; FIBER 4.6g; CHOL 8mg; IRON 4.9mg; SODIUM 627mg; CALC 24mg

INGREDIENT TIP

Also known as boletes, cèpes, or steinpilz, porcini mushrooms are most often found dried in the United States. If you find fresh porcinis, choose those that are pale to tan in color, and avoid those that crumble easily.

Basic Marinara

Rely on a large Dutch oven or stockpot because this recipe makes enough sauce for several meals. Cook at a low simmer—just a few bubbles every few seconds will yield the deepest taste.

Yield: about 12 cups (serving size: ½ cup)

3 tablespoons olive oil

3 cups chopped yellow onion (about 3 medium)

1 tablespoon sugar

3 tablespoons minced garlic (about 6 cloves)

2 teaspoons salt

2 teaspoons dried basil

1½ teaspoons dried oregano

1 teaspoon dried thyme

1 teaspoon freshly ground black pepper

½ teaspoon fennel seeds, crushed

2 tablespoons balsamic vinegar

2 cups fat-free, lower-sodium chicken broth

3 (28-ounce) cans no-salt-added crushed tomatoes, undrained

1. Heat oil in a large Dutch oven over medium heat. Add onion to pan; cook 4 minutes, stirring frequently. Add sugar and next 7 ingredients; cook 1 minute, stirring constantly. Stir in vinegar; cook 30 seconds. Add broth and tomatoes; bring to a simmer. Cook over low heat 55 minutes or until sauce thickens, stirring occasionally.

CALORIES 50; FAT 1.8g (sat 0.2g, mono 1.3g, poly 0.2g); PROTEIN 1.3g; CARB 8g; FIBER 2.1g; CHOL 0mg; IRON 0.5mg; SODIUM 270mg; CALC 28mg

FREEZER TIP

Ladle room-temperature or chilled sauce into plastic containers or zip-top plastic freezer bags. Seal and freeze for up to four months. Consider freezing the sauce in 1-cup increments (two servings' worth). That way, you can pull out exactly as much as you want for future meals.

Sage, Bay, and Garlic Dipping Oil

Bay and sage permeate this garlicky oil, infusing it with wonderful earthy, woodsy flavors. Serve this oil, Basil Dipping Oil or Three-Pepper Dipping Oil (page 398), with Ciabatta (page 339), a purchased focaccia, or a loaf of Italian bread. Pour the oil into small, wide bowls to facilitate dipping, and garnish each oil with its seasonings. Refrigerate oils up to a week in glass containers. Toss leftover oil with pasta, or use it in salad dressing.

Yield: 12 servings (serving size: 2 teaspoons)

½ cup olive oil

2 garlic cloves, crushed

2 fresh sage leaves

1 bay leaf

1. Combine all ingredients in a small, heavy saucepan. Cook over medium-low heat until thermometer registers 180°. Reduce heat to low, and cook 20 minutes (do not allow temperature to rise above 200°). Cool to room temperature. Drain oil mixture through a sieve into a bowl, and discard solids.

CALORIES 80; FAT 9g (sat 1.2g, mono 6.6g, poly 0.8g); PROTEIN 0g; CARB 0g; FIBER 0g; CHOL 0mg; IRON 0mg; SODIUM 0mg; CALC 0mg

Basil Dipping Oil

Yield: 12 servings (serving size: 2 teaspoons)

2 cups chopped fresh basil leaves
(about 2 [¾-ounce] packages)

½ cup olive oil

1. Combine basil and oil in a small, heavy saucepan. Cook over medium-low heat until thermometer registers 180°. Reduce heat to low; cook 20 minutes (do not allow temperature to rise above 200°). Cool to room temperature. Drain oil mixture through a sieve into a bowl; discard solids.

CALORIES 80; FAT 9g (sat 1.2g, mono 6.6g, poly 0.8g); PROTEIN 0g; CARB 0g; FIBER 0g; CHOL 0mg; IRON 0mg; SODIUM 0mg; CALC 0mg

Three-Pepper Dipping Oil

Yield: 12 servings (serving size: 2 teaspoons)

½ cup olive oil

1 pepperoncini pepper, halved lengthwise

1 whole dried hot red chile, crushed

2 whole black peppercorns

1. Combine all ingredients in a small, heavy saucepan. Cook mixture over medium-low heat until thermometer registers 180°. Reduce heat to low, and cook 20 minutes (do not allow temperature to rise above 200°). Cool mixture to room temperature. Drain oil mixture through a sieve into a bowl, and discard solids.

CALORIES 80; FAT 9g (sat 1.2g, mono 6.6g, poly 0.8g); PROTEIN 0g; CARB 0g; FIBER 0g; CHOL 0mg; IRON 0mg; SODIUM 0mg; CALC 0mg

Pesto

We reduced the amount of oil, pine nuts, cheese, and butter usually found in a classic pesto, cutting 28 grams of fat per serving without losing any flavor. Avoid packing the basil leaves when you measure them so you won't use too many.

Yield: 4 servings (serving size: about 1 cup pasta)

4 cups fresh basil leaves

2 tablespoons pine nuts

2 tablespoons extra-virgin olive oil

¼ teaspoon salt

2 garlic cloves, peeled

½ cup (2 ounces) grated fresh Parmesan cheese

2 tablespoons grated fresh Romano cheese

2 teaspoons butter, softened

2 cups uncooked penne (about 8 ounces)

1. Combine first 5 ingredients in a food processor; process until finely minced. Place in a large bowl. Stir in cheeses and butter until blended.

2. Cook pasta according to package directions, omitting salt and fat. Drain in a colander over a bowl, reserving 3 tablespoons cooking liquid. Add pasta and reserved cooking liquid to pesto, tossing to coat.

CALORIES 390; FAT 17g (sat 5.4g, mono 6.5g, poly 2.1g); PROTEIN 14.5g; CARB 45.3g; FIBER 3.2g; CHOL 18mg; IRON 4mg; SODIUM 352mg; CALC 281mg

Sherried Zabaglione with Berries

Serve this light custard sauce immediately to enjoy its frothy texture. A double boiler cooks the delicate custard gently and eliminates the chance of curdling. The water that heats the custard must simmer, not boil. Regulate the water before placing the custard on top, and be conservative; once the top is in place, the water tends to heat up. Any berries will work with this tasty sauce.

Yield: 4 servings (serving size: ½ cup berries and about ¼ cup zabaglione)

5 tablespoons sugar

3 tablespoons cream sherry

2 large eggs

3 tablespoons reduced-fat sour cream

2 cups fresh blackberries

Mint sprigs (optional)

1. Combine first 3 ingredients in top of a double boiler. Cook over simmering water until thick (about 4 minutes) and a thermometer registers 160°, stirring mixture constantly with a whisk. Remove top pan from heat; whisk the mixture an additional 2 minutes. Gently whisk in sour cream. Serve zabaglione immediately over berries. Garnish with mint sprigs, if desired.

CALORIES 157; FAT 4.2g (sat 1.7g, mono 1.4g, poly 0.6g); PROTEIN 4.2g; CARB 25.9g; FIBER 3.8g; CHOL 112mg; IRON 0.8mg; SODIUM 39mg; CALC 55mg

Tuscan Almond Biscotti

These crunchy, light cookies are a specialty of Prato, a city in Tuscany, where they are called cantucci. The biscotti will keep in airtight tins for up to a week.

Yield: 2 dozen (serving size: 1 biscotto)

7.9 ounces all-purpose flour (about 1¾ cups)

1 cup sugar

1 teaspoon baking powder

¼ teaspoon salt

1 cup whole almonds, toasted

2 large eggs

½ teaspoon almond extract

Cooking spray

1. Preheat oven to 375°.
2. Weigh or lightly spoon flour into dry measuring cups; level with a knife. Combine flour, sugar, baking powder, and salt in a large bowl. Place almonds in a food processor; pulse 10 times. Stir nuts into flour mixture.
3. Combine eggs and extract, stirring well with a whisk. Add egg mixture to flour mixture, stirring just until blended (dough will be crumbly). Turn dough out onto a lightly floured surface; knead lightly 7 or 8 times. Divide dough into 2 equal portions. Shape each portion into a 6-inch-long roll. Place rolls 6 inches apart on a baking sheet coated with cooking spray, and pat to 1-inch thickness. Bake at 375° for 25 minutes or until lightly browned. Cool 5 minutes on a wire rack.
4. Cut each roll crosswise into 12 (½-inch) slices. Stand slices upright on baking sheet.
5. Bake 14 minutes (cookies will be slightly soft in center but will harden as they cool). Remove from baking sheet, and cool completely on wire rack.

CALORIES 102; FAT 3.4g (sat 0.4g, mono 2.1g, poly 0.8g); PROTEIN 2.7g; CARB 15.7g; FIBER 0.9g; CHOL 18mg; IRON 0.8mg; SODIUM 51mg; CALC 28mg

WINE TIP

In Italy, this type of biscotti is typically served at the end of a meal with a glass of Vin Santo, *a sweet dessert wine.*

Honey Gelato

Store the gelato in an airtight container in the freezer for up to one week; it won't freeze solid but will maintain a soft texture. Purchased rolled wafer cookies make a delicate accompaniment to this rich dessert.

Yield: 8 servings (serving size: ½ cup)

½ cup honey

⅓ cup nonfat dry milk

1 (12-ounce) can evaporated fat-free milk

⅛ teaspoon salt

4 large egg yolks

1 cup 2% reduced-fat milk

Mint sprigs (optional)

1. Combine first 3 ingredients in a medium, heavy saucepan. Heat mixture over medium heat until honey dissolves, stirring frequently (do not boil). Remove from heat.
2. Combine salt and egg yolks in a large bowl, stirring with a whisk. Gradually add honey mixture to egg mixture, stirring constantly with a whisk. Place honey mixture in pan; cook over medium heat until mixture reaches 180° (about 3 minutes), stirring constantly (do not boil). Remove from heat; stir in reduced-fat milk. Cool completely.
3. Pour mixture into freezer can of an ice-cream freezer; freeze according to manufacturer's instructions. Spoon gelato into a freezer-safe container. Cover and freeze 2 hours or until firm. Garnish with mint sprigs, if desired.

CALORIES 153; FAT 3.3g (sat 1.2g, mono 1.2g, poly 0.4g); PROTEIN 6.7g; CARB 25.4g; FIBER 0g; CHOL 111mg; IRON 0.5mg; SODIUM 121mg; CALC 208mg

INGREDIENT TIP

Honey is a good choice for gelato— its resistance to freezing ensures creaminess. We like mild clover and lavender honeys in this recipe.

Spiced Poached Pears

Yield: 6 servings (serving size: 2 pear halves and about 3 tablespoons sauce)

6 firm ripe Anjou pears (2¾ pounds), peeled

1 (500-milliliter) bottle Vin Santo or other sweet dessert wine

½ cup sugar

⅓ cup fresh orange juice

1 (3-inch) vanilla bean, split lengthwise

¼ teaspoon juniper berries

1 (3-inch) cinnamon stick

6 tablespoons crème fraîche (optional)

Ground cinnamon (optional)

1. Remove cores from blossom ends of pears, leaving stem end intact. If necessary, cut about ¼ inch from base of each pear so it sits flat. Place wine, sugar, and orange juice in an oval 5-quart electric slow cooker; stir until sugar dissolves. Scrape seeds from vanilla bean; stir seeds and bean into wine mixture. Add juniper berries and cinnamon stick. Set pears in wine mixture. Cover and cook on HIGH for 3 hours or until pears are tender.

2. Remove pears from cooking liquid. Cut pears in half. Place pear halves in dessert dishes.

3. Pour cooking liquid into a sieve over a medium saucepan; discard solids. Bring to a boil; boil 20 minutes or until reduced to 1 cup. Drizzle sauce evenly over pears. Top with crème fraîche and sprinkle with cinnamon, if desired.

CALORIES 257; FAT 0.2g (sat 0g, mono 0.1g, poly 0.1g); PROTEIN 0.9g; CARB 53g; FIBER 6.2g; CHOL 0mg; IRON 2.8mg; SODIUM 7mg; CALC 23mg

Strawberries with Crunchy Almond Topping

This easy but stylish dessert is best made early in the day to let the strawberries macerate in the sweetened almond liqueur.

Yield: 6 servings (serving size: ½ cup strawberries, 1 crushed cookie, and 1 tablespoon sour cream)

6 cups sliced strawberries

½ cup sugar

2 tablespoons amaretto (almond-flavored liqueur)

6 amaretti cookies, crushed

6 tablespoons reduced-fat sour cream

1. Combine first 3 ingredients in a bowl. Cover and chill 4 to 8 hours. Spoon into individual dessert dishes. Sprinkle with crushed cookies; top with sour cream.

CALORIES 207; FAT 2.6g (sat 0.4g, mono 0.3g, poly 0.3g); PROTEIN 2.8g; CARB 44g; FIBER 4.8g; CHOL 2mg; IRON 0.7mg; SODIUM 29mg; CALC 32mg

Tiramisu Bread Pudding

Drizzled with a rich mascarpone sauce, this moist, coffee- and Kahlúa-flavored bread pudding offers the flavors of a favorite Italian dessert.

Yield: 10 servings (serving size: ½ cup pudding, about 1 tablespoon sauce, and about ¼ teaspoon cocoa)

½ cup water

⅓ cup sugar

1½ tablespoons instant espresso granules

2 tablespoons Kahlúa (coffee-flavored liqueur)

2 cups 1% low-fat milk, divided

2 large eggs, lightly beaten

8 cups (1-inch) cubed French bread (about 8 ounces)

Cooking spray

⅓ cup mascarpone cheese

1 teaspoon vanilla extract

2 teaspoons unsweetened cocoa

1. Combine first 3 ingredients in a small saucepan. Bring to a boil; boil 1 minute, stirring occasionally. Remove from heat; stir in liqueur.

2. Combine 1¾ cups milk and eggs in a large bowl, stirring with a whisk. Add espresso mixture, stirring with whisk. Add bread, stirring to coat. Pour bread mixture into a 2½-quart round casserole coated with cooking spray. Place dish in an oval 7-quart electric slow cooker. Cover and cook on LOW for 2 hours or until set.

3. Combine remaining ¼ cup milk, mascarpone cheese, and vanilla in a small bowl, stirring with a whisk until smooth. Spoon bread pudding into dessert dishes; top each with mascarpone sauce, and sprinkle with cocoa.

CALORIES 199; FAT 9g (sat 4.5g, mono 1.9g, poly 0.4g); PROTEIN 6.7g; CARB 23.5g; FIBER 0.7g; CHOL 63mg; IRON 1.1mg; SODIUM 191mg; CALC 95mg

Tiramisu

Place toothpicks in the center and in each corner of the dish to prevent the plastic wrap from sticking to the tiramisu as it chills.

Yield: 8 servings

Espresso Drizzle:

½ cup water

2 tablespoons granulated sugar

2 tablespoons instant espresso granules

2 tablespoons Kahlúa (coffee-flavored liqueur)

Filling:

1 (8-ounce) block fat-free cream cheese, softened

1 (3.5-ounce) carton mascarpone cheese

⅓ cup granulated sugar

¼ cup packed brown sugar

2 tablespoons Kahlúa

Remaining Ingredients:

24 cakelike ladyfingers (2 [3-ounce] packages)

1½ teaspoons unsweetened cocoa

½ ounce bittersweet chocolate, grated

Chocolate curls (optional)

1. To prepare espresso drizzle, combine first 3 ingredients in a small saucepan over medium-high heat; bring to a boil. Cook 1 minute, stirring occasionally. Remove from heat; stir in 2 tablespoons liqueur. Cool completely.

2. To prepare filling, combine cheeses in a large bowl, and beat with a mixer at medium speed until smooth. Add ⅓ cup granulated sugar, brown sugar, and 2 tablespoons liqueur; beat at medium speed until well blended.

3. Split ladyfingers in half lengthwise. Arrange 24 ladyfinger halves, cut sides up, in bottom of an 8-inch square baking dish. Drizzle half of espresso drizzle over ladyfinger halves. Spread half of filling over ladyfinger halves, and repeat procedure with remaining ladyfinger halves, espresso drizzle, and filling. Combine 1½ teaspoons cocoa and chocolate; sprinkle evenly over top of filling. Cover and chill 2 hours. Garnish with chocolate curls, if desired.

CALORIES 260; FAT 8g (sat 4.1g, mono 2.2g, poly 0.5g); PROTEIN 7.1g; CARB 38.4g; FIBER 0.5g; CHOL 55mg; IRON 0.8mg; SODIUM 317mg; CALC 104mg

INGREDIENT TIP

Find ladyfingers in the bakery section of your supermarket. Most come

already split in half lengthwise, but you can split them yourself with a serrated knife, if needed.

Brandied Plum–Vanilla Bread Pudding

Brandy-spiked dried plums bejewel this delicious vanilla-infused bread pudding, putting a decadent spin on comfort.

Yield: 8 servings (serving size: ⅔ cup)

¾ cup pitted dried plums, quartered

⅓ cup brandy

1½ cups 2% reduced-fat milk

½ cup sugar

1 tablespoon vanilla extract

⅛ teaspoon salt

3 large eggs

5 cups (½-inch) cubed dry French bread (6 ounces)

Cooking spray

½ cup vanilla light ice cream (optional)

1. Place plums and brandy in a bowl. Let stand 30 minutes. Pour mixture into a sieve over a bowl, reserving soaking liquid. Set plums aside.

2. Combine reserved soaking liquid, milk, and next 4 ingredients in a large bowl, stirring well with a whisk. Add bread, tossing gently to coat. Stir in plums. Spoon mixture into a 1½-quart round casserole coated with cooking spray. (Dish will be full.) Cover with foil; let rest 30 minutes to absorb liquid. Remove foil.

3. Place dish in a 5-quart round electric slow cooker; add enough hot water to cooker to come halfway up sides of dish. Place several layers of paper towels across top of slow cooker. Cover and cook on LOW for 4 hours or until a wooden pick inserted in center comes out clean.

4. Remove dish from slow cooker. Serve bread pudding warm. Top with ice cream, if desired.

CALORIES 212; FAT 3.3g (sat 1.3g, mono 1g, poly 0.5g); PROTEIN 6.7g; CARB 33.9g; FIBER 1.4g; CHOL 83mg; IRON 1.2mg; SODIUM 222mg; CALC 79mg

Vanilla Bean Baked Custard

Using evaporated milk helps the custard stabilize and not curdle.

Yield: 4 servings (serving size: 1 custard)

1 (12-ounce) can evaporated low-fat milk

½ cup 1% low-fat milk

1 teaspoon vanilla bean paste

1 large egg, lightly beaten

2 large egg yolks

⅓ cup sugar

1. Combine milks in a medium saucepan. Bring to a simmer over medium heat, about 4 minutes. Remove from heat; add vanilla bean paste, stirring with a whisk until blended.

2. Combine egg, egg yolks, and sugar in a medium bowl, stirring with a whisk until blended. Gradually add hot milk, stirring vigorously with a whisk. Pour egg mixture through a sieve into a bowl.

3. Place 4 metal canning jar bands in bottom of a 6-quart oval electric slow cooker. Ladle egg mixture evenly into 4 (8-ounce) ramekins. Cover ramekins with foil. Set 1 ramekin on each band, making sure ramekins do not touch each other or sides of slow cooker. Carefully pour hot water into slow cooker to depth of 1 inch up sides of ramekins.

4. Cover and cook on HIGH for 1 hour and 45 minutes or until a knife inserted in center of custards comes out clean. Remove ramekins from slow cooker, and cool on a wire rack. Serve warm or chilled.

CALORIES 193; FAT 5.2g (sat 2.7g, mono 1.6g, poly 0.6g); PROTEIN 9.3g; CARB 27.4g; FIBER 0g; CHOL 173mg; IRON 0.5mg; SODIUM 130mg; CALC 269mg

Pineapple-Coconut Tapioca

Small pearl tapioca combined with coconut milk and fresh pineapple makes a simple tropics-inspired treat. The key to success is using small pearl tapioca, not instant or minute tapioca. Fresh mango or papaya works equally well as a substitute for the fresh pineapple.

Yield: 9 servings (serving size: ½ cup tapioca and about 1 tablespoon coconut)

Cooking spray

¾ cup sugar

½ cup regular small pearl tapioca

2 (13.5-ounce) cans light coconut milk

1 large egg

½ cup finely chopped fresh pineapple

½ cup flaked sweetened coconut, toasted

1. Coat a 4-quart electric slow cooker with cooking spray. Combine sugar, tapioca, and coconut milk in slow cooker, stirring with a whisk. Cover and cook on LOW for 2 hours or until most of tapioca is transparent. (Pudding will be thin.)

2. Place egg in a medium bowl; stir with a whisk. Add ½ cup hot tapioca mixture to egg, stirring constantly with a whisk. Stir egg mixture into remaining tapioca mixture in slow cooker. Cover and cook on LOW for 30 minutes. Turn off slow cooker. Stir pineapple into tapioca mixture; cover and let stand 30 minutes. Serve warm or chilled. Top each serving with toasted coconut.

CALORIES 141; FAT 3g (sat 2.3g, mono 0.3g, poly 0.1g); PROTEIN 1.1g; CARB 28.4g; FIBER 0.7g; CHOL 24mg; IRON 0.3mg; SODIUM 25mg; CALC 7mg

Angel Food Cake with Mixed Berry Compote

Slow-cooked sauce made from three types of berries dresses up store-bought angel food cake.

Yield: 8 servings (serving size: 1 cake slice and about ⅔ cup berry compote)

Cooking spray

2 cups blueberries

2 cups blackberries

2 cups raspberries

1 cup orange juice

½ cup sugar

3 tablespoons cornstarch

6 tablespoons water

1 (8-ounce) angel food cake, cut into 8 slices

1. Coat a 5-quart electric slow cooker with cooking spray. Combine berries, orange juice, and sugar in slow cooker. Cover and cook on HIGH for 2 hours.

2. Combine cornstarch and water in a small bowl, stirring until smooth. Stir cornstarch mixture into berry mixture. Cover and cook on HIGH for 15 minutes or until sauce thickens. Serve compote over angel food cake.

CALORIES 201; FAT 0.9g (sat 0.1g, mono 0.1g, poly 0.4g); PROTEIN 3g; CARB 47.4g; FIBER 5.2g; CHOL 0mg; IRON 0.8mg; SODIUM 214mg; CALC 64mg

INGREDIENT TIP

If you only have one or two types of berries, you can still make this compote. Just make sure the berries add up to a total of 6 cups.

Rum-Raisin Arborio Pudding

Soaking the raisins in rum allows them to absorb the flavor and plump up before you stir them into the pudding.

Yield: 6 servings (serving size: about ½ cup)

½ cup raisins

¼ cup dark rum

1 (12-ounce) can evaporated low-fat milk

1½ cups water

⅓ cup sugar

¾ cup Arborio rice

¼ teaspoon salt

¼ teaspoon freshly grated nutmeg

1. Combine raisins and rum. Cover and set aside.

2. Combine evaporated milk and 1½ cups water in a medium saucepan. Bring to a simmer over medium heat. Add sugar, stirring to dissolve. Remove from heat.

3. Pour milk mixture into a 3-quart electric slow cooker. Stir in rice and salt. Cover and cook on LOW for 4 hours or just until pudding is set in center, stirring after 1 hour and again after 3 hours.

4. Stir in raisin mixture and nutmeg; let stand, uncovered, 10 minutes. Serve warm.

CALORIES 232; FAT 1.2g (sat 0.9g, mono 0g, poly 0g); PROTEIN 5.9g; CARB 45.1g; FIBER 1.8g; CHOL 9mg; IRON 0.4mg; SODIUM 167mg; CALC 147mg

Amaretti Cheesecake

To prevent the pan from touching the bottom of the slow cooker, you'll need a small rack that fits inside your cooker. If you don't have one, make a ring out of foil.

Yield: 10 servings (serving size: 1 wedge)

Crust:

⅔ cup amaretti cookie crumbs (about 16 cookies)

2 tablespoons butter, melted

1 tablespoon sugar

Cooking spray

Filling:

2 (8-ounce) blocks fat-free cream cheese, softened and divided

1 (8-ounce) block ⅓-less-fat cream cheese, softened

⅔ cup sugar

1 tablespoon all-purpose flour

2 large eggs

¾ teaspoon almond extract

Raspberries (optional)

1. To prepare crust, combine first 3 ingredients, tossing with a fork until moist and crumbly. Gently press mixture into bottom of a 7-inch springform pan coated with cooking spray.

2. To prepare filling, beat 1 block fat-free cream cheese and ⅓-less-fat cream cheese with a mixer at medium speed until smooth. Add remaining 1 block fat-free cream cheese; beat until blended. Add ⅔ cup sugar and flour; beat well. Add eggs, one at a time, beating well after each addition. Stir in almond extract. Pour batter over crust in pan.

3. Pour 1 cup hot water into bottom of a 5-quart electric slow cooker. Place a rack in slow cooker (rack should be taller than water level). Place pan on rack. Place several layers of paper towels over slow cooker insert. Cover and cook on HIGH for 2 hours or until center of cheesecake barely moves when pan is touched. Remove lid from slow cooker; turn off heat, and run a knife around outside edge. Let cheesecake stand in slow cooker 1 hour. Remove cheesecake from slow cooker. Cool to room temperature in pan on a wire rack. Cover and chill at least 6 hours. Cut into wedges. Garnish with raspberries, if desired.

CALORIES 232; FAT 24.3g (sat 5.3g, mono 2.6g, poly 0.9g); PROTEIN 11.2g; CARB 31.7g; FIBER 0.4g; CHOL 120mg; IRON 0.5mg; SODIUM 390mg; CALC 168mg

Brownie Pudding Cake

Rich and decadent from both Dutch process cocoa and bittersweet chocolate, this dessert is part cake and part pudding. Top with vanilla light ice cream, if desired.

Yield: 8 servings (serving size: ⅛ of cake)

4.5 ounces all purpose flour (about 1 cup)

1¼ cups sugar

¼ cup Dutch process cocoa

¼ teaspoon salt

¼ cup canola oil

1 teaspoon vanilla extract

3 large egg whites

2 large eggs

2 ounces bittersweet chocolate, melted

¼ cup coarsely chopped walnuts, toasted

Cooking spray

1 teaspoon powdered sugar (optional)

1. Weigh or lightly spoon flour into a dry measuring cup; level with a knife. Combine flour, sugar, cocoa, and salt, stirring with a whisk.
2. Combine canola oil and next 3 ingredients, stirring with a whisk. Add to dry ingredients, stirring until blended. Stir in melted chocolate. Stir in walnuts.
3. Coat a 3-quart electric slow cooker with cooking spray. Pour batter into slow cooker. Cover and cook on LOW for 2 to 2½ hours or until set around edges but still soft in the center. Turn off slow cooker. Let stand, covered, 30 minutes before serving. Sprinkle with powdered sugar, if desired.

CALORIES 324; FAT 14.6g (sat 2.7g, mono 5.5g, poly 3.9g); PROTEIN 5.2g; CARB 48.7g; FIBER 1.4g; CHOL 30mg; IRON 1.6mg; SODIUM 105mg; CALC 11mg

Nutritional Analysis

How to Use It and Why

Glance at the end of any *Cooking Light* recipe, and you'll see how committed we are to helping you make the best of today's light cooking. With chefs, registered dietitians, home economists, and a computer system that analyzes every ingredient we use, *Cooking Light* gives you authoritative dietary detail like no other magazine. We go to such lengths so you can see how our recipes fit into your healthful eating plan. If you're trying to lose weight, the calorie and fat figures will probably help most. But if you're keeping a close eye on the sodium, cholesterol, and saturated fat in your diet, we provide those num-bers, too. And because many women don't get enough iron or calcium, we can help there, as well. Finally, there's a fiber analysis for those of us who don't get enough roughage.

Here's a helpful guide to put our nutritional analysis numbers into perspective. Remember, one size doesn't fit all, so take your lifestyle, age, and circumstances into consideration when determining your nutrition needs. For example, pregnant or breast-feeding women need more protein, calories, and calcium. And women older than 50 need 1,200mg of calcium daily, 200mg more than the amount recommended for younger women.

In Our Nutritional Analysis, We Use These Abbreviations

sat	saturated fat	**CHOL**	cholesterol
mono	monounsaturated fat	**CALC**	calcium
poly	polyunsaturated fat	**g**	gram
CARB	carbohydrates	**mg**	milligram

Daily Nutrition Guide

	Women ages 25 to 50	Women over 50	Men ages 24 to 50	Men over 50
Calories	2,000	2,000 or less	2,700	2,500
Protein	50g	50g or less	63g	60g
Fat	65g or less	65g or less	88g or less	83g or less
Saturated Fat	20g or less	20g or less	27g or less	25g or less
Carbohydrates	304g	304g	410g	375g
Fiber	25g to 35g	25g to 35g	25g to 35g	25g to 35g
Cholesterol	300mg or less	300mg or less	300mg or less	300mg or less
Iron	18mg	8mg	8mg	8mg
Sodium	2,300mg or less	1,500mg or less	2,300mg or less	1,500mg or less
Calcium	1,000mg	1,200mg	1,000mg	1,000mg

The nutritional values used in our calculations either come from The Food Processor, Version 8.9 (ESHA Research), or are provided by food manufacturers.

Metric Equivalents

The information in the following charts is provided to help cooks outside the United States successfully use the recipes in this book. All equivalents are approximate.

Cooking/Oven Temperatures

	Fahrenheit	Celsius	Gas Mark
Freeze Water	32° F	0° C	
Room Temp.	68° F	20° C	
Boil Water	212° F	100° C	
Bake	325° F	160° C	3
	350° F	180° C	4
	375° F	190° C	5
	400° F	200° C	6
	425° F	220° C	7
	450° F	230° C	8
Broil			Grill

Liquid Ingredients by Volume

¼ tsp	=					1 ml
½ tsp	=					2 ml
1 tsp	=					5 ml
3 tsp	=	1 tbl	=	½ fl oz	=	15 ml
2 tbls	=	⅛ cup	=	1 fl oz	=	30 ml
4 tbls	=	¼ cup	=	2 fl oz	=	60 ml
5⅓ tbls	=	⅓ cup	=	3 fl oz	=	80 ml
8 tbls	=	½ cup	=	4 fl oz	=	120 ml
10⅔ tbls	=	⅔ cup	=	5 fl oz	=	160 ml
12 tbls	=	¾ cup	=	6 fl oz	=	180 ml
16 tbls	=	1 cup	=	8 fl oz	=	240 ml
1 pt	=	2 cups	=	16 fl oz	=	480 ml
1 qt	=	4 cups	=	32 fl oz	=	960 ml
				33 fl oz	=	1000 ml = 1 l

Dry Ingredients by Weight

(To convert ounces to grams, multiply the number of ounces by 30.)

1 oz	=	¹⁄₁₆ lb	=	30 g
4 oz	=	¼ lb	=	120 g
8 oz	=	½ lb	=	240 g
12 oz	=	¾ lb	=	360 g
16 oz	=	1 lb	=	480 g

Length

(To convert inches to centimeters, multiply the number of inches by 2.5.)

1 in	=				2.5 cm	
6 in	=	½ ft		=	15 cm	
12 in	=	1 ft		=	30 cm	
36 in	=	3 ft	= 1 yd	=	90 cm	
40 in	=				100 cm	= 1 m

Equivalents for Different Types of Ingredients

Standard Cup	Fine Powder (ex. flour)	Grain (ex. rice)	Granular (ex. sugar)	Liquid Solids (ex. butter)	Liquid (ex. milk)
1	140 g	150 g	190 g	200 g	240 ml
¾	105 g	113 g	143 g	150 g	180 ml
⅔	93 g	100 g	125 g	133 g	160 ml
½	70 g	75 g	95 g	100 g	120 ml
⅓	47 g	50 g	63 g	67 g	80 ml
¼	35 g	38 g	48 g	50 g	60 ml
⅛	18 g	19 g	24 g	25 g	30 ml

Index